T0265255

With his new book, *Disrupting Corporate Culture: How Cognitive Science Alters Accepted Beliefs About Culture and Culture Change and Its Impact on Leaders and Change Agents*, David White has joined the short list of those truly challenging organizations to be better than they are. The more we learn about neuroscience and how it helps us understand the complexity of humankind, the more some of us have become motivated to evolve and reach new heights of knowledge, feelings, connectedness, and purpose.

David's core contention is that new science also allows us to bring the same possibilities to organizations through truly understanding this heretofore elusive thing called, 'culture' to bring about real, as opposed to, skin-deep, feel good, check the-box change. And, his warning that true, deep change will be necessary to succeed in the Fourth Industrial Revolution is the clarion call all organizations should heed. As with all opportunities for organizations to lift their game through sustained, human-focused hard work rather than offsites and bromides, the real challenge is how many will be up for it. For most, the managerial age has allowed them to pay lip service to culture in one form or another while focusing on finance driven KPI's to satisfy shareholders. For those organizations that see mastering their culture as the next frontier, however, White's book is a must-read, and offers the potential to pull ahead in the race to unleash new possibilities. Truly forward-leaning organizations should get on board quickly.

Paul Kinsinger
Thunderbird School of Global Management (emeritus)
Central Intelligence Agency

This book will challenge the perspective of any leader who thinks culture will automatically be what they want it to be. It will remind you culture is carried every day in the practices of your organization and in the minds and actions of your people and leaders. The cognitive science explains why, and this book leverages that science to help you transform your organization in a practical and meaningful way.

Mark Aslett
Chief Executive Officer, Mercury Systems

We inhabit a very complex and rapidly changing world which constantly asks us to innovate, adapt, but doesn't give us the intellectual and practical tools to do so. Taking seriously what transformation entails is what David White's groundbreaking book is about. In *Disrupting Corporate Culture*, White proposes an entirely new way of looking at how corporate culture is constituted. "Culture", he argues, is fundamentally what governs change, and only those who will be able to use it as a resource will be able to adapt. Using cutting edge scholarship on cognition as well as his own expertise as a leading consultant in the business world, Dr. White debunks the most pervasive myths about culture and allows us to understand the multiple layers that structure the way we see "our world," a product of our intimate (embodied) engagement with the objects we manipulate, the spaces we inhabit, and the products we create. We also understand why it is impossible to transform an environment from outside, but only by making visible and recognizing the invisible structures, the "schemas," that make us act the way we do. This book will be of great interest for leaders, managers, or anyone who is not looking for easy and quick answers, but has the curiosity and the courage to rethink how they think and act on the eve of the most challenging industrial revolution to come.

Hélène Mialet
Associate Professor of Science and Technology Studies
York University

We're between worlds, one foot in the past, the other perched on the edge of the new: global pandemics, revolutions in AI, robotics, manufacturing, human-machine interfaces, and communications have—or are in the process of—disrupting how we make things, how we work, what (and how) we buy, the ways we talk (and listen) to one another, the skills and knowledge we need to get by, and even how we feel, desire and love. The pivot point between these two worlds is culture. Culture is at the heart of everything—it "governs" change, makes the possible thinkable, and the impossible a possibility. David White's *Disrupting Corporate Culture* begins by dismantling the myths, misunderstandings, fables and fairytales defining our notions of culture, to show his readers what culture looks like through the eyes of a cognitive scientist: a "shared mental operating system" of schemas that guide, delimit, pattern and channel the ways we understand, signify, give meaning to and interact with the world. White's questions are both big and small; he not only asks us to think about revolutionary transformations in the global economy, but about the day-to-day activities that define organizational cultures locally: how to budget, to allocate resources, to plan, and to define goals. He thus challenges his readers to observe culture in action, on the ground, and in the wild. Culture as it is lived and made, he tells us, is not a uniform and static resource that can be changed by executive fiat, nor is it a reflection of what a company truly cares about, or the stage upon which the well-being of its employees is performed. Rather, White's *Disrupting Corporate Culture* disrupts, reveals, and challenges business leaders to move beyond the hackneyed advice and outmoded clichés of organizational theorist and business gurus, to look instead to the dispositions, the logics, the habits and the rituals that structure how organizations actually do the work that they do.

Michael Wintroub
Professor, Department of Rhetoric
University of California, Berkeley

Disrupting Corporate Culture

Disrupting Corporate Culture

How Cognitive Science Alters
Accepted Beliefs About Culture
and Culture Change and Its Impact
on Leaders and Change Agents

David G. White, Jr.

A PRODUCTIVITY PRESS BOOK

First published 2021
by Routledge
52 Vanderbilt Avenue, New York, NY 10017

and by Routledge
2 Park Square, Milton Park, Abingdon, Oxon, OX14 4RN

Routledge is an imprint of the Taylor & Francis Group, an informa business

Library of Congress Cataloging-in-Publication Data

Names: White, David G., Jr., author.
Title: Disrupting corporate culture : how cognitive science alters accepted beliefs about culture and culture change and its impact on leaders and change agents / David G. White, Jr.
Description: New York, NY : Routledge, 2020. | Includes bibliographical references and index.
Identifiers: LCCN 2020011945 (print) | LCCN 2020011946 (ebook) | ISBN 9780367280864 (hardback) | ISBN 9780429316357 (ebook)
Subjects: LCSH: Corporate culture. | Organizational change. | Cognitive science.
Classification: LCC HD58.7 .W46 2020 (print) | LCC HD58.7 (ebook) | DDC 306.3--dc23
LC record available at https://lccn.loc.gov/2020011945
LC ebook record available at https://lccn.loc.gov/2020011946

ISBN: 978-0-367-28086-4 (hbk)
ISBN: 978-0-429-31635-7 (ebk)

Typeset in Minion
by Deanta Global Publishing Services, Chennai, India

Contents

Acknowledgments

Bringing the new science of culture from the many interdisciplinary strands of theory and research in the cognitive sciences to a wider business audience has been one of the most difficult intellectual challenges I have ever confronted. Whether or not it proves successful in the end, I know it would not have been possible without the help of many colleagues, clients, mentors, family, and friends along the way. Some of my mentors I have not met but have nonetheless towered over this work and to whom I owe a huge debt: Philippe Descola, Roy D'Andrade, Naomi Quinn, David Kronenfeld, Ed Hutchins, Penn Handwerker, Mark Johnson, Giovanni Bennardo, Victor De Munck, Ed Schein, and Stanley Harris. Some have been at each step along the way, patiently listening, nudging, and clarifying my thinking to allow me to get to this book. For this I thank Bob Silverman, Fred Steier, Dorothy Agger-Gupta, Claudia Strauss, Eric Rait, Michael Wintroub, Helene Mialet, Bob Kegan, and Paul Kinsinger. I owe a huge debt of gratitude to my clients: without their input and clarifications, many of the insights in this book would not have been possible. Even though I cannot mention you by name, you know who you are. And lastly, to Adriana, Chris, and Lisa, my collaborators at Ontos who helped in invaluable ways with the research, and to Elizabeth, my Dad, and especially to Lisa: you constantly pushed for more clarity and connection. I couldn't have gotten here without you.

Introduction

In a world deluged by irrelevant information, clarity is power.

– Yuval Noah Harari

This book is about dilemmas. Although its title is *Disrupting Corporate Culture*, on the eve of the Fourth Industrial Revolution culture may not be in any need of disrupting. This is because the world of work and organization as we know it may be gone within 50 years. The convergence of biotechnology, nanotechnology, artificial intelligence, and robotics may render the idea of corporate culture a quaint artifact of the late 20th century as workers turn into robots, or become robot-like on account of the "steady stripping of human judgment" from work.[1] Corporations as we know them won't need to exist because robots and brain–machine interfaces will perform most of the work, and what's left will be done by highly skilled human free agents collaborating across constantly evolving global networks in a hyperconnected world.[2]

On the other hand, consider that on the eve of the Fourth Industrial Revolution, culture, as the natural byproduct of what happens when humans form into groups and communities to accomplish a task, may be the single most important phenomenon of organizational life. This is not just because that in all of the social-media–fanned hyperventilation the concept in mainstream use is not well understood, or perhaps, profoundly misunderstood. As we arrive at the first quarter of the 21st century, the corporatization of our world is being assailed by some as the end of freedom and democracy, the takeover and corruptor of governments, and the primary perpetrator of global warming, among other social and environmental evils attributed to the modern enterprise. Today we live in a world ruptured by Cambridge Analytica and Equifax scandals, where Google is linked to enabling child pornography, and where companies like Facebook are accused of creating platforms based on "amoral" algorithms.[3] Without a better understanding of *why* humans in organizations think and act as they do and how that leads to specific outcomes, how can we possibly help corporations and the people who lead them find their way to the emancipating future that the Fourth Industrial Revolution, in its finest hoped-for incarnation anyway, represents for humankind?[4] To even approach doing that, we will need a much better – *more sophisticated, more precise, more complete* – understanding of culture in organizations than we have today. *Dilemma.*

We are living in a time when the difference between one second and half a second in booking an airline reservation online may mean a $500 difference in airfare. Data scientists at Walmart have found every half second added in on-line transaction time results in 2 or more percentage points lost in transactions among the millions it completes each day.[5] As Thomas L. Friedman writes, we live in an age of acceleration where "under a second" is just too slow (2016, p. 122). The cumulative effect of these daily and hourly experiences as consumers and knowledge workers have reset our expectations and tolerances. So much so that simplicity is now widely considered a corporate virtue. We have little patience for anything that cannot be digested in a quick scan of a blog post or in about three bullet points.

On the other hand, as managers and practitioners, we sense and often acknowledge culture's importance, yet we routinely settle for boiled down, half-baked, and much-less-than-adequate solutions to the questions and challenges it presents. In this age of digital everything, we want our organizations to be agile, our leaders to be risk-takers, and our managers to be decisive. And yet when it comes to culture, arguably the most complex domain of organizational life, we have low tolerance for any but the most saccharine answers. What we want from culture (a lot) and what we are willing to give to get from it (not so much) are incompatible. This makes a book on disrupting corporate culture problematic: to fully appreciate how cognitive science disrupts nearly everything we thought we knew about culture takes a bit more than a blog post and few bullets. *Dilemma.*

At home I have trouble hammering a nail, yet thanks to the wonders of YouTube, I can make reasonable repairs of our espresso machine after watching a three-minute video. So I empathize with all the managers and practitioners who seek the same simplicity and expediency in understanding culture as they endeavor to lead and transform 21st-century enterprises. The problem is the culture field today is incapable of adequately answering that crucible question: why *do* humans in organizations think and act as they do, and how *does* that lead to specific outcomes? Part of the reason why is that, for too long, the field has trafficked in expediency at the expense of efficacy. Until it can resolve this tension and begin to more completely address this question, achieving any sustainable success through planned organizational transformation in large enterprises is in doubt. *Dilemma.*

This book will not help you "fix" your culture in the way I do my espresso machine. It will not tell you how to unleash the power of your workforce for competitive advantage, give you the *5 Secrets of Great Cultures*, or show you *How to Use Culture to Ensure Unlimited Corporate Profit*. It cannot do these things because in order to address that crucible question with any serious engagement with the cognitive science of culture, more time, space, and appreciation of nuance is needed.[6] That's not to under-appreciate how much "content" competes for your attention, even at this very moment. One need only peruse Amazon to see how many books on corporate culture were published in the last few years alone (see Chapter 2). But to get at what's different here, and why it matters, this book will ask more of you. I do provide help: there are shortcuts, an outline of the basic ideas, and a chapter guide (this Introduction). The chapters themselves contain tips and pictures summarizing key points. Like cairns on a misty trail, these tools will help you get the gist of the thesis. But I will caution some of the arguments in this book – for example, that leaders don't directly create culture, or that culture doesn't cause us to *do* anything – may sound strange and counter to what you might have been led to believe. They may even be counter to your own experience. By taking shortcuts, you might miss key points: it so happens there's a lot to the new science.

WHY THIS BOOK?

The reasons for this book is best summed up by historian Yuval Harari's quote at the beginning of this Introduction. In the world of corporate culture, we are deluged with information, much of it misleading, outdated, naïve, or just plain wrong. That's not to say it isn't well-intended, but much of what masquerades as the latest and greatest insight is based on outdated science, a single case study, a compelling personal experience, or is simply wishful thinking. Our traditional sources aren't very reliable, either: much of the misleading work on culture is coming directly from MBA programs and reputable consulting firms. A good chunk of it confuses culture with employee well-being. This is understandable given the science of well-being, in the form of employee engagement, has made considerable contributions to what we know about the relationship between emotional states and business outcomes. It's easy to see why the culture pundits might have hitched their wagon to the employee engagement star.

It's also understandable why many of us have not noticed. We are too busy trying to make the numbers for the quarter, bring the new product to market, solve that hard engineering problem, or figure out how to move from manufacturing stuff to selling information. We can't afford the luxury of thinking about issues with culture because we have more immediate and pressing needs. We can't afford it, that is, until we notice what we want isn't happening. Or it's happening in a way we didn't expect and don't much like. It is then we tend to notice culture and try to do something about it. It is then we tend to reach for the expedient solution. We buy that airport book or try to find the compelling blog we read a month ago which outlined that five-step change program. Or we try and recreate what we did at our last company which seemed to work. Or, like hiring a plumber to finally address the leaky faucet, we just hire someone to fix it.

To borrow another phrase from Harari: unfortunately, culture, like history, doesn't give discounts.[7] If the future of your company or division, or that of your clients, is set into place while you were too busy solving its immediate problems in the most expedient way, you may find one day what you want to change is impossible. The forces for sameness, like an overwhelming lethargy or the relentless outflow of a tidal estuary, will be too much to overcome. Your strategies won't work, or will backfire. You may make promises to your boss, the board of directors, or your shareholders of better profits or increased market share on the basis of culture that you cannot possibly deliver. Or worse, you may think you made change happen when in fact nothing in the actual lived experience of the people in your organization will have changed at all. Failing at culture may not be fatal. Then again, how many jobs have been lost or executive careers discarded into the no-credibility landfill because of a failure to recognize or take into account some critical aspect of culture or for trying to change a culture through naïve means? We will never know for sure. What we do know is managers are dealing with culture and culture change every day with inadequate theories and ineffective tools, whether they know it or not.

Ironically, however, these are boom times for those of us in the culture business. Organizational culture according to the *Economist* is a fad, the word of the day.[8] The concept seems to explain everything, from Uber's rapaciousness to Amazon's intensity to GM's ethical lapses to Enron's greed. Start-ups now have "VPs of Culture". "Failures of culture" are the reason for executive malfeasance, poor performance, low morale, failed strategy, and many other corporate shortcomings. The term is so firmly in the mainstream that sportswriters use it to explain the (up-until-recent) success of basketball's Golden State Warriors or the perpetual underachievement of my dear Arsenal in the English Premier League. There are corporate culture conferences sponsored by mainstream media like the *New York Times*, and a seemingly never-ending stream of books, Ted Talks, videos, blogs, and podcasts from pundits of all stripes.

Unfortunately for cognitive anthropologists, culture is like Dr. Frankenstein's monster escaped from the lab to wreak havoc on the countryside: a well-intended and promising invention gone alarmingly awry. And most of us in the lab are partially to blame. The organizational researchers John Van Maanen and Stephen Barley once famously characterized the study of human behavior in organizations as a field "already choking on assorted frameworks, hypotheses, methods, variables, and other objects of intellectual passion".[9] Culture is their poster child.

Culture has been a major topic of interest, both in business and in academia, since the late 1970s (Kunda, 1992). And yet, as I will argue, the field is immature. Academic research is still characterized by debates over methods, assumptions, basic definitions, or struggles for relevancy. Managers and consultants, meanwhile, proceed blithely unencumbered by any of these difficulties despite the fact there is very little empirical evidence to show culture can be deliberately shaped in any organization larger than about 150 people. This is ironic but not surprising: given competing or contradictory theory, culture in practice has devolved into a mish-mash of ideology, belief, and folksy wisdom. It seems one need only recite the famous quip, *culture eats strategy for breakfast* as evidence for why a culture investment is justified.[10] The popular Corner Office column in the *Sunday New York Times* bore witness to how passionately managers believe culture can and should be shaped, like clay, as an expression and projection of their own values and ideologies (Bryant, 2009–2015).[11] Which brings me back to the opening question, *why this book?*

The late great musician Frank Zappa is well known among musicians for composing *The Black Page*, a devilishly difficult piece to play originally written as a drum solo (the name of the piece refers to the massive amounts of notes blackening the musical score). As Zappa said in one of his live performances, the problem is few non-musicians could appreciate what he called the piece's "statistical density", so in response he re-arranged it to convey the same material over a catchy disco beat to appeal to a wider audience. This book is a kind of *Black Page* 2.0 for the wider audience. It bridges the cognitive science of culture, which has emerged well out of sight of business and business schools, with the practice of culture in organizations.[12] My previous book, *Rethinking Culture: Embodied Cognition and the Origin of Culture in Organizations*, was written for academics and scholar-practitioners. It described in detail the theory, research, and epistemology supporting the cognitive science of culture. This book conveys the essentials of the new science but emphasizes what it all means for managers and practitioners.

What We Know Is Woefully Inadequate to Deal with What's Coming

But there's a more important answer as well. The real reason I wrote this book is that most of what corporate executives, change leaders, human resources (HR), organizational development (OD) practitioners, and consultants know about culture is woefully inadequate to support the massive upheavals already upon us on the leading edge of the Fourth Industrial Revolution. The new science of culture changes almost everything we thought we knew about culture, and this matters now more than ever. This is because every industry on the planet is or will soon be fundamentally disrupted by digital technology, artificial intelligence, robotics, human–machine interfaces, and related technologies, not to mention the massive global upheavals wrought by pandemics like Covid-19. These forces are already or will soon transform every aspect of our lives, from how we live, communicate, work, travel, eat, buy, love, and so on. The convergence of technologies alone, in the form of chip- and sensor-enabled devices – from jet engines to coffee makers to a cow's vital signs – with cheap computer processors powering machine learning algorithms, so-called "ubiquitous computing",[13] are putting enormous pressure on traditional sources of corporate earnings as value is transferred directly to consumers and end-users. Advanced technologies enable companies to forge into adjacent markets or invent entirely new markets, allowing, for example, legacy industrial manufacturers to offer digital platforms for predictive analytics, or tech to allow companies to become global transportation, supply chain, and logistics juggernauts. These forays are already eating into the profits of legacy players and changing entire value chains, forever reshaping traditional industries and altering who makes money and what share of the pie they capture. The slow, risk-averse, unimaginative, and inefficient are now, or will soon be left behind, competing for scraps.[14]

Culture Is the Governor of Change

What this means for managers and practitioners is that you are on the front lines of corporate transformation like never before. As organizations try to position themselves to take advantage of digital transformation and all it implies, they are running headlong into that invisible wall called culture. *Culture governs change.* It is the great enabler or limiter, that hidden force that can empower or derail the most well-thought-out corporate transformation. Companies who understand this and can wisely harness culture as a resource will be more likely to survive the tsunami of the Fourth Industrial Revolution. Those that can't will be left behind. Of course, pundits have been saying this for decades since corporate culture first came into mass consciousness in the early 1980s. The problem is the data suggests most of what we have been doing with culture in all of that time hasn't worked. Moreover, corporate and societal transformation of this magnitude has not been seen since the development of mass production, the Second Industrial Revolution. Culturally speaking, transforming a 100-year-old industrial company into a digital platform, or an internet commerce company into an airline (and such), is, as they say, non-trivial. It is impossible without a much better understanding of how culture actually works, and why.

The problem is the culture industry – and it is a billion-dollar industry made up of business-school academics, consultants, journalists, publishers, HR, and OD practitioners – for the most part peddles ideas and approaches based largely on myth. Not for lack of good intention, but as with all myths, they stay with us because their explanations are expedient. They provide a convenient way to think about and work with culture, and keeps purveyors and consumers engaged in a cycle of mutual collusion. Purveyors – consultants and pundits – sell "solutions" based on approaches and tools that consumers – executives, HR, and change agents – say they want. But both sides put forward overly simplified and boiled down approaches because it maintains the appearance that something is being done about culture, which keeps bosses and boards happy, while at the same time adhering to the inconvenient truth that corporate and board tolerance for any idea that is not easy to digest and quick to implement is alarmingly low. This is the collusion. Business and management academics exacerbate the problem by promulgating reductive theories from intellectual silos that break little new ground. With no academic consensus, consultants and managers are free to define and operationalize culture in any way that suits their needs and interests, as if culture was a completely fungible and arbitrary construct, and as if what applies to organizations is somehow different than what has applied to societies over millennia. This keeps the buying cycle moving, even if actual efficacy is low.

This amounts to a crisis: organizations have been trying to deal with culture and culture change for a long time with little to show for it. The field has been tinkering at the margins with naïve theories and blunt tools. Until we can bring a more well-informed and sophisticated understanding of culture to bear on these gargantuan organizational and societal upheavals, we will fail the organizations we help and lead. Which brings me to the goal of this book.

The cognitive science of culture shakes all this up. It offers an entirely new way to think about and work with culture, one based not on myth, but one that tracks closely to intuition. It is a game-changer. Not because of any single idea (other than, maybe, culture has a neurochemical basis in the brain, a notion that shouldn't sound radical given the popularity of neuroscience in mainstream media). The game change is what it all means. Where culture comes from; what it consists of as "source code" and an "operating system"; how pervasive it is; how to distinguish cultural signals from cultural noise; how to intervene at the cultural root cause rather than a symptom; how to make interventions sustainable: all of this is what changes the game. This book presents a framework where all of this is understood and leveraged.

But this is not a "how-to" book. The cognitive science of culture is barely three decades old and we are still at the dawn of application in the business world. It is not a panacea or a silver bullet. Much of how culture actually works – how it is experienced inside organizations, and why – is explained by the science. And because it accounts for virtually everything we take as culture, this book will help you understand, work with, and make use of it in more productive and sustainable ways than what you currently have at your disposal.

Curiosity and Courage

This matters because the transformation and societal challenges of today and tomorrow raise the stakes considerably on your ability and willingness to become a more sophisticated change leader. By definition that means becoming a more sophisticated culture change leader. By exposing you to the myths of culture and where they come from, I hope to help you see why current approaches don't work. When we stop chasing false prophets, we can start to focus on what really matters. Admittedly, this takes curiosity and courage. Curiosity because cognitive science challenges conventional wisdoms (aka "myths"). Curiosity because the science exposes why culture is so pervasive, as much an invisible wall as an invisible hand. Courage because the science isn't a watered-down recipe for success or a playbook guaranteeing anything. Courage because the science deals with what is unspoken and implied, the taken-for-granted "stuff" that makes up culture. Which will mean designing interventions that challenge prevailing assumptions and dare to change the things that leaders hold most dear, like how they budget, allocate resources, plan, or define success. Along with self-awareness and psychological flexibility, curiosity and courage are the two most important personal orientations for change leaders in the Fourth Industrial Revolution. The stakes are higher now than at any point in our careers for those of us that lead change, or help those that do.

THE NEW SCIENCE OF CULTURE – IN BRIEF

Hardly anything in life is ever truly "new". Take artificial intelligence (AI), one of the most promising technologies of our time. For all its promise, AI requires millions of instances of training data supplied by humans for the machine learning algorithms that power AI to "learn" a particular domain, whether it recognizes traffic signals, sensor data from a jet engine, or makes a medical diagnosis. And so with the new science of culture, the "training" data here are the many strands of theory and research woven from the cognitive subdisciplines of anthropology, sociology, psychology, linguistics, and cultural neuroscience. For reasons I explain in the first two chapters, with some notable exceptions, little of it comes from business schools or the fields of management science, economics, or industrial/organizational (I/O) psychology, the traditional provinces of corporate cultural knowledge.[15]

What Is Culture?

What does "culture" mean to you? Is it how people feel? What they do? What they like and don't like? What they believe or value? What they say?

Or does it have something to do with things like free food and foosball? Or some combination of all of the above?

In popular usage, the word is a mash-up. As we can never be sure what it means, let's take a short quiz. Read through each question below and try to answer from the perspective of your own organization, or one you know well. Pick the answer that is *most* like your organization, even if it doesn't completely match (it's not an exhaustive list). You might answer "it depends", "none of the above", or "all of the above" for many of these items, and that's OK. But try to think about what your organization *typically* does. If what it typically does is not on the list, think about what else it does ("you" here is the typical response of most people in the organization you have in mind):

1. How do you plan?
    a. Do you gather your top lieutenants into a two day offsite and map out the next five years?
    b. Do you go through a thorough bottoms-up exercise once a year where every business submits its plan and financial forecast, which you then vet and approve with a core group of leaders?
    c. Do you not bother to plan out more than six months because your world moves too fast?
2. How do you define success?
    a. Is it exceeding revenue and operating income targets, or similar financial measures?
    b. Is it productivity?
    c. Is it how you accomplished your goals?
    d. Is it innovation and technical brilliance?
3. How do you prioritize?
    a. Do you want to do everything at the same time?
    b. Do you change direction at the first hint of trouble?
    c. Do you have a clear "north star", a set of guiding principles you stick to no matter what?
4. How do you deal with risk?
    a. Do you believe in "failing fast"?
    b. Do you fund multiple competing projects at the same time to see which one succeeds?
    c. Do you require any new project or initiative have a clearly spelled-out return on investment before any green light is given?
5. How do you delegate authority?
    a. Does each business unit or function have the autonomy to make its owns strategic decisions?

    b. Do the top executives personally make every major decision in their business or function?

    c. What is the lowest level in the organization in which a manager controls his or her own budget?

6. How do you handle reporting?

    a. Are your team meetings essentially free-flowing brainstorming sessions?

    b. Are your meetings formal report-outs on the performance of each person's business or functional area?

    c. Do you like to keep informal tabs on the business by "walking around", or through spontaneous drop-in visits to offices?

7. Who is *most* respected?

    a. The person who reliably delivers whatever it is they said they would deliver?

    b. The person who knows the ins and outs of his or her business in intimate detail?

    c. The visionary and brilliant strategist?

    d. The team builder?

    e. The person who gets along with everyone?

8. Given two equally qualified candidates for promotion with all other variables equal:

    a. Do you tend to select the known hard worker?

    b. Do you tend to select the one with the raw intellectual horsepower?

    c. Do you tend to select the one with the proven track record?

    d. Do you tend to select the one that will shake up the status quo?

9. How do you handle conflict?

    a. Do you immediately have it out with the person one-to-one and not move forward until you have agreement?

    b. Are you deferentially polite in person but openly critical when the other person is not around?

    c. Do you argue in public?

    d. Do you not say anything but escalate the issue up the chain of command?

10. What is your tolerance for abstraction?

    a. Do you need a new idea spelled out with real-world examples and practical benefits before you can understand or appreciate it?

    b. Do you prefer conceptual models and theories over action plans?

    c. Does brainstorming bore you?

    d. Unless an idea has a clear monetary return, it doesn't interest you?

Now: what do these questions have to do with culture? If your answer is "everything", then you intuitively grasp what the cognitive science of culture is all about.[16]

Culture Is Knowledge

From the perspective of cognitive science, culture, or some aspect of it, influenced every one of your answers. This is because culture is *knowledge* – shared knowledge distributed within a social community. Much of it is *implicit* – we know it but don't know we know it until it is brought into our awareness.

This is quite different than saying culture is beliefs, values, attitudes, or norms. It would be quite reasonable to suggest that your answers were, in fact, expression of your beliefs, values, attitudes, or norms. And while that would be true, it would miss the key point: you most likely didn't know the answers to some or all of these questions until triggered by the question (or the actual event). This distinction is key. The crucial difference between current mainstream thinking and this approach is that beliefs, values, attitudes, and norms (and such) are the products of conscious awareness and choice, whereas most of culture is actually *preconscious* and the product of *reflex*, at least until brought into awareness.[17] This is not a semantic or technical distinction. It may be difficult to grasp or accept this because we tend to believe everything we do is based on conscious choice and free will. This does explain, however, why culture feels so pervasive and automatic. It speaks to how and where culture originates, and it points to how and where to intervene.

Cultural knowledge at its core consists of basic, simplified mental models that anchor a "reference system", a shared mental operating system running in the background of our daily lives. There are many names for these models, but cognitive anthropologists know them as cultural schemas. Schemas structure – meaning, they pattern, delimit, and provide a kind of logic or rationale – for everything understood as culture in any group or community. For the purposes of this book I refer to schemas as *shared dominant logics*, or SDLs, because the term "logic" conveys the essence of what a schema is all about, and is a more intuitive label for most managers and practitioners to grab on to. What underlies the answers to all of the questions above are logics (schemas). When we put a shared logic into words we call it an "assumption".[18] These logics show up in many ways: as assumptions and implicit beliefs that structure more elaborate and complex logics; as implicit standards of what is taken as "good" or ideal; as ways of justifying a course of action; as rationalizations for why something happened or will happen; and as repeated patterns in processes or practices.

What the cultural reference system is *not* is something that forces us to do anything. It is background knowledge; an operating system people *can* use to make sense of to function in the world around them. It can be a wall, or a hand, but it's not a magical force. This is another of the many myths of culture that executives and practitioners often get confused by, thinking culture is the *cause* of this or that. Cultural knowledge is preconscious and we use it reflexively, yes, but the more aware we are of it, the more choice we have in how to use it. This is a key to unlocking the power of culture in organizational transformation.

What cultural reference systems are, where they come from, why they operate as they do, and how to leverage them is what the rest of this book is about.

SUMMARY OF CHAPTERS

The opening chapter begins with a thought experiment: what would you do as the CEO of a medium-sized global company keen on changing your culture? The most popular methods you might employ would in all likelihood be based on what I call the 5 *Myths of Culture*. These are: (1) *Culture Starts at the Top*; (2) *Culture is a Physical Thing*; (3) *One Company, One Culture*; (4) *Culture is What We Say We Care About*; and (5) *Culture is Employee Well-Being*. From the perspective of cognitive science, each of these myths are based on assumptions or theories that are outmoded, incomplete, limited, or, as is most often the case, not based on any theory at all but instead reliant upon some kind of managerial wishful thinking. And yet, as mentioned, these theories prevail. Why?

The second chapter addresses that question. I begin by showing how we are in a corporate culture "crisis". Despite millions of dollars, thousands of books, and decades of interest, most corporate culture change fails to produce desired results. The myths explain why. I show where the myths originate: siloed and narrow academic perspectives in business schools and a culture industry too willing to supply simplistic solutions to highly complex challenges in the name of expediency. And, yes, profit.

Against this current state, Chapter 3 introduces the new science. The cognitive branches of anthropology, cultural psychology, sociology, linguistics, and the emerging field of cultural neuroscience have developed major new paradigms for culture, with big implications. It begins with the idea that how we think is deeply patterned by our ecological, social, and cultural environments of which we are a part from birth. *Regular, sustained,* and *meaningful* patterns of interaction with *regularities* in our environments form the basis for *what, how,* and *why* we collectively think as we do. What the science shows is that our minds extract mental images (logics) based on these interactions, and that over time these become foundational for the formation of culture. The way in which this happens is obviously complex, but the key mechanism is adaptation: humans are structure-seeking creatures. We are always trying to adapt and make sense of the ecologies around us. Culture is an evolutionary adaptive response to this process of natural sense-making. And it is basic for group functioning and survival.

In organizations, this means culture is born out of a firm's dominant occupational group(s); from how it has gone about solving or adapting to hard problems or environmental challenges (especially existential problems of survival); from a clearly differentiated core purpose that goes well beyond ordinary commercial ambitions; or some combination of all three. These sources provide a firm with its dominant logics, the cognitive foundations of a firm's *cultural reference system*. Reference systems are anchored by SDLs that structure practices as well as conscious beliefs and attitudes, many of which are "adaptations" – compensations for or reactions to dominant logics. That tech firms "move fast and break things" but manufacturers can't release "beta versions of refrigerators" is a much deeper cultural truth than these clichés might suggest.[19]

In other words, task shapes culture. Chapter 4 shows how this works by showcasing an archetypal Fortune 1000 industrial manufacturer's reference system. It shows how layers of culture extend from shared preconscious logics to practices and adaptations, and depicts the extent to which a reference system pervades every day business practices embedded deep within the firm, and how those practices reinforce the reference system. Reference systems are "perfect" for their current environment but "perfectly constraining" for transformation. Understanding how and why this is so is pivotal to successful organizational change.

In Chapter 5 we shift our focus to how managers and practitioners intervene using the new science. I show how exposing the reference system and its workings is essential to successful transformation. Once exposed, the next question is what to do? To change culture requires changing logics. But this is tricky. After all, dominant logics are dominant for good reason: they have worked well as ways of adapting the organization to the ecological and existential threats in its environment. They also reside in people's brains, in their so-called "unthought knowns" (what they don't know they know). This makes change doubly hard, and is one reason why so many culture change programs fail. To change culture, in essence, means intervening in the collective's *preconscious*. How does one do that? The key is practices. Changing logics requires new habits and routines – *practices* – that induce new neural pathways. This is how the logics got there to begin with, from meaningful adaptive practices growing out of the dominant profession, shared tasks, or core purpose of the enterprise. And while leaders don't create culture – cultures form just as well without obvious leaders in any group based on the group's inherent need to adapt and make meaning – leaders do play a vital role in molding it. This is because they control resources and set agendas that determine which practices matter most, and why. This chapter ends by describing two frameworks for how leaders do this. One is a Process Framework for identifying and intervening in SDLs through practices. The other is a Leadership Framework that speaks to the emotional and psychological orientations leaders must have to lead this kind of change for their organizations as well as for themselves.

The book closes with a short epilogue. It summarizes the main points of the book in four new laws of culture for organizations. It also describes how the new science addresses common culture change scenarios, such as improving collaboration.

BRINGING LIGHT TO DARK MATTER

Much of the known world is made up of atoms and other types of normal matter. But most of the universe, by some accounts up to 85 percent, is made up of dark energy and dark matter, stuff only detectable via its gravitational effects. Astronomers believe dark matter keeps galaxies intact and holds galaxy clusters together.[20] In many ways, culture is like dark matter: we have a hard time detecting it directly except via its effects, and yet it appears to hold entities, like organizations, together. Many managers intuitively understand this, yet management academics and consultants tend to operate as if the analogy is reversed: culture is readily detectable, a dependent variable, easily manageable, and eminently changeable.

This view is obviously at odds with my own experience. I have been a student of organizational culture and change since the early 1990s. We may not have always called it that, but whether it was trying to help Lotus Development (now a part of IBM) transform itself into a services and solution provider, help Bayer Pharmaceuticals in the Americas implement an integrated system for managing talent, or trying to bring my own technology company to profitability, virtually my entire career has been spent working inside, or alongside, organizations in the service of culture transformation.

My thinking on culture accelerated exponentially when I arrived at Microsoft in the early 2000s to work with a talented group of OD practitioners and I/O psychologists. At that time, Microsoft was embarking on a major transition to augment its Windows and Office-dominant strategy with one that was more customer and service-centric, a move which entailed a significant shift in culture. This change emphasized greater collaboration across internal functions, since the premium now was on developing solutions determined by customers rather than by engineering teams used to coming up with new and advanced software features. Our team was tasked with creating the model, strategy, and tools to enable this change.

We approached the problem by first identifying a "go-to" culture that leaders felt would help drive the strategy, and then identifying the behaviors and attitudes to enable the change. Our way of operationalizing culture, thus, was through the talent management system, a very common and reasonable approach to culture change.[21] After several employee engagement surveys and a huge undertaking to build competency and career path models that contained the aspired values for virtually the entire workforce (approximately 90,000 employees at the time), after five years of effort we found disappointingly little change. We had moved the employee engagement needle, sure: the emphasis on creating competencies associated with success as well as dual-track career paths helped employees feel the company was invested in their careers. But had the company become more customer and service-centric? Had engineering teams stopped creating cool features just because they could? Hardly. With the best of intentions, we failed. By the standards of the new science, we did too much and not enough: we over-emphasized a talent solution at the expense of more impactful interventions beyond the realm of HR (Chapter 2 describes why this approach is flawed).[22]

My experiences at Microsoft led to this book – albeit crossing a few streams to get here. It also led me back to school at the tender age of 48 to try to answer a burning research question: *what is wrong with culture?* Why have virtually all of the approaches to culture and culture change I have been a party to in almost 30 years of work in global corporations, consulting firms, and start-ups, despite burning platforms, great intentions, and a wealth of talented bosses, mentors, and colleagues all failed? One could argue bad luck or bad timing. My instincts, and later my doctorate research, told me otherwise.

That research led me to the cognitive science of culture. It also led me to a realization: the current lack of efficacy in the culture field means a new generation of work with fresh ideas and methods is badly needed. Working the problem from outside the typical ways in which business schools approach culture, using the multi-disciplinary vantage points of cultural neuroscience, cognitive psychology, cognitive linguistics, cognitive anthropology, and sociology, forced me to synthesize. I am not an expert in all of these fields, of course. I am a cognitive anthropologist who has worked in business for three decades, and an OD practitioner who has done extensive research resulting in a dissertation and two books. This makes me a generalist. I have relied on thinking from these disciplines with their own ontologies and epistemologies, and triangulated their research and perspectives through an extended process of distillation and comparison against those of my own discipline. That cocktail is now poured into this book. I believe it takes working in this way to escape the vortex of the many narrowly drawn orthodoxies on culture found in the mainstream to arrive at something more impactful.

But whether I am a practitioner with a scholarly bent or a researcher who consults, either way I'm an odd duck swimming in multiple ponds. This has advantages and disadvantages. What it does provide is relatively few intellectual sacred cows, and no departmental or academic tenure concerns. On the other hand, like anyone, I bring my own biases and baggage to the material. One bias, of course, is that I make a living as a practitioner. While some might accuse me of trying to sell consulting gigs, I suspect readers will be assured upon reading the rest of this book that what I care about most is efficacy. I'm interested in helping complex organizations transform. I'm not interested in what is expedient or easy in order to sell another project or a few more books. As much as I care about helping people and organizations, I am equally committed to advancing the science of culture. These goals are not mutually exclusive: they are, in fact, inseparable. What we are doing today in our field is not working. The new science over the horizon just out of sight of the mainstream has a better alternative. And yet that alternative only will prove truly helpful when tested, refined, and improved in the laboratory of real-world interventions.

As with Vera Rubin's (Figure I.1) pioneering work on dark matter, we are still in the early days of corporate culture despite the fact we have been at it for almost 50 years. Things will only get worse as jobs, work, and the very meaning of the corporation as we know it are radically transformed in the coming revolution. Many legacy companies that exist today will not be around in ten years. They will not because they will not have been able

FIGURE I.1
Vera Rubin, source: https://pressfrom.info/us/news/science-and-technology/-14389-vera-rubin-who-did-pioneering-work-on-dark-matter-dies.html. *Source: Carnegie Institution of Washington*

to adopt a more sophisticated approach to organizational transformation, one that made use of the latest science rather than pseudo-science and myth. As the culture researchers Joanne Martin and Peter Frost (2011) pointed out, what the organizational culture field needs most right now is imagination and courage. Perhaps you will be inspired to bring more imagination and courage to your work after reading this book.

NOTES

1. Scheiber, *The New York Times.*
2. Michelman (2017).
3. As put by Kyle Dent (2019) writing about artificial intelligence (AI): "AI is being used in a surprising number of applications, making judgments about job performance, hiring, loans, and criminal justice among many others. Most people are not aware of the potential risks in these judgments. They should be. There is a general feeling that technology is inherently neutral – even among many of those developing AI solutions. But AI developers make decisions and choose trade-offs that affect outcomes. Developers are embedding ethical choices within the technology but without thinking about their decisions in those terms".
4. Klaus Schwab, World Economic Forum, 2019. As he writes: "The First Industrial Revolution used water and steam power to mechanize production. The Second used electric power to create mass production. The Third used electronics and information technology to automate production. Now a Fourth Industrial Revolution is building on the Third, the digital revolution that has been occurring since the middle of the last century. It is characterized by a fusion of technologies that is blurring the lines between the physical, digital, and biological spheres".
5. From Thomas L. Friedman (2016).
6. This is not a formal "school" of academic research or practice as much as a convenient way to refer to the body of knowledge making up the ideas in this book. The term was coined by the cognitive anthropologist Bradd Shore.
7. Yuval Harari (2018).
8. *The Economist* (January 11, 2014). It might be more aptly thought of as fashion, discussed in Chapter 2.
9. Van Maanen and Barley (1984, Chapter 1).
10. The famous phrase is attributed to Peter Drucker, but an actual reference is hard to find. I first heard it at a talk given by Stanford's Charles O'Reilly.
11. And see Alvesson and Sveningsson (2008), Kunda (1992), or Martin and Frost (2011). The Corner Office column was renamed and shifted in focus in 2018.
12. The term "cognitive science" used throughout this book is to be distinguished from traditional cognitive science, which used the metaphor of the computer to explain cognitive processes. That is, cognition is mental computation and the mind is a processing system that manipulates symbolic representations impervious to context (de Bruin & Kastner, 2012). The use of the term here is quite different. It refers to the modern "embodied" view of cognitive science, explained fully in Chapter 3.
13. *The Economist* (September 14, 2019).

14. Bughin, Catlin, and LaBerge, *McKinsey Quarterly* (June 2019).
15. The "notable exceptions" can be found in the work of Edgar Schein, Peter Senge, Mats Alvesson, Stan Harris and a few others.
16. This list, of course, is a sample intended to illustrate the point. It is not meant as a definitive survey of culture.
17. This is different than the unconscious. "Preconscious" means the knowledge lies dormant but is available to our conscious mind when triggered by context cues – such as this questionnaire.
18. This idea was first articulated by Ed Schein in 1984.
19. *The Economist* (September 14, 2019).
20. Cowen (2002).
21. Interested readers should refer to Olesen, White, and Lemmer (2007).
22. Arguably, the shift we envisioned has only recently started to take hold as a product or byproduct of changes to the company's customer practices. *The Economist* (July 6, 2019).

1

The 5 Myths of Culture

Changing hemlines, the pronunciation of words, or the style of pop songs does not change the underlying system of clothing, language, and musical intervals...Cultures are systems larger than the individual. No one individual controls all the knowledge and practices, which are distributed throughout the population in a complex division of labor and cognition.

– Stephen C. Levinson

Imagine you are the CEO of a medium-sized, global industrial company who wants to change your company's culture. Let's say you want to do so because your world is changing: product and service disruption by digitization, the Internet of Things, sensors, machine learning, big data, changing customer demands, the risk of global pandemics, environmental concerns, the rise of emerging markets, the needs of a younger workforce, and on. You believe your organization needs to shed old ways of doing things, move faster, and be more innovative and collaborative in order to avoid becoming irrelevant in this rapidly changing post-industrial world. You believe a change in your culture is the key to avoiding this fate.

Where would you begin?

You might begin by impressing upon your senior managers that they need to be more innovative and collaborative. You might say something like, "Culture change starts at the top". Some of your managers might wonder what you mean, to which you would say, "You set the tone. If you are more this way the rest of the organization will be more this way too". You might invest in internal marketing. This would mean creating a statement of your desired norms and values for every employee, a kind of corporate manifesto similar to Netflix's famous "Culture" document.[1] It could mean a clever branding campaign with tag lines such as *Connect* or *Go Big* or *Do Something New!* to fill posters in conference rooms, tent cards in cafeterias, and new hire collateral. These themes become the centerpieces of your town halls as you evangelize the benefits of upping the collective innovation and collaboration quotient of your company.

Depending on the size of your budget, you might create training that teaches people how to behave in more collaborative and innovative ways. A sizable chunk of your workforce will be required to take these classes, with everyone receiving a tchotchke reminding what innovation and collaboration really mean. Rightfully you will be concerned these efforts are making a difference, so you will ensure the next employee engagement survey measures innovation and collaboration. In fact, a year passes, and you are pleased to see the relevant survey questions have improved by a couple of percentage points from previous surveys.

So, after all this, have you changed your culture?

You might say you have, pointing to the survey results. To which I would ask, is your organization truly more collaborative and innovative? Or, might you be measuring the effects of priming by a marketing and training exercise? You might have improved your employee engagement scores, but is engagement the same as culture?

YOUR PLATFORM IS ALREADY BURNING

The scenario above, with minor variations, is the most commonly used approach and evidentiary standard for culture change in organizations today. Here's the problem: in modern cognitive science terms, and more importantly the lived experience of most people in your organization, nothing much will have changed. And this means the success of your corporate transformation, whether it's an attempt to double or triple in size in two years, become a digital disruptor as a pre-digital player, execute a turnaround or any other major change, is already in doubt. It's in doubt because you will have tried to get beyond that invisible wall called culture with naïve methods. Not for lack of trying, but for lack of knowledge for what culture is and how it really works.

Viewed through the lens of the last 30 years in cognitive anthropology, psychology, linguistics, sociology, cultural neuroscience, and artificial intelligence – every aspect of our thought experiment is flawed. The assumptions behind it are based on theories that are outmoded, incomplete, limited, or as is most often the case, not based on any theory at all but instead reliant upon some kind of gut feel or wishful thinking. In other words, much of how businesses typically approach culture is based on myth. There are five popular myths in particular that need close scrutiny. Understanding what they are and why they are myths is the first step toward becoming a more sophisticated culture and change leader.

MYTH 1: CULTURE STARTS AT THE TOP

This myth is so deeply entrenched in the pop-culture-of-culture that few of us ever stop and ask where this idea comes from or whether it is supported by any theory, research, or independent evidence. We take for granted that leaders, especially the CEO, "set" the culture. Even corporate boards now take this as conventional wisdom.[2] This idea tends to play out in two ways: leaders set the culture by "setting the tone", that is, saying the culturally desired things in the culturally desired way, or by demonstrating behavior that people will emulate and somehow, as if by osmosis, pass down through the organization.

Leadership and culture are related. The question is whether they are related in the way we think they are, which is to presume a causal link between them. The cognitive science suggests not. As with all things with culture, the relationship between leadership and culture is complex. One could say leadership is necessary but not sufficient for culture, but even that is not true: cultures form just as well without leaders.

Value Engineering and Self-Enhancement

The mythology that connects leadership and culture has two major origins. The first one is the idea of *value engineering*, the desire of leaders to leave their legacies imprinted on their organizations by projecting their own ideologies, beliefs, and values (Martin & Frost, 2011). The need for legacy fuels a belief that organizational productivity can be achieved without overt intervention, as if by magic. ING Bank founder Arkadi Kuhlmann epitomizes this belief: "With the right culture, the problems of commitment, alignment, and motivation go away and hierarchy becomes irrelevant" (from Heskett, 2011, p. 42). Leaders like Kuhlmann make the connection between leadership and culture an article of faith. A recent study of how CEOs and CFOs think about culture conducted by John Graham of Duke University and his colleagues bears this out. They found that the majority believe culture to be an "invisible hand" at "work inside of each of the employees that helps to guide their decisions and judgments in a way that the overall corporation would desire it to be" (Graham et al., 2017, p. 1).

This belief owes its origin in part to the work of Douglas McGregor, one of the most influential thinkers in modern management the late 1950s and early 1960s and father of "Theory X" and "Theory Y". Drawing on the work of Kurt Lewin and Lewin's students, Lippitt and White and their ideas about autocratic versus democratic management (Adelman, 1993), McGregor's Theory X is the idea that employees are inherently unmotivated and dislike work, so managerial control, coercion, manipulation, and close supervision are needed to achieve business outcomes. Theory Y is the antidote: the creative capacity of people and their human potential is underutilized. People inherently want autonomy and responsibility in problem-solving and accomplishing goals; therefore, the leader's job is to create the conditions by which people can do and be at their best. McGregor's groundbreaking work helped fuel a corresponding interest in corporate culture in the 1970s; culture was the vehicle by which Theory Y could be realized, a view popular to this day (Kunda, 1992). Culture, thus, is *how* you drive employee productivity. Therefore, it must be central to the CEO's agenda. Or so the logic goes.

It's What Good Leaders Do

Another explanation resides in the wider social history of the United States and how that has shaped views of leadership. Because U.S. business ideas and values figure so prominently in Western conceptions of business, certain features of U.S. social history are relevant. We *want* to believe leaders shape culture because it is deeply consistent with socio-historical ideals of what good leaders are *supposed* to do. Mental models of individualism, self-reliance, and self-perfection prevalent since the 17th century from Calvinist, Quaker, and Scot immigrant groups, forged through the experience of survival and colonization of a wild continent, have evolved into dominant U.S. American cultural assumptions about leadership.[3] The American ideal of what Stanford's Joanne Martin (2002) calls leader "self-enhancement" is fused with an idealized and popularly reinforced belief in great individual leadership as the key variable that maximizes profits. It's accomplished through the creation of an organization molded in the leader's benevolent and striving self-image. This compelling logic reinforces the CEO and top management's creativity, humanism and technical brilliance while perpetuating the general exultation of leadership that dominates U.S. business and popular culture – and fuels a $14 billion dollar industry in the U.S.[4]

Mainstream conceptions of corporate culture allow these popular narratives to persist unchecked by contrary evidence or unclouded by epistemic doubt. It is simply conventional wisdom that leaders directly shape culture with their own beliefs, values, and ideologies, like molding clay.

From the perspective of modern cognitive science, this is naïve. There are five big problems with this view, and each needs to be unpacked to fully debunk the leader-culture myth. These are: *(1) leaders overestimate their own influence; (2) complex social change is much more a function of social ties and network characteristics than individual leader influence; (3) a leader's beliefs or ideologies need to be already present in a social system for those ideas to take hold; (4) culture is not personality writ large;* and *(5) language alone does not change culture.*

Problem 1: Leaders Overestimate Their Own Influence

Leaders tend to believe they are much more influential than they really are. This is part of a well-studied broader phenomenon of optimistic and egocentric bias in individual decision-making famously documented by Daniel Kahneman and Amos Tversky in 1973. Because individuals expect that their own behavior will produce success, they are more likely to attribute good outcomes to their actions, and bad outcomes to bad luck. For example, 94 percent of men rate themselves in the top half of male athletic ability. A vast majority of people say they are above average drivers.[5]

Executives are particularly prone to overconfidence (Ormerod, 2005). For example, in a study of Forbes 500 CEOs, researchers demonstrated that CEOs systematically overestimate the return of their investment projects when sufficient internal funds are available, and are not held back by capital markets or corporate governance constraints. But when funds are insufficient, they are reluctant to issue new equity because they perceive their company's stock is undervalued (Malmendier & Tate, 2005). Similarly, in a marketing strategy exercise, a group of corporate presidents consistently overestimated their abilities to overtake established competition (Larwood & Whittaker, 1977).[6] It extends to hiring: leaders overstate the features and benefits of their own cultures to job applicants.[7] And as if this point needed further proof, a recent Gartner survey with over 7500 employees and 190 HR leaders shows that what leaders say and how they behave impacts only 1 percent of the alignment between the workforce and culture.[8]

Leadership overconfidence tends to be most prevalent when tasks are difficult, when competition is based on one's own perceived skill, and in situations lacking quick and clear feedback.[9] It's no wonder in the realm of culture, CEO's feel as if they have inordinate influence: it's prone to all of these conditions.

Problem 2: Complex Change Does Not Happen through Individual Influence

Malcolm Gladwell's bestseller, *The Tipping Point* (2000) suggested that exceptional and highly connected people change the world. Certainly, individual influencing skills play a role in change. But the real story is quite a bit more complicated.

The research on social diffusion makes clear that key influencers are no more likely to be influential in complex change than average employees. Without sufficient social structure to bring people together – offices, functions, departments, project teams, affinity groups, and similar formal and informal organizational structures – the spread of cultural norms and practices is highly unlikely. Damon Centola (2018, 2015) at the University of Pennsylvania has done what amounts to the most extensive research to date on how complex social change, such as a change to cultural norms and practices, occurs. Using sophisticated modeling algorithms, he shows how social networks are the product of relationships formed by individuals based on common interests and motivations, as well as by institutional factors such as roles and organizational structures. Social ties are not random: we affiliate with those who share our interests and concerns, as well as those who live and work in physical or organizational proximity to us. This directs as well as limits our everyday interactions. The diffusion of complex change requires opportunity for interaction; the greater the social distance between people, the fewer opportunities they will have to form ties.[10] And complex change requires that networks enable rather than preclude diffusion. Social systems that are too siloed, like islands, preclude diffusion, as do networks in systems with too many weak social ties. Complex social change requires social "contagion" effects, which Centola labels as complementarity, credibility, legitimacy, and emotional contagion.[11]

While it might take an influential leader to establish the idea of a movement, complex change is not possible without these network dynamics. In none of these scenarios is a key leader or influencer the central change diffusion agent.

Problem 3: For a Leader's Beliefs to Take Hold in the Organization, They Have to Be There to Begin With

The extent to which a leader's own beliefs influence the behavior of the majority depends on the pre-existing distribution of those beliefs among employees.[12] Research on the impact of norms on behavior shows that descriptive norms – what people actually do – impacts a target group only when most individuals in the group already behave in the desired way (Cialdini, 1991). For example, more littering occurs in already-littered environments than in clean environments.[13] The dynamics of this process are the same as for values and beliefs in general, discussed later in this chapter.

In cases where it appears as if a leader's beliefs are widely adopted, what actually may be happening is better explained by the cognitive science of culture: shared cognitions adopted because of the influence of a dominant occupational group – software engineers in software companies, lawyers in law firms – or because the organization successfully overcame a tough challenge (see Chapter 3 onward). What appears to be the adoption of the leader's belief in the organization may have more to do with the alignment between the organization's task focus and the leader's professional background, or the fact the leader's strategy or vision proved successful (Schein, 1992).

Problem 4: Culture Is Not the Sum of Personalities (The Leaders' or Anyone Else)

Culture and Personality theorists from the first half of the 20th century believed cultures could be analyzed based on personality type.[14] But whereas culture and personality theorists saw this relationship as a complex system, managers, consultants, and business-school academics have tended to view this relationship literally, suggesting that over time organizations adopt the personalities of their leaders.[15] These positions tend to be based on a set of assumptions that seem reasonable on the face of it but become more problematic the closer one examines them.

Take the need for achievement. If CEOs did not need to achieve they wouldn't be CEOs. So the idea that somehow organizations manifest "achievement" orientations within their own strategies and structures, as some researchers suggest, is circular (Wood & Vilkinas, 2004). And the idea that a collective of personalities can produce a corresponding culture seems plausible, but it is based on a couple of shaky assumptions. The first is that organizations tend to recruit their own such that "organizations actually end up choosing people who share many common personal attributes ... In other words accountants in YMCAs should share many personal attributes with YMCA social workers, while they share only some very specific competencies with accountants in banks" (Schneider, 1987, p. 448). Cognitive science suggests the exact *opposite*: what you habitually do and how you have been professionally socialized shape how you think. Accountants will generally always have more in common with fellow accountants than with social workers because their own professionalization process will neurologically induce shared logics and values with other accountants. The same is true for pilots, engineers, lawyers, biologists, marketers, nurses, construction workers, and every other occupational group where professional socialization plays a role (see Chapter 3).

The second is that the structures and processes in organizations come about because the people in them want to "facilitate the accomplishments of the goals of the founder" (p. 448). It is unclear how this would actually work in any large organization: the relationship between CEO personality and culture has not been systematically observed in any organization larger than a start-up. In fact, the relationship is often in the other direction: cultures can exert a profound influence on how leaders are socialized. One of the few longitudinal studies that bears this out was conducted in the 1980s at an electronics manufacturer in Silicon Valley. Researchers there found many of the concerns and interpretations of company founders were not shared over time by employees. Those that were could be explained by other contingent factors, such as constraints due to business cycles, or salience and attribution bias by employees.[16]

There is yet another problem with the culture-is-personality view. To empirically establish a connection between personality and culture, stable and observable constructs must exist for both. If one or both cannot be reliably measured, the idea of a personality–culture link remains an urban myth. To make this link requires several leaps of faith. One is that categorization schemes – the basis of most personality and culture assessments – are universal. Anthropologists and cultural psychologists have known for years that systems of categorization – names for colors, plants, next of kin, navigation references, conceptualizations of the self – all vary across cultures.[17] So asking people from multiple social or cultural groups to judge a given culture based on a personality type is unreliable (this is a general problem in all externally derived culture assessments). Another is the presumption that personality traits (e.g., agreeableness, extroversion, conscientiousness) are reliable across cultures. Cognitive anthropologists raised doubts as to whether personality factors in assessments such as the "Big 5" and Minnesota Multiphasic Personality Inventory (MMPI) actually measure personality rather than similarities in the meaning of the tested terms (e.g., *friendly* positively correlated with *sociable*; *cleverness* correlated with *inventiveness*).[18] This also has to do with the level of abstraction used to define the construct in question: the greater the degree of abstraction (*"prepared"*, *"team player"*, *"smart"*) the more "universal" a trait can appear to be (Hui & Triandis, 1986). They concluded that individual personality traits cannot be reliably described in language free of context, so broader assertions about culture based on them is dubious (Shweder, 1991).[19]

It's seductive and facile to think the personality of the leader can be imprinted onto her own organization. It's easy thinking because it reduces the complexities of culture to individuals and their traits, which proves convenient for an industry trying to sell culture consulting services, as well as for industrial-organizational (I/O) psychologists who have outsize influence in business schools (see next chapter).

Problem 5: Language Alone Does Not Change Culture

When the President of the United States can make racist and inflammatory comments on Twitter one day and a mass shooting related to racism occurs on the next, it's tempting to claim language impacts culture. The emphasis on internal marketing in our thought experiment, on leaders "setting" culture by what they say, is based on this same assumption. We assume if we just get the words right, *that* will produce the behavior we want. This belief is so deeply embedded in the pop-culture-of-culture that even American football coaches and sportswriters extol the virtues of motivational slogans on T-shirts to instill a culture.[20] This is one reason why culture change is often approached as a problem for the corporate communications team.

Organizations do need leaders to establish compelling visions and purpose, and evangelize desired values and behaviors. Leaders should indeed set aspirational goals or inspire a desired future state, for that is something leaders are uniquely positioned to do. But is that the same thing, or enough, to directly cause a culture to come about? Most companies assume it is.

Words can incite behavior. But the question is not whether some words compel action, but whether language alone can permanently change culture. This emphasis on language reflects a decades-old debate in cognitive science about whether language shapes, rather than reflects, how people think.[21] But this debate has been largely resolved: cognitive linguists have demonstrated convincingly we have many more thoughts, ideas, and feelings than we can speak or write. Cultural knowledge is more than what can be conveyed through words alone.[22] Language may reflect some aspect of a culture, yes, but it should not be assumed language *is* culture. Language plays a role in what is collectively meaningful, as we shall see in later chapters. But to assume language is the same as culture is to assume the tip is the whole iceberg. The prevailing view now is that language and culture in any society are *parallel* systems with overlaps and touch points that reflect, support, or at times serve as adaptations to each other.[23] How language operates, and how it evolves or resists change often gives clues to culture itself. Language can be a valuable window into culture. In fact, many of the research methods used by cognitive anthropologists to study cultural logics are based on language. But to expect slogans or posters or beautiful speeches will shift a culture is nowhere near enough. It's like putting a sail on the tip of your iceberg and hoping the iceberg goes in the direction you want.[24]

> Tip: Language matters, but less than you might think. Without reinforcing practices, clever pronouncements or marketing campaigns amount to little in culture change.

Leadership and Culture: There Is a Connection

My point is not to contest the importance of leadership, relieve CEOs of setting aspirational goals, or absolve them of the responsibility for creating humane and psychologically safe environments where people can bring their whole selves to do their best work. I do mean to cast doubt on the idea of a linear and causal relationship between leadership and culture. Leaders have *something* to do with culture. It's just more complicated than the myth.

A more precise way to think about the relationship between leadership and culture is through the constructs of *purpose* and *power*. Leaders frame the organization's core mission and purpose. The extent that purpose motivates the majority (itself a complex process and never a given) will contribute to the formation of shared logics among the majority. Leaders set agendas and priorities, allocate capital, set aside resources, establish accountability structures, and determine rewards. These actions influence organizational *practices* that shape how people think and act. Practices are key to culture change because they change brain chemistry. Even in the most well-publicized cases of charismatic leadership ostensibly shaping culture (for example, Ray Dalio at Bridgewater, Herb Kelleher at Southwest), on closer examination one sees organizational practices at the heart of the shaping.

The bottom line: leaders are *one input* into culture, albeit a *potentially* important one.

> Tip: Leaders would see a lot more ROI for their culture investment if they prioritized holding their organizations accountable for prac-tices supportive of a desired future state than simply evangelizing their beliefs.

MYTH 2: CULTURE IS A PHYSICAL THING

If I were to say, "culture is a box" or "culture is a machine", you would know what I'm really trying to say is "culture is *like* a box", or "culture is *like* a machine". You would automatically supply the missing simile because these expressions make no sense otherwise. We know culture is, literally, not a box. Yet we commonly think of culture as a physical object with shape, size, defining characteristics, force, or even a character that compels us to do or not do certain things. Think of the many ways in which we talk about culture: *we need to put it in the culture; we are a male-dominated culture; our culture drove our success; our culture won't allow us to do that*, and hundreds of expressions like these common in business. They're not just figures of speech: consulting and market research firms routinely come out with reports such as *Creating a Culture that Performs*.[25] We know cultures aren't literally performers, but we speak and act as if they are. But where, exactly, *is* that culture? Can you touch it? Can you make it perform, like a trained animal? Can you trim the parts you don't want, like pruning a tree? Can you fine-tune it, like a sports car? Can you talk to it? Can it talk to you? You get the point. Why do we do this?

Problem: Culture Doesn't Exist – or Does It?

Culture does not actually exist. At least that's the contemporary cognitive anthropological view. It has visible manifestations – symbols, stories, jargon, behavior, rituals, physical artifacts, and so on, but these are the products of culture, not culture itself. Culture in the modern cognitive view is a phenomenon of mind, a so-called *epiphenomenon* – a mental state caused by and accompanying something that happens in the physical world. But we take it as real, thinking, and acting as if it has power over us. This is due, in part, to a fundamental feature of cognition: *we think in analogies*. We make sense of abstract things in terms of what we have physically experienced, and a large part of that knowledge is built up analogically over time from childhood.[26] Which is why we talk and act as if much of the world around us – "the economy", "society", "the organization" – are actual, physical things. Think of the way we characterize corporate mergers – *fighting, mating,* or *marriage* – as if a merger literally is one of these things. So with culture. You might observe its effects, but this does not make culture real in the same way as machinery, or even money.

Yet, as a mental state, culture has a vital function. This is because maintaining social cohesion amid multiple fragmentary and potentially conflicting social groups requires a regulating function. Culture, in fact, is an evolutionary adaptation for ensuring biological survival (Lehmann & Dunbar, 2009). It is believed that the evolutionary ability for humans to integrate cultural knowledge into a cohesive worldview may have allowed the development of self- and other identities as well as kinship systems, among other cultural phenomena (Vorhees, Read, and Gabora, 2020). The evolutionary anthropologist Stephen Levinson outlines this idea brilliantly in his 2006 account of the culture of Rossel Islanders. Rossel Island lies about 500 km off the coast of New Guinea, the easternmost island in the Louisiade Archipelago of which New Guinea is the largest. By virtue of its location and being surrounded by dangerous reefs, the population had little contact with Western shipping until the mid-1900s, and a resident Catholic mission was only established in 1953. This makes it culturally distinct (although by no means frozen in time) and ideal for studying cultural evolution and change in a relatively isolated society. Levinson records how many aspects of Rossel cultural knowledge, such as practices related to food cultivation and storage, helped the islanders recover from the devastating effects of cyclone Justin in March 1997 with almost no outside help. This is a clear example of how cultural practices help a society recover from catastrophe and ensure its own survival.[27]

Culture Doesn't Make Us Do Anything

But a key distinction needs to be made. Culture doesn't make us *do* anything. Culture is background knowledge; a tacit system people use as a resource, one available to be made use of at any time – like knowing what to do to recover from a devasting cyclone. What it is not is a causal force. At any given moment an individual might consciously or unconsciously think or act in ways contrary to the prevailing system, as when we land in a foreign country and before we even leave the airport discover how hailing a taxi is very different from anything experienced before. At that moment we have a choice: act in the ways we know how to get a cab, or try to "read" the scene to act in accordance with what seems to be happening (how many culturally awkward moments have been observed by foreigners who attempt to behave as they would at home in the face of very different local norms?).

By *essentializing* culture – thinking of it as something tangible and real that makes us do or not do certain things – we diminish its true value as a resource. We fool ourselves into thinking we can manage culture like any other asset: "target" what you want to "fix" (e.g. more collaboration) and then fix it. This leads us to conceive of culture as no different than inventory, something to catalog, box up, warehouse, and manage its supply and demand. Thinking of culture in this way leads to a host of other problems, discussed below. When we stop thinking of culture as a physical thing and start understanding it as a resource of knowledge, we begin to see how, where, and why it can be as influential as it is. Much like Rossel Islanders rebuilding their communities.

MYTH 3: ONE COMPANY, ONE CULTURE

One problem in thinking of culture as a real thing is that it leads us to the idea of "one company, one culture". The classic ethnographers of the early 20th century studying so-called "simple societies", such as Margaret Mead's work on Samoa or Ruth Benedict's on the Zuni, realized early on that the concept of rigid cultural boundaries was of limited use. Yet many leaders, consultants and management scholars persist with literal interpretations of this idea to this day, assuming any "society" such as an organization has a single culture (Sewell, 1999). There are three major problems with this view.

FIGURE 1.1
Margaret Mead in Samoa with Fa'amotu. *Source: Mead, 1995/1972, p. 149.*

Problem 1: Cultural Boundaries Overlap

Consider the case of a Bengali chemical engineer living and working in Houston.[28] This person simultaneously participates in multiple cultures: in U.S. American culture when going to the supermarket or dealing with the internet provider or commuting to work; in Bengali culture when with his family or raising his children; in engineering culture when at work or in the broader professional community of chemical engineers. Each of these cultures has its own language, symbols, judgments, authority figures, norms, and underlying dominant logics. The physical, social, or political boundaries of each is blurred and overlapping, such as when our engineer is at home with his wife watching a basketball game on TV while responding to his employer's corporate culture survey on his laptop. The question is, which of the many cultures in which he participates will this culture survey actually be measuring? And how would those administering the survey know? More importantly, how could any such assessment based on his input be considered useful in light of this fact?

The issue is one of boundaries. Humans exist in environments already considerably shaped by culture; people belong at once to multiple cultures and communities.[29] So it is difficult to presuppose corporate cultural boundaries, especially in diverse, multi-region, or global organizations. Cultural boundaries are highly permeable and changing; people in organizations inhabit multiple pre-existing cultural systems (ethnic, regional, occupational, site, or division-specific, etc.). So much so that some anthropologists doubt the concept of discrete cultures altogether. To think of any sizable organization having a single culture, or a collection of sub-cultures nested within a larger culture, is usually an invention of management or founders promulgated for the reasons stated in the previous section.

Problem 2: Region, Nation, and Language

Not only are cultural boundaries overlapping, they are also highly porous. For example, Meric Gertler (2004) showed how so-called "Silicon Valley culture" in the San Francisco Bay Area contributed to a general environment of cooperation and labor mobility among firms in that region, as opposed to "Route 128 culture" in the greater Boston area in Massachusetts, which discouraged information sharing and labor mobility. Similarly, firms in Emilia-Romagna in Italy share an artisan culture with longstanding social interaction across firms and mutual trust built up over centuries. In Baden-Wurttemberg, Germany, an old, predominant culture of engineering excellence and problem solving allows small and mid-sized *Mittelstand* firms to compete worldwide with much larger ones.

Culture does not end once you step across borders or off corporate property. People bring their "outside" values and cultural knowledge with them wherever they go. Systems of values are not unchanging; they are in flux as people draw from different repertoires of knowledge to make sense of and function within their environments. Therefore, it is no surprise that studies which attempt to show how various organizational behaviors are interpreted across cultures, such as motivation, goal attainment, feedback, rewards, job satisfaction, organizational commitment, teaming, and leadership have trouble replicating consistent results across national boundaries.[30]

Nowhere is this better illustrated than the debate over Geert Hofstede's (1998) famous research on national culture. Hofstede's work was based on attitude surveys conducted between 1967 and 1983 with 88,000 IBM employees. These surveys yielded 117,000 responses and resulted in the development of four dimensions of national culture: *power distance, individual–collectivism, uncertainty avoidance,* and *masculinity–femininity.* His indices have been among the most influential in measuring organizational culture as well (Baskerville, 2003). Not surprisingly, researchers have had difficulties replicating them globally. Among them: Hofstede's *uncertainty avoidance* was not observed in China (Smith & Dugan, 1996). Chanchani (1998) tried to replicate Hofstede's indices in India and New Zealand, but found three out of the five dimensions were opposite to Hofstede's original. And his *Individualist–Collectivist* scale has been shown to not be empirically equivalent – *Individualist* is not the opposite of *Collectivist* (Fiske, 2002).[31]

There are many reasons for these difficulties. One is the simplicity of his measures. Triandis (1996), for example, found over 60 attributes that make up *Individualist* or *Collectivist* cultures. Another is that most cross-cultural measures of culture are based on values, but actual cultural differences (national, regional, or organizational) are a function of many factors such as social norms, occupational roles, basic beliefs, assumptions and theories about the world, and so on.[32] Broad generalizations about culture ignore differences of race, class, gender, or professional orientation. And people interpret rating scales differently across cultures, which produce systematic differences in results, as discussed above. Yet another issue is majority groups in nations (linguistic, ethnic, or religious) develop a stronger sense of attachment to the concept of a nation as a whole than minorities.[33] I have observed this same phenomenon in organizations: top managers typically identify with the cultural norms and values espoused by the top of the house more than the rank and file. Cultural identification is biased in the direction of where one "sits" (in the society or organization), and perhaps as well by an affiliation motive (to affiliate, or at least appear to) with top management.

Problem 3: Network Size Limits Culture

Social networks are constrained by how many individual relationships any human brain can hold and process at one time. This idea was made famous (or infamous depending on who you read) by Gladwell's *Tipping Point* for his take on the evolutionary psychologist Robin Dunbar's so-called "Dunbar's Number". Dunbar's work came from extensive study of social grooming behavior in primates, the study of human social networks, as well as from census data from tribal and traditional societies. Taken together the evidence suggested to Dunbar that the number of actual human relationships any individual can maintain at any one time is about 150 (Dunbar, 1992, 1993).[34] Dunbar and his number have been co-opted and applied to organizational and office design (most notably the Swedish Tax Authority), and, with some justification, criticized for being indiscriminately applied (for example, suggesting anyone with more than 150 Facebook friends can't have that many "true" friends).[35] That said, Dunbar's body of work over four decades is compelling. He readily admits primates can circumvent the limit of 150 to create "multilevel sociality based on weak and strong ties", but that nonetheless the time available for social grooming (the human equivalent is paying attention to one's friends), as well as the number of relationships one can hold in mind at any one time, impose a natural limit on group size (2018, p. 2).

This raises the distinct possibility that cognitive constraints govern how cultures form. Beyond a certain group size, the sense of a single culture may be impossible to attain or sustain. It may be easier to engineer an experience of a common culture in groups of less than 150, which is one reason why smaller companies often appear to have more tangible and cohesive cultures than larger ones.[36] As a company grows, the sense of cohesion morphs into a nostalgic myth that outlives actual lived experience. Founders and executives may hold on to the belief in a cohesive culture based on their experience of the early days even though the company is well beyond the size where a sense of a single culture is the experience of the majority of the people in the company.

In sum, "one company, one culture", may be convenient shorthand to characterize a company or help managers rally the troops, but it has little support in the science, or even in lived cultural reality, in any enterprise larger than a start-up.

MYTH 4: CULTURE IS WHAT WE SAY WE CARE ABOUT

A well-known corporate culture consultant (who shall remain nameless) is famous for publishing posters and wallet-sized cards with catchy and colorful phrases meant to convey the company's values (or perhaps his own). According to those who have been his clients, these phrases mainly serve to generate a lot of off-color bathroom stall humor. Nonetheless, almost every company believes it necessary to publish their desired values, norms, beliefs, tenets, or philosophies in the form of manifestos, such as Netflix's mentioned earlier, or like one of our clients, below (see Figure 1.2).

Organizational norms and values have been a focus for management scholars since it was first suggested in the early 1950s that they pertain to organizations.[37] Most companies put tremendous stock in these things. To be clear, coming up with desired values (or norms, etc.) can often be very beneficial and instructive for a management team to signal what it cares about. The effort is, in fact, one element in creating psychological safety to enable high performing teams.[38] Publishing aspired values when they are meaningful and inspirational for employees is an important part of

Integrity and Respect
Doing the right thing, always.

Accountability
Focusing on results; doing what you say you are going to do.

Continuous Improvement & Innovation
Maintaining a customer focus; improving every day.

Transparency
Demonstrating candor and openly sharing information.

FIGURE 1.2
Example of a statement of beliefs by a corporation.

the change process (see Chapter 5). And they can help with new hires in signaling what is important, or in a merger integration.

Having said that, in my 30 years of corporate experience I am slightly embarrassed to admit I have never read any one of these documents (and if I have I can't remember it).[39] When it comes to instilling culture at the enterprise level, there are many problems with a *tell 'em what we care about* approach, not the least of which is employee cynicism fostered when any one of the espoused items are found wanting in practice.[40] The myth that we can set in place culture by stating what we care about runs deep as corporate orthodoxy. It rests on three assumptions. The first two were already mentioned: cultures are singular wholes, and language shapes culture. The third is that norms and values (and such) are *the* culture. As with many ideas about corporate culture, the relationship between norms, values, and culture has been muddled and oversimplified. A thorough review would take a separate book. The issues extend to all espoused tenets, so only norms and values are discussed here.

Problem 1: Norms Aren't the Whole Story

Shared norms are one important aspect of a culture. But some scholars claim norms *are* culture, and that by solely focusing on them one can shape or manage culture (Chatman & O'Reilly, 2016). This reduces culture to a single variable and leaves a lot of cultural "stuff" out of the picture. And attempting to use norms to define culture comes with several major caveats.

Caveat 1: Context Matters

Leaving aside that most research on norms has been conducted with university students or in the public sphere (e.g., littering) rather than in corporate settings, the first problem is that norms influence behavior under certain conditions, but not in others. And the interplay is complex. For example, Asians are stereotypically known to possess a norm of modesty. But Asians, like U.S. Americans and some Western Europeans also have a need for positive self-regard. In situations where the norm of modesty is not enforced (such as in an anonymous survey response), or where the context provides clear goals (such as winning a tennis match), the Japanese, for one, tend not to adhere to the modesty norm (Takata, 2003). While modesty may be pervasive in Japan, in certain contexts it can be overwritten by individual needs or goals. There is a dynamic interaction between individual motives and cultural knowledge, and that interaction is difficult to prescribe, let alone engineer.[41] When a cultural norm is aligned with individual motives or goals, the norm can push behavior in the desired direction in some contexts. But that same norm aligned with different motives or in a different context can push behavior in the opposite direction.

As we saw with leadership pronouncements, the degree to which a given norm influences behavior depends on the preexistence of the desired norm in the organization. If what is desired is foreign, or foreign for some, the chance of instilling it throughout your company will be low.

Caveat 2: Group Membership Matters

There is a complex interplay between injunctive norms (what we should do) and descriptive norms (what we actually do) relating to what the norm is about and group membership. When norms originate from a group of which one is not a member, they have a minimal influence on behavior and attitudes (Smith & Louis, 2008).[42] So if group membership is a factor in determining whether a given norm drives behavior, this presents problems. What constitutes an ingroup or outgroup? Simply assuming everyone in the organization identifies as part of the ingroup is naïve and inconsistent with our discussion on cultural boundaries, or the lived experience of people in an organization of any size. On the other hand, when the norm originates from a group of which one is a member, it can impact behavior. This idea is entirely consistent with the notion that occupational norms (anchored by shared logics) coming from occupational groups who wield power and influence can be a foundational element of culture (e.g., software engineers in software firms, doctors in HMOs).

Caveat 3: Task Matters

When the physical task is highly congruent with the norm, there is a higher likelihood that behavior will follow the norm (Handwerker, 2009). For example, tribes like the Shoshone of North America's Great Basin or the San of the Kalahari suffered from an inability to control the location and timing of a relatively small food supply, requiring them to live in small, mobile camps and move frequently. Sharing – of food and other resources – was a vitally important norm because of the lack of assurance any family or clan would survive solely on their own. As a result, rules concerning visitation and marriage arose between camps which, upon marriage, compelled people to move to different camps from where they had been raised, further solidifying the sharing norm. This might seem like an anecdote far removed from corporate life, yet numerous studies show how norms follow task and necessity, from airline pilots to architects to construction workers.[43] Daley (2001), for example, showed how the attitudes of lawyers, nurses, social workers, and adult educators were shaped by the normative expectations of their own professional roles and tasks, which is highly consistent with research on how culture relates to profession and task.

The problem is most executives publish what they wish for without thinking through how their wishes relate to or are aligned with the core business. A good example of this comes from one of our manufacturing clients that wants to speed up how it does business, from decision-making to customer responses to overall management. This worthy goal is accompanied by a catchy phrase, *"speed is the new IP!"* Unfortunately, when overlaid onto the realities of a manufacturing company with extensive financial controls and hierarchical decision-making, this norm has no impact. People repeat the phrase like a mantra, but the time it takes to make a decision, fulfill an order, or run any other part of the business is virtually unchanged. The desired norm is not aligned in any way with company practices, which are still tightly coupled, necessarily so, with the core tasks of manufacturing.

For all of these reasons, reducing culture to norms is highly problematic. It pushes a lot of what constitutes culture out of the picture and leaves many unanswered questions: how do norms account for other kinds of cultural knowledge, such as standards of "good", or idealizations? How do norms account for cultural practices, such as how to allocate budgets? How do norms account for cultural symbols, stories, or jargon? How do norms explain what people find meaningful? And how do norms explain why cultures are so hard to change? If it was simply a matter of putting forward injunctive norms (the norms we want), it would have been done and documented long ago.

The Problem with Culture as Values

Research on values has a long tradition in cross-cultural psychology and anthropology.[44] As such, many business-school academics tend to think of values as *the* defining element of a culture (for example, Chatman & Jehn, 1994). Values and beliefs are the basis for several influential culture frameworks, such as the Competing Values Framework (Cameron & Quinn, 1999), and those focused on person–organization fit, such as the Organizational Culture Profile (O'Reilly, Chatman, & Caldwell, 1991). Values are relatively easy to understand and apply. Managers believe they can gain leverage over the workforce by substituting one set of values for another. And common values can be seen as a way to ensure harmony and employee engagement. If we supply the "right" values, people will be happier and more productive.

Values matter. But can culture be described *exclusively* in terms of them? Can we change culture simply by telling people what they should value – through posters, training programs, rewards, evangelism, or other entreaties?[45] There are many problems with this.

Problem 1: "Values" Means Different Things to Different People

The word can mean "goodness", "preference", "price", "worth", or "moral right" (D'Andrade, 2008, pp. 8–11). In some languages like Japanese or Vietnamese, there are no translations of the term (Maltseva & D'Andrade, 2011). Different cultures ascribe different meanings to particular values. For example, an African American might think of equality in terms of race, whereas a Chinese might think of equality as social equality. Reliability studies focusing on how value importance ratings are interpreted by Chinese, Singaporean Chinese, and U.S. Americans show low agreement across these groups, and low test-retest reliability for Chinese participants.[46] While such studies have not been conducted across all national groups, similar to the difficulties replicating Hofstede's scales, making generalizations about corporate values based on values assessments may not be globally replicable. This is problematic for any international or global organization that thinks its "culture" applies to everyone. This problem shows up in academic research on culture as well: some define values as "basic concepts" and "beliefs", a lack of precision that muddies the concept and dilutes the efficacy of the research.[47]

Problem 2: Values Are Expectations, Not Behaviors

Values are *idealized* notions about how the world *should* be, not how it is actually perceived (D'Andrade, 2008). Differences in values have to do with differences in what one is *expected* to hold as a member of a particular institution or society rather than personal and subjective experience (Maltseva & D'Andrade, 2011). Thus, scales such as *individual–collectivism* measure the ways one should live, not necessarily the way things are, so evaluations about organizations based on this scale, or others like it, need to be interpreted as expectations.

For this reason, similar values often lead to different behaviors. For example, values of egalitarianism and social equality held by the Democratic party in the U.S., such as whether members of the LGBTQ community have the same rights as other minorities, will manifest differently when applied in the deep South versus New England. Thus, when a company claims that it values, say, collaboration (as most do), what it is really saying is that it believes collaboration *should* matter. This is quite different than saying the company is collaborative.[48]

Problem 3: Values Need to Be Already Socialized to Be Adopted

Similar to norms, for values to function as *shoulds*, the values need to already be present in the target population (D'Andrade, 2006). The more diverse and heterogeneous an organization is in terms of professional groups, technology, market segments, industries, or regions of the world in which it operates, the likelihood of values being universally shared and already socialized will be low. One study from the health care industry showed that organizational values *congruent* with employee values did increase employee satisfaction, commitment, and performance (Fitzgerald & Desjardins, 2010). But the key word is "congruent". When the values of leaders or founders happen to overlap with employee values, the chances of those values being adopted increases. Which is one reason why common values appear to be more easily instilled in smaller organizations.

Problem 4: Some Values Are Compensations for Deeper Cultural Forces

Yet another issue is mistaking the symptom for the cause. Making assumptions about any community's culture based on the values it publicly advocates misses the fact values may be reactions to or compensations for unconscious beliefs or orientations, or even opposite to actual behaviors or practices. One example comes from the Baktaman of western New Guinea. The Baktaman are known for their sharing norms which lead, more or less, to equal living standards. But they lack any publicly stated value of generosity. The Balinese, on the other hand, have large differences in wealth, but explicitly value generosity.[49]

A given set of values may be so accepted and routine within a community that they reside below conscious awareness. Societies often have dominant ideologies, but rarely do these present a "single, clearly defined, well-integrated reality" (Strauss, 1992, p. 11). One of the best examples of ideology lacking a "well-integrated reality" is in the United States, a country with an espoused ideology of equality enshrined into the Declaration of Independence but where the wealthiest 10 percent of American households control nearly 75 percent of household net worth. The U.S. is ranked among the top ten most *un*equal countries in the world.[50] Or, take a corporate example: a technology client of ours states it values open communication and goodwill. In our research there, however, we observe "robust" thinking and mastery of one's "craft" to be widely held implicit attitudes on what is considered "good". In practice, this gets in the way of "goodwill": it's difficult to have goodwill when your default mode is to judge whether a coworker actually knows his stuff. Nonetheless, these public values are expressed because the organization believes they *should* be important (what organization wouldn't?). They are a socially acceptable way to address and compensate for a perceived deficit. This is why publicly expressed values should never be confused with actual values in lived experience; they are likely compensations or the idealizations of top management (Schein, 1992).

Problem 5: Values Cannot Be Instilled by Telling People What to Value

Many companies and consultants (like our friend whose work is immortalized in the men's room) believe culture can be transmitted, basically, by telling people what to believe and how to behave. Societies do inculcate dominant values in its members, for this is critical to the survival and continuity of the society. But their transmission is never straightforward. As every parent knows, getting a child to buy-in to desired values or beliefs is not simply a matter of communicating them. Transmission is more complicated because the realities of the social order are more complicated. If the social environment of the child was hermetically sealed so that somehow it was forever unchanging and unambiguous, there would be no need to study how social messages are understood and appropriated. The meaning of the society's messages would be immediately clear to any child that learned them (Strauss, 1992). Alas, the world, organizations included, doesn't work that way. What the receiver receives is always mediated and filtered by individual life experience and context at the moment of reception.

For example, one of our clients, a Fortune 1000 industrial, explicitly values integrity and expects this value to be held by all employees. The value is communicated in written artifacts and public statements both internally and externally, and the company has an active social responsibility arm and an environmental non-profit subsidiary, reinforcing the public perception that the company cares about integrity. And yet, surveys show mixed results on measures of trust, a surprising result for a company espousing integrity.[51] On the face of it, a company that values integrity might be expected to be one where adequate trust is discernable.[52] Here is yet another example of the complexities involved in trying to inculcate a value by expressing it as an expectation. This simple idea is among the most often missed when we think culture equals values.

Lived Culture

What all this amounts to is a sharp divide between what is *espoused* – what we say we want – and what is actually lived and practiced in organizations. Published organizational values can only be read as what is wished for by management, not what is lived by employees. Values cannot be commanded. You don't need a professional ethnographer to see this: a short visit to websites such as Glassdoor, or a few pointed and candid conversations with employees will often reveal a distinct gap between espoused values and lived culture. Yet we persist in thinking that what we espouse *is* the culture. This might be, in part, because some organizations appear to have expressed values that are indeed aligned with lived experience. These are oft-cited cases like Southwest Airlines, Netflix, Nucor, and more recently (and problematically) Amazon (see Kantor & Streitfeld, 2015), among others. While these examples can often be overblown – conversations with insiders typically reveal a much more complex and nuanced story, it is often claimed that values are *the* reason for a company's success.[53] The attribution is misplaced. Values don't drive success; rather, it's a set of organizational practices highly congruent and aligned with the organization's overarching mission or purpose. Practices are hard to "see" and "read", however, so we fall back to what is easier to think about and attempt to engineer – espoused values.

Tip: There is nothing wrong with establishing a desired set of norms and values. The problem is most companies stop there. They either expect people will somehow magically "get it" and behave accordingly, or they expend significant resources trying to drive conformance. The modern science of the brain shows why this is so often wasted effort, and points to a better way.

MYTH 5: CULTURE IS EMPLOYEE WELL-BEING

Consultants, managers, and pundits will insist that "a company's culture has a direct impact on employee turnover, which affects productivity, and therefore success".[54] This assertion is based on the assumption that culture is synonymous with, or closely linked to how people feel and their attitudes. Understanding how employees feel, in the form of attitudes and opinions, is important; attitudes make up a part of employee engagement, and engagement has been empirically linked to positive business outcomes.[55] But is employee well-being the same as culture? Not so much. There are several problems here.

Problem 1: Attitudes and Opinions Are Not Culture

One of the biggest mistakes managers and practitioners make is confusing culture with employee attitudes and general well-being. This is not semantics. As with language, how employees feel may reflect *some* aspect of a culture, or, as with values, might be compensations *for* something missing or not socially acceptable to express (such as lack of respect). To see this, one need only reflect on one's own feelings as a member of any company, group, or institution.

For example, at Microsoft, I often felt pressure and anxiety to perform at my best in many different situations (giving a presentation, writing an email, formulating an opinion in a meeting, and so forth), because the standards for what constitutes competence and excellence at Microsoft were, at the time, very high. Sloppy work, half-baked ideas, unfounded opinions – these things tended to not get one very far, and reputations of competence mattered greatly even though competence was not explicitly expressed as a value.[56] Feeling anxious was therefore often my emotional state in reaction to this unspoken but widely shared standard. But to characterize Microsoft culture as "anxious" would be flat-out wrong: my reactions were one among 90,000 others, one person's reaction to a dominant logic. Other employees had different reactions to this same standard (excitement, competitiveness, exhilaration, antagonism, and so on). Their feelings, like mine, would be subject to change based on specific context, events, individual motives, needs, and goals evolving over time. Attitudes, opinions, states of well-being, feelings – all of these matter in leadership and change, but they are not culture. Culture may be what is giving rise to these personal emotional states to begin with. At Microsoft, competence was (and is) a dominant logic anchoring many cultural practices. But when we zero in on attitudes as our definition of culture, we are liable to be registering attitudes *about* culture, not measuring culture itself.

Problem 2: How We Behave Does Not Reflect How We Feel (or Think)

The other major problem with confusing feelings, attitudes, and such (as well as norms or values) for culture is that the way someone behaves may not actually reflect their attitudes, beliefs, or how they feel.[57] Studies on the relationship between people's self-reports about their own attitudes and observed behavior show, at best, low or weak correlations.[58] People's predictions about how they will behave in the future are inaccurate; hypothetical decisions do not reliably match actual ones. For example, in hypothetical scenarios about risk and money, people tend to be moderately risk-averse when the amount of money at stake is hypothetical, but dramatically more risk-averse when actual money is used.[59] Tim Wilson and Dan Gilbert (2003) have shown through numerous studies on impact bias that people have a tendency to overestimate the impact future events will have on how they feel. Memory for past emotional states is also poor: people tend to overestimate the impact a past event had on their emotions at the time: they reconstruct how they felt in the past based on how they feel about the event in the present. The implications for culture are significant: if the memory of past emotions or expectations of feelings in the future are systematically subject to bias and distortion, then reliably asserting anything about a given culture based on self-reports about how people feel, felt, or will feel, is nearly impossible.

Problem 3: Measuring Items Out of Range

There are still more problems with thinking attitudes are culture. One is that a survey cannot test for items out of range. What makes it on to the survey to begin with is a function of the survey giver's own assumptions and biases. If an item is not on a survey, it can't be measured. But who is to say non-tested items are not equally or more important than those being tested? This is a problem for all attitude and culture survey instruments in general, especially those that impose measures of culture divined by the researcher based on absolute types (*Individualist–Collectivist*; *clan-adhocracy*, etc., so-called "etic" measures).[60,61]

When we mistake attitudes, opinions, or employee well-being for culture we chase the wrong variable. This is one reason why so many culture interventions don't deliver on expected results. The good news, I suppose, is that the direction of bias on self-evaluations of emotional states or attitudes, while not very predictive of behavior, is not random: it's in the direction of some kind of norm. People seem to remember a system of underlying rules or a pattern better than actual facts or events. This is highly consistent with the cognitive view of culture.[62]

> *Tip: Culture is not how people feel. One of the biggest mistakes change leaders and practitioners make is in thinking employee well-being and happiness is culture. How employees feel does relate to business outcomes, but those feelings may be a reaction to or a compensation for some deeper aspect of culture.*

The Gap between Myth and Science

The great French anthropologist Claude Levi-Strauss wrote that the aim of mythology is to ensure the future remains faithful to the present and the past.[63] In many respects these culture myths are no different. They are well-intended endeavors to predict and mitigate the future, something every corporate leader would give up a lot to know. So deconstructing them may feel de-stabilizing, a heretical challenge, akin to claiming in the 15th century that the ships you commissioned to explore the new world would not fall off the edge of the earth.

You might respond by dismissing these issues as narrow objections. Arguing whether values or attitude surveys are predictive, for example, or how social networks really function, taken individually may seem

FIGURE 1.3
Deconstructing popular myths about culture is like claiming the ships you commissioned to explore the new world will not fall off the edge of the earth. *Source: Shutterstock.com.*

like technical objections. The problem is, there are a lot of objections. When you add them all up based on what the modern science has to say, the myths fall apart. Complicating things is the fact culture shaping is usually well-intended: happier employees, better productivity, improved financial performance, and satisfied shareholders. We want these myths to be true because our intentions are honorable. We want to predict the future and bring order and predictability to what is a very complex and dynamic world, one only getting more so by the day. And we don't like to be reminded that our honorable intentions aren't having much of an impact. But when you add up these objections it becomes clear our popular notions of culture are built on seismic fault lines, much like houses in the San Francisco Bay Area. Sooner or later these faults rip. Each and everyone one of these myths is founded on outdated science, misconceptions, half-truths, over-simplification, or just plain wishful thinking. Which explains why so much culture change and shaping doesn't go according to plan or deliver the hoped-for financial results. The next chapter explores where these myths come from and why they have stuck with us as long as they have.

In this era of massive disruption and social change forcing organizations to fundamentally rethink business models and transform or risk obsolescence, there is a material cost to holding on to myths. There is a cost to ignorance. The cost is deferred, in the same way continuing to smoke relieves stress in the moment even though it will eventually kill you.

So the bigger question is, what does it take to give up on myths?

NOTES

1. This is Netflix's description of the traits and behaviors it desires in its employees. Like thousands of other artifacts in other companies, it consists of statements such as "You are good at using data to inform your intuition" and "You inspire others with your thirst for excellence". This is, of course, a recruitment tool and self-selection reference. It also sounds like thousands of other companies (Source: https://jobs.netflix.com/culture).
2. The law firm Wachtel, Lipton, Rosen, & Katz in their *Spotlight on Boards* newsletter states the board of directors role is to "establish the appropriate 'Tone at the Top' to actively cultivate a corporate culture that gives high priority to ethical standards, principles of fair dealing, professionalism, integrity, full compliance with legal requirements and ethically sound strategic goals".
3. From Handwerker (2009).
4. According to McKinsey (as cited in Pfeffer, 2015, p. 10).
5. See Keller and Aiken (2009); Svenson (1981).
6. This phenomenon has also been demonstrated in professions from clinical psychology to law to entrepreneurs and engineers (Barber & Odean, 2001).
7. See Cable, Aiman-Smith, Mulvey, and Edwards (2000); also Camerer and Lovallo (1999).
8. CEB 2017 Workplace Culture Benchmarking Survey, as cited in the Gartner CHRO Quarterly Forum (2017).
9. Researchers attribute these findings to three factors: CEO illusions of control, a high degree of commitment to good outcomes, and abstract points of reference that make it hard to compare performance with others (Malmendier & Tate, 2005). See also Yates (1990); Griffin and Tversky (1992).
10. This is one reason why creating coalitions and networks of cohesive leadership groups is important for culture change, discussed in later chapters.
11. See Centola (2018, 2015).
12. See Schultz, Nolan, Cialdini, Goldstein, and Griskevicius (2007).
13. This was demonstrated experimentally by Cialdini and colleagues (1991).
14. Lindholm (2007).

15. For example, Schneider and Smith (2004) proposed that organizations become homogenous based on the personalities of the people in them, and this process produces culture. Miller and Droge (1986) suggested the personality traits of the CEO, such as the need for achievement, manifest within the strategy and structures their organizations adopt.

16. See Martin, Sitkin, and Boehm (1985). For similar studies, see Gregory (1983); Van Maanen & Kunda (1989).

17. For example, frames of reference for interpreting rating scales on surveys have been found to be quite different between Koreans and Americans, and Japanese and Americans (Chun, Campbell, & Yoo; Stening & Everett, 1984; Hui & Triandis, 1989). For more, see D'Andrade (1995); Hallowell (1976); Hutchins (1995); Lakoff (1987); Rogoff (1990); Shweder (1991); Beuckelaer, Lievens, and Swinnen (2007).

18. What cognitive anthropologists contest is not the existence of personality traits per se, but whether these ratings measure features of behavior rather than language. It turns out taking personality assessments, cognitively speaking, is quite challenging. Inferring the meaning of a word based on its association (e.g., "smiles easily" with "likes parties") or exclusions (e.g., "gentle" as not related to "managerial") dominate the test taker's thought process so that concepts deemed alike based on language are judged to go together even when they may not in actual behavior.

19. This leads to speculation on whether items in well-known trait studies of culture such as the GLOBE study of national leadership profiles (e.g., *visionary: foresighted, prepared, anticipatory, plans ahead*; *performance oriented: improvement oriented, excellence-oriented*) are measuring observed leadership traits or simply capturing semantic similarity (from Koopman, Den Hartog, Konrad et al., 1999).

20. For example, see Jamison Hensley (2019), writing about John Harbaugh and the Baltimore Ravens.

21. Known as the linguistic relativity problem outline by Edward Sapir and Benjamin Lee Whorf. See Duranti (2009).

22. For more on this see Kronenfeld (2018), or Keller (2011). As put by Keller: "while there is some evidence suggesting language plays a role in shaping thinking, there is no definitive evidence that language is a dominant or even significant influence on conceptual categorization. Language may play a structuring role in some encounters, may support alternative modes of thought and action in others, or may be sidelined, or even contradicted by other modalities such as imagery, emotion or embodied actions" (p. 75).

23. Kronenfeld (2018).

24. In fact, based on how the brain processes figurative language, it is likely that using typical business jargon may not have any impact at all in change scenarios. Studies using fMRI techniques on the location of language comprehension in the brain demonstrate that conventional metaphors (e.g., *sweet dreams*) show more activity in the left hemisphere, while novel metaphors and figurative language (e.g., *our bone density is not like theirs*) show greater activation in the right. Because the right hemisphere is not typically involved in language comprehension, the fact it is being recruited in comprehension of unusual and figurative language suggests such language is more memorable because it takes more integration processing resources (Diaz, Barrett, & Hogstrom, 2011).

25. From Gartner. Not to pick on one firm, but to point out how common and embedded these phrases are in nearly everything we read and discuss on culture. Chapter 2 cites the content of this report in some detail.

26. For a complete review I suggest readers consult my first book, *Rethinking Culture* (2017), which has an entire chapter devoted to embodied cognition. A wonderful, easy to digest primer on this topic is also Lakoff and Johnson's *Metaphor's We Live By* (1980, 2003).
27. See Levinson (2006) for more detail.
28. Adapted from Sewell (2005, pp. 203–204).
29. See Handwerker (2002); Quinn (2011); Strauss (2012).
30. See Gelfand, Erez, and Aycan (2007).
31. As Alan Fiske states, "the samples from the nations that have been studied… (show) no correlation between sample means on IND and COL. Clearly, IND is not the opposite of COL or empirically related at all. Residents of the United States and Canada…are a bit more individualistic and less collectivistic than most others but nowhere near the end of either range" (2002, p. 78).
32. Gelfand et al. (2007).
33. Perhaps the most significant issue with culture interpreted as a whole is language. English-speaking regions are the only ones where empirical evidence for the measurement equivalence of national culture types as observed in organizations is found. Maybe the take-away from all this is the concept of a single culture existing in any sizable organization is being artificially supported by the prevalence of English in the business world. For more, see Sidanius, Feshbach, Levin, and Pratto (1997).
34. Social grooming is the process by which relationships are built up and attended to over time. Individuals invest disproportionately in a small number of close relationships, most likely so as to ensure their effective functioning as a group. In both nonhumans and humans, the quality of a relationship is determined by the amount of time an individual invests in it (Dunbar, 2018).
35. See De Ruiter, Weston, and Lyon (2011).
36. There is empirical evidence that smaller groups perceive social cohesion more than larger ones (Chang & Bordia, 2001).
37. Particularly in the work of Elliot Jaques(1951).
38. For more on this process, see Kepner (1980).
39. Today I read corporate manifestos and values statements with keen interest.
40. Chris Argyris (1995) was one of the first to illustrate the difference between espoused and lived values.
41. See Chiu and Hong (2007); also Pool and Schwegler (2007).
42. On the other hand, Smith and Louis' research suggests injunctive norms exert greater influence on public behaviors, such as overt political action, rather than more private or discreet ones. Left open is the question of whether behavior inside an organization is public or private. The answer most likely is it's both.
43. For example, see Guzman, Stam, and Stanton (2008); Caballero (2006); Gertler (2004); Elliott and Scacchi (2003); Merritt (2000); Abrahamson and Fombrun (1994); Dougherty (1992); Applebaum (1981); Bucher and Stelling (1977).
44. For example, differences in values between U.S. Americans and East Asians have been shown to be based on differences in the way these groups understand causality: U.S. Americans tend to attribute cause to individual traits such as individual initiative and hard work, while East Asians to social obligations and situational factors such as the wishes or needs of the team. This is thought to lead to differences in values. For more on this see Peng, Ames, and Knowles, 2000. These differences extend even to the way East Asians and Americans visually perceive the world. For example, in visual and memory processing experiments, Park and Huang (2012)

found that Westerners process information in the visual field by focusing on central objects, as well as by rules and categories. East Asians tend to view scenes holistically, where the context and the object itself are jointly encoded in memory.

45. I am intentionally omitting a discussion of ethics here as it takes us down a side road. The question of whether a corporation can or should impose its values on an individual is a complex question that veers into the nature of contracts, the moral status of the corporation, the nature of market-based economies, and individual agency. Readers interested in this topic should refer to my first book, *Rethinking Culture* (2017).

46. See Peng, Nisbett, and Wong (1997). This is a measure of convergence between two sets of results of the same measurement for the same sample.

47. For example, see Denison (1990).

48. Another problem with values is that some researchers believe judgments about one's own values are always made in relation to beliefs about the values of others, such as the woman who values the respect of her elders because she believes she cares more about this than her siblings.

49. Example taken from Claudia Strauss (2012) and her example from Fredrik Barth.

50. Suneson and Stebbins, *USA Today* (2019). Inequality measures include Gini coefficient; unemployment rate; GDP per capita; and poverty rate per total population.

51. On an internal survey of trust conducted with 428 global managers and employees, several key markers of trust scored low producing majority "Disagree" or "Neither Agree or Disagree answers.

52. Obviously many factors contribute to this result (many of which have been discussed in this chapter), not the least of which the term *integrity* means different things to different people.

53. Another reason may have to do with our tendency to be loose with language, such that when we say "values" we actually mean "culture".

54. From Eric Siu's blog, *The Statistical Case for Company Culture* (2019).

55. See Huselid (1995). As with findings about culture, the employee engagement literature is also characterized by differences of opinion on the meaning, measurement, and theory of employee engagement. It is difficult to draw clear conclusions about the direction of causality in the engagement literature due to a number of research limitations (Saks & Gruman, 2014).

56. "Intellectual Horsepower" was a Microsoft competency in the late 1990s and early 2000s. But this competency was about intellect and insight.

57. See Peng, Nisbett, and Wong (1997).

58. See the landmark work by Bernard and his associates (1984), or work by Tim Wilson and colleagues (1984). From the latter: three studies were conducted with 39 college couples involved in dating relationships. In the first two studies, 58 undergraduates were shown "attitude objects" (puzzle or photographs), and half were instructed to analyze why they felt the way they did about them. Both self-report and behavioral measures of attitudes toward the objects were then analyzed. In the third study, couples were or were not asked to analyze their own relationship. Self-reports and behavioral measures of adjustment, such as whether the couples were still dating several months later, were then assessed. In all three studies, subjects who explained reasons for their attitudes had significantly lower correlations between their attitudes and behavior than subjects who did not explain reasons for their attitudes (the control condition) (Wilson, Dunn, Bybee, Hyman, & Rotondo, 1984).

59. See Baumeister, Vohs, and Funder (2007).
60. This is a problem for all survey instruments, including those testing for schemas. However, schema research addresses this by ensuring the surveyed items are developed based on interviews with informants from the culture being assessed.
61. Another problem is one of *satisficing,* the tendency to provide a satisfactory answer rather than an answer that requires more cognitive effort. According to Krosnick and colleagues (1991), "satisficing may lead respondents to employ a variety of response strategies, including choosing the first response alternative that seems to constitute a reasonable answer, agreeing with an assertion made by a question, endorsing the *status quo* instead of endorsing social change, failing to differentiate among a set of diverse objects in ratings, saying 'don't know' instead of reporting an opinion, and randomly choosing among the response alternatives offered" (p. 213).
62. See D'Andrade (1995), or Freeman, Romney, and Freeman (1987).
63. *Myth and Meaning* (1978).

2

What's Wrong With Corporate Culture?

Objectivity is a relative term because what is objectively perceived is by definition to some extent subjectively conceived of.

– D.W. Winnicott

We are in a corporate culture crisis. It may not seem that way given the concept's popularity, but if you look beyond the high-gloss conferences, Ted talks, YouTube videos, bestsellers, and VPs of Culture, you can spot a disturbing trend:

- According to Gallup's most recent State of the American Workplace report, a majority (51 percent) of the U.S. workforce is not engaged.[1] Other recent studies by Gallup have put that number as high as 68 percent.[2]
- Two-thirds of Canadian and U.S. employees are either actively looking for or would consider a new job opportunity if approached, with only 27 percent saying they would have no interest in a job outside of their current company.[3]
- Surveys suggest global employee engagement is only 29 percent, with North America at 39 percent and Europe at 27 percent.[4]
- Forty-six percent of nonunion workers say they would like to be in a union, up 32 percent since 1995.[5]
- Consider the many well-documented cases of toxic work environments and corporate scandal, such as Kay Jeweler's decades of sexual abuse,[6] Volkswagen and Audi's emission scandals, Boeing's issues with the 737MAX, or Wells Fargo's and Enron's institutionalized cheating of customers and entire markets, to name just a few.
- Consider that 40 percent of Fortune 1000 CEOs engaged in some kind of misconduct between 2000 and 2005.[7]

For all our preoccupations with corporate culture over the last 40 years (not to mention leadership) this is what we have to show for it: un-engaged employees, dissatisfied workers, and corporate scandal.[8] And it gets worse.

The consultancy Booz and Company cites a recent survey of 2000 executives from across industries and geographies where 84 percent of respondents think culture is critically important but less than half believe their companies do a good job of managing it.[9] These same executives say culture isn't a priority in their companies' transformation initiatives. A recent survey by Duke University of 933 North American CEOs and CFOs revealed that 91 percent believe that improving their own culture would increase their firm's overall value.[10] Similarly, Gartner found in 2017 that earnings calls with shareholders since 2010 show culture to be "by far the most discussed *talent* issue, and that mentions of culture have increased by 12% annually" (italics mine).[11] At the same time, only 10 percent of human resource leaders agree their organizations have the necessary culture to drive future business performance, or that their organizations understand their culture.[12] The consultancy Grant Thornton reports that 57 percent of surveyed executives believe a pleasing physical workplace environment is essential for employee loyalty, but only 31 of surveyed employees agree. From a related perspective, consider that two-thirds of all mergers fail, that is, they do not deliver on the benefits promised at the time the deal is struck (Clark & Mills, 2013). When culture is the direct object of change, as in a merger or acquisition, success rates are low (Smith, 2003). As Emmanuel Ogbonna and Barry Wilkinson put it in their study of grocery retailing change in the United Kingdom, what is more commonly seen in culture change programs is "instrumental compliance" and "skillful parodying" by middle managers and employees rather than any "transformation of managerial values" (2003, p. 1151).

When you consider that most interventions in culture are explicitly targeted at employee engagement, ethics, talent management, or ensuring people "do the right thing on their own", the current state of affairs is abysmal. We've been toiling with culture in one way or another for a long time with very little progress. This amounts to a crisis.

And we throw a lot of money at it. Gartner estimates 80 percent of surveyed firms spend on average $2200 per employee per year on "culture management". If those two figures were applied to the Fortune 1000, given an average employee population of 35,000, the annual spend on culture is in the billions.[13] Despite decades of interest and literally billions of dollars of investment, we're not close to cracking the code on culture.

From all the above, one could say the culture field is ripe for disruption.

It's not clear how long corporations will continue to justify spending this kind of money given these results. Sooner or later the fad or fashion of culture will pass (it's a surprise it hasn't already). Some anthropologists already believe the concept has outlived its usefulness (Bennardo & de Munck, 2014). For businesses this would be a loss: the many insights available through the cognitive science of culture would not find their way into the mainstream. We may have to wait another generation, which means those who toil in toxic work environments under ignorant leaders and boards will continue to suffer. Moreover, those working in environments and ecosystems where culture is misunderstood and misappropriated, where inordinate amounts of time, energy and resources are wasted on misguided efforts will soldier on in silence.

The mother of all culture problems, as stated in the Introduction, is the invisible wall culture represents for those leading corporate transformations. Every organizational transformation involves culture. On the eve of the Fourth Industrial Revolution, many companies that exist today will not in ten years. They will not because they were unable to adopt a more sophisticated approach to organizational transformation, one that made use of the latest science of culture rather than relied on pseudo-science and myth, which leads to suboptimal approaches that burn through significant resources, with huge opportunity costs.

So why, after decades of interest and big money, do companies continue to proliferate naïve and misguided approaches? This chapter explores those questions. If you feel satisfied with your understanding of how we got to this state and want to get to the new science, you might skip the rest of this chapter and move to Chapter 3. But by understanding how the myths originated – untangling the fictions from the facts embedded within them – we can develop a more sophisticated, clear-eyed, and contemporary understanding of organizational culture and why the cultural mind's approach is a disruptor.

THE GREAT REDUCTIONS

Unearthing the origins of the 5 Myths requires a short journey down two parallel and overlapping tracks. One has to do with how culture has been researched and taught in MBA programs over the last four decades. The other is how culture is practiced in business. Problems in each contribute to problems in the other, but both tracks arrive at the same place: a culture construct reduced to the most basic terms so it can be easily consumed by an impatient and pragmatic audience interested primarily in expedience.[14] As the famous saying in anthropology goes, *cultures don't stand still for their portraits.* Unfortunately, culture doesn't lend itself easily to reduction. These next sections explain.

Reduction #1: The Problem in MBA Programs

As early as the 1950s scholars were writing about organizational culture, and a steady stream of books and articles have appeared since the 1980s. Yet corporate culture is hardly a mature field. While business executives tend to think much of what happens inside companies is because of culture, beyond superficial agreement that culture is something shared, business and management academics still can't agree on the basics: what culture is (*Values? Beliefs? Norms? Symbols? Stories? All of the above? None of the above? The same or different as climate? An instrument of domination? Etc.*); how to measure it (*Quantitatively? Qualitatively? Empirically knowable? Inherently subjective? Etc.*); what are its boundaries (*Monolithic? Fragmented? Porous? Identifiable through typologies? Related to national culture? Etc.*); where it comes from (*Founders and leaders? National culture? Occupational groups? Whatever we want, i.e., willfully engineered?*); is it eligible to be changed, and if so, how (*By leaders? By teaching people new values? Through marketing campaigns? Through cataclysmic events?*); and so on.[15] All of these questions are contested, with no consensus, which gives the field the whiff of immaturity.[16] The cognitive science of culture answers these questions, but as it is virtually unknown in the mainstream, no consensus on what culture is or how to work with it has been available for managers and practitioners.

But there is a deeper problem. An alarming amount of business-school research is characterized by serious flaws. Worse, these flaws tend to be ignored by those doing the research, lending much of this work a false air of certainty borne from a collective ignorance of its own limitations. Issues include problematic or unexamined assumptions, claims not supported by the evidence presented, and fundamental misconceptions about the nature of culture itself, known as *ontological* issues.[17] I am not the first to cite these challenges: Joanne Martin (2002), among others, has written compellingly about the problems in organizational culture research. But her voice has been drowned out amid the din of competing ideas and the pop-culture-of-culture that dominates the mainstream business press. Her work has no visibility in the business world.

Consider, for example, seven popular works from business school or management-oriented academics written primarily for business audiences since the 1980s: Deal and Kennedy's *Corporate Cultures* (1982); Peters and Waterman's *In Search of Excellence* (1982); Denison's *Corporate Culture and Organizational Effectiveness* (1990); Schein's *Organizational Culture and Leadership* (1992); Kotter and Heskett's *Corporate Culture and Performance* (1992); Cameron and Quinn's *Diagnosing and Changing Organizational Culture* (1999); and Collin's *Good to Great* (2001). Collin's work is not about culture per se, but its central claim rests on the concept of core values. While this list by no means encompasses all culture research coming out of business schools, I chose these titles because they are among the most cited.[18] While all have made contributions, and some even define culture in ways compatible with cognitive science, owing to their popularity all but one can be said to be guilty of originating or perpetuating the culture myths. The exception is Ed Schein's *Organizational Culture and Leadership*. Schein's ideas were prescient: his model and theory was concurrent with modern cognitive anthropology. Schein's work echoed the earliest thinker in the organizational culture field, Eliot Jaques, who in 1951 foreshadowed the modern cognitive view by defining culture as the "customary and traditional way of *thinking* and of doing things, shared to a degree by all" (1951/2013, p. 251, italics mine). Jaques's work is obscure, but Schein's is well known. That his ideas and model remain one among equals rather than the consensus view, however, underscores the point. Amid all the noise, the best ideas struggle to gain ground.[19]

Outdated Theory, Problematic Assumptions, Leaps of Faith, and Anecdotes

Myths seem plausible when you don't examine them too closely. Some of the assumptions within the *5 Myths* are, in fact, consistent with or borne out by cognitive science (see later chapters). But what remains remarkable about these influential works is the extent to which the bulk of their theses rest on outdated theory, problematic assumptions, leaps of faith, or simply anecdote. They perpetuate the mythology, for example, by claiming:

- Organizations are like primitive societies (Deal and Kennedy) (*outdated theory*).

- Culture is dependent on leaders (Denison) (*problematic assumption*).
- Values are conflated with "basic concepts and beliefs" (Deal and Kennedy; Kotter and Heskett) (*problematic assumption*).
- Culture, as values, beliefs, and principles, are foundational to the management system of a company (Denison) (*leap of faith*).
- Shared values provide a sense of consistency for employees (Denison) (*problematic assumption; leap of faith*).
- Espoused values (what management says it wants) are synonymous with how employees actually behave (Peters and Waterman; Deal and Kennedy; Kotter and Heskett) (*outdated theory; problematic assumption; leap of faith*).
- The way to build culture and unify a company is to emphasize values (Peters and Waterman; Kotter and Heskett; Collins) (*outdated theory; problematic assumption; leap of faith*).
- Culture can make people feel a certain way, such as conferring a sense of personal responsibility (Cameron and Quinn; Deal and Kennedy) (*anecdotal evidence; leap of faith*).
- So-called "strong" cultures motivate people (Deal and Kennedy) (*problematic assumption; leap of faith*).
- Culture shapes behavior (Kotter and Heskett) (*outdated theory; problematic assumption; leap of faith*).
- Culture can be assessed through employee behavior (Denison) (*problematic assumption*).
- When cultural patterns "mirror the environment, all is well" (Deal and Kennedy, p. v) (*leap of faith; problematic assumption*).
- Culture is changed through communication – stories, myths, and natural process of identification, as in a tribe (Kotter and Heskett) (*outdated theory; problematic assumption; leap of faith*).

The Big Assumption: Culture Drives Business Performance

The central idea in these texts is that culture drives business performance. This claim is what has made the concept of culture so popular today. Unfortunately, it doesn't hold up to critical assessment.

First, there is the rather important problem of causation. For example, Peters and Waterman see the key to corporate financial success as a strongly unified culture. The evidence for this comes from examining the values of companies with strong financial performance and claiming that these values, one way or another, lead to positive financial results (cultural "cohesion" in Deal and Kennedy's case; core principles in Collins'). This confuses correlation with causation; the actual drivers of financial performance documented in these works are unsubstantiated. That financial performance and culture may be related doesn't mean they are. What drives what? Corporate success may actually drive culture formation, as the science now suggests (see Chapters 3 and 4; also Schein, 1992). Further, in Peters and Waterman's sample of companies with so-called "strong cultures", 14 out of their original 62 subsequently suffered significant earnings declines and even bankruptcy. The same phenomenon can be seen in Deal and Kennedy and Kotter and Heskett's samples.[20] How do "strong" cultures explain earnings declines, or bankruptcy? In addition, there is what I call a *temporal equivalency* problem: all measures of financial performance require establishing some arbitrary time interval in which to assess performance. This assumes culture in the target organizations is somehow static and measurable *during that same time*.

Kotter and Heskett's refinement to the culture-performance argument is to introduce the idea of strategic appropriateness. This is the idea that organizations have to have cultures appropriate to their competitive environments, which explains why some so-called "strong" cultures failed (they claim culture *can* impact long term performance). This is a reasonable refinement of the argument. But it falls apart in method. Their assessment was built off of letters written to executives at 207 companies asking about the strength of their *competitors'* cultures, which they operationalized as "style", "credo", and "longstanding policies and practices". Kotter and Heskett then created a "culture strength index" by "computing the average response" for each firm to these questions and testing this index through interviews (p. 159). While the research is comprehensive, one does not need to go any further to see the methodology problem: asking executives to evaluate competitor cultures from afar, using the operational definition provided, and then using that to build a strength index by which to compare financial performance is flawed from the outset. Assuming the executive hasn't worked in the evaluated company, on what basis can an executive at company A judge a culture at company B? Using criteria that is publicly available is exceedingly difficult.[21] How would one evaluate "credo" or "practices" except on hearsay and general impressions?[22] To assume a competitor can evaluate the culture of another company is to assume anecdote – what has been heard, read, and observed from afar – somehow *is* culture. Furthermore, it violates Kotter and Heskett's own definition (offered via Webster's) of culture as a "totality of socially transmitted behavior patterns ..." (p. 4). How would an outside observer possibly know such a "totality"? With a flawed "strength index", their claim of financial performance falls apart, not to mention suffering from the same causation-correlation problems noted above.

Denison tried to work around these issues. He created an index of behavioral data related to organizational climate, job design, supervisor quality, and tried to tie these to performance data such as income, net sales, invested capital, income-to-sales, and income-to-investment ratios.[23] The problem is the items used as the basis for his index were attitudes and opinions. For example, questions such as "does the organization have goals and objectives that are both clear cut and reasonable?"; "are the persons affected by decisions asked for their ideas?"; and "overall, are you satisfied with your job?" are measures of attitude (p. 210–212). They may be valid as measures of employee engagement, but they are not of culture. If one operationalizes culture as assumptions, asking employees to evaluate it on the basis of how they feel about their job or goal-setting practices (etc.) misses the mark by a wide margin. Attitudes are not assumptions. It's like asking a German to describe Germany by asking about how they feel about bratwurst. As seen in the previous chapter, attitudes and opinions may be as much reactions to some aspect of a culture as reflections of it. Again, a flawed comparator leads to a flawed claim about financial performance, with all the issues about causation versus correlation applicable as well.

If these well-known and oft-cited texts cannot substantiate a link between culture and business performance, why do scholars, pundits, and consultants continue to push the idea? Wouldn't a more modest suggestion be that *some* aspects of culture *might* aid in generating profit by, for example, enabling a reputation of high integrity manifested in practices that lead to enhanced or increased customer loyalty? Or, that the basis upon which decisions are made – the standard for "good" – is implicitly understood throughout the organization, from the board to the shop floor, which increases decision-making speed which in turn leads to greater productivity? These kinds of variables can be measured empirically; the cognitive framework in this book shows how. The problem is most studies do not adequately operationalize measures like these or document their supporting practices in order to empirically establish a link with financial outcomes. Admittedly, this is difficult. But maybe one reason the link continues to be pushed is that we want there to be one. Myths, after all, remain myths because they are in line with our aspirations.

Reducing Culture to a Dependent Variable

In order to claim culture drives financial performance, or any other desired outcome, several assumptions must be made. These are that cultures are singular, monolithic, and stable wholes characterized by a single variable, such as values or norms, which can be measured so that any state change is therefore "proven".[24] These assumptions are generally not supported by researchers outside of management, or disciplines closely associated with it.[25]

At issue is not the scientific method or the nature of empiricism. Making valid and verifiable claims is essential to advancing our knowledge of culture in organizations (the cognitive science approach provides numerous methods for how to do this). But construct validity means little when the construct is vague or poorly defined to begin with. This is pure research sleight of hand, and the fundamental problem with many quantitative studies of culture. The basic premise about what culture is in these studies is flawed from the outset, rendering any truth-claims derived from them pseudo-science.[26]

Academic Myopia: Drawing From Too Few Wells

Behind the tendency to reduce culture to a single variable in order to link it to business performance is the problem of intellectual silos. The assumptions, methods, and theories put forth in the popular books, as in many other studies, are drawn from within the field of management itself or its close siblings, economics, social psychology, and industrial-organizational (I/O) psychology. Denison admits this readily; you can see this in others' work as well by the many anecdotes and thin cases.[27] The problem is these disciplines have historically not placed culture at the center of their intellectual agendas.

Culture was not invented by management scholars. It was appropriated from cultural anthropology (Stewart & Aldrich, 2015) with an end in mind: to provide a way for academics and consultant to actualize the management philosophy of Theory Y, and to do so in a way that could be quantified with clear financial benefits.

Consider how economists think about culture. For example, here's economist Benjamin Hermalin's (1999) take:

> To the extent that corporate culture is a choice variable for the firm, the level or intensity of a firm's culture depends on both the costs and ben-efits of a strong corporate culture. Whereas the costs can be reasonably

understood by looking at the firm only, the benefits depend significantly on the firm's competitive environment.

(1999, p. 42)

The assumption that culture is a "choice", a dependent variable, is directly at odds with cultural and cognitive anthropology and related disciplines. But economists believe culture leads to value creation.[28] In Hermalin's words:

> Like any "input" used by the firm, corporate culture would seem subject to the make-or-buy decision. Does a firm essentially rely on the prevailing (i.e., national, regional, or professional) cultural norms or does it craft its own?
>
> **(1999, p. 9)**

The reduction is clear. It is based on the idea that culture is a choice, a dependent variable. But this is difficult to apply to real people in real social systems. The economist Paul Ormerod (2005) argues that the reason for this is because economics regards the natural state of the world as static and unchanging. Their solutions are based on the principle that the world in which their theories and models apply is perpetually at rest:

> The business school gurus … are by no means immune to the temptation to reduce highly complex problems to a set of easy formulas. Leading figures like Tom Peters offer beguiling sets of simple rules. Business-school thinking has fallen into the trap of standard economics: everyone can use the same rules and prosper. But most of the firms in Tom Peters' *In Search of Excellence* later failed to maintain their excellence, to say the least.
>
> **(2005, pp. 17–18)**

The root problem with economics and management science-based approaches to corporate culture is that the *very nature of culture is misunderstood*. From this all errors stem. The late Peter Drucker, perhaps the foremost management thinker of his generation (and at one time an economist), as early as 1973 was aware of this problem:

> What this indicates is a serious misunderstanding on the part of the management scientist of what "scientific" means. Scientific is not – as many management scientists naively seem to think – synonymous with

quantification. If this were true, astrology would be the queen of the sciences…the first task for management science, if it is to be able to contribute rather than distort or mislead, is therefore to define the specific nature of its subject matter … this might include as a basic definition the insight that business enterprise is made up of human beings.

(p. 510)

Social systems are made up of human beings. Because humans are not static and unchanging creatures, nor can social systems ever be. This is one reason why sociologists and anthropologists developed other metaphors and heuristics to study them.[29] Cultures do exhibit patterns and tendencies that can be subjected to careful empirical study, as I show in later chapters. But a more advanced and multi-faceted model is needed to explain these phenomena, one that does not begin with the distorted and incorrect assumption of culture as static and stable, easily reduced to single variables such as values, norms, attitudes, beliefs, leadership behavior, and such. Unfortunately, it is much simpler and expedient to do so.

> Tip: *The more culture can be made to appear as a rational, choice-dependent input to behavior, the more appealing it is to managers who seek rational, choice-dependent inputs to drive business outcomes. Unfortunately, this assumes cultures are simple and static, which they are not. Culture comes from human beings. Human beings are anything but simple and static.*

Psychology's perspective on culture also leans toward reductionism, for similar reasons. Psychology, however, is much closer to anthropology in its shared concern with human experience (Lindholm, 2007). The differences lie in the former's concern with the individual, and its focus (in experimental and social psychology) on hypothesis testing and evaluation, much of it within the controlled confines of the lab or with the captive population of university students (Lindholm, 2007).

"Culture" was first identified as a target of psychological inquiry as early as 1888, and appears in Freud's work (Misra & Gergen, 1993). But as put by the cross-cultural psychologist Harry Triandis, "psychologists are interested in cultural data if and only if the data challenge one of their findings" (in Fiske, 2002, p. 78). At the highest level of abstraction, psychologists care about universal patterns of behavior and thinking.

As such, the social psychology of culture mainly deals with cultural differences, not directly with culture itself. It is characterized by the creation and testing of cultural types that can be empirically assessed across cultures.[30] It's not surprising that this same orientation emerges in some corporate culture research, such as in the work of Cameron and Quinn.

The core paradigm of I/O psychology is the individual, not culture. As described in Chapter 1, I/O psychologists tend to view culture as static, based on the idea that people within organizations share common psychological traits.[31] As put by Zeynep Aycan, I/O research on culture "is dominated by a reductionist perspective in which behavior is examined in isolation from multiple forces of the environment" (2000, p. 111). This orientation has inhibited I/O research on culture itself (Erez, 1994).[32]

Whether culture is thought of as psychological syndromes, the projection of early childhood experiences of leaders, or the sum total of the personalities in the organization, all of these moves reduce culture to something fixed and stable, again fundamentally missing the point that human systems are anything but. To address this error, anthropology and psychology produced two offspring: *cultural psychology* and *psychological anthropology*, subdisciplines that put the individual in the center of cultural experience (the former), or posit that cultural experience, while shared, is shaped by individual experience (the latter).[33] The cognitive science of culture presented in this book draws from both subdisciplines.

Cultural anthropologists have studied culture in all its manifestations for over a century. Historically, however, they have not concerned themselves with business (Stewart & Aldrich, 2015). As well, their methods of studying culture on its own terms rather than imposing external types have not readily lent themselves to management science's concerns with quantifiable data, or managerial thirst for quick and easy answers. This has limited anthropology's influence in business.[34]

But this is also a failure of MBA programs. Their failure to take a more multi-disciplinary approach and look farther afield for new theories of culture with greater explanatory valence means many of the insights being generated in modern cognitive anthropology and related disciplines, with a few exceptions, are not getting to managers. Business schools promulgate simplistic and reductive ideas that appeal to their market (MBA students), which perpetuates the mutual collusion I talked about earlier. This follows a model proposed by Eric Abrahamson and Greg Fairchild (1999), who argue that management ideas become fashionable when proponents reinforce the belief that one's own organization will benefit because other, similar organizations have benefited. A good example was seen in the 1980s with the claim that all U.S. organizations should adopt Japanese management techniques such as Quality Circles. Management consultants picked up this idea and ran with it, while executives and other management academics believed they might be discredited or viewed as behind the times by not adopting it (Abrahamson, 1996). When academics, consultants and executives believe they have to keep up with the fashion, there is little incentive to teach or adopt something new or different. There are exceptions, but in general this has proved a major limitation to advancing work on culture. One CEO I know, a Harvard Business School graduate, puts it bluntly: "business schools do a terrible job of teaching culture".

Tip: Business schools shoulder blame for putting forward simplistic solutions to culture to appeal to their market (MBAs) rather than searching further afield for more robust and sophisticated frameworks with greater explanatory power.

Reduction #2: Dumbing Down for Business

Jennifer Chatman and Charles O'Reilly, two well-known academics from the University of California Haas School of Business and Stanford Graduate School of Business, respectively, make the argument that practitioners have retarded the science of culture (2016). In their view, the reason why there isn't a consensus theory of culture is because consultants popularized the construct to the point where academics were distracted by lucrative consulting opportunities, which hindered research. One need only scan the top ten current best sellers on Amazon or look at how the major consulting firms frame culture to see their point.[35] As a scholar-practitioner who spends equal time researching and consulting, I do acknowledge my potential bias in appreciating this point.[36] But there is also a curious paradox to their argument: what is happening in business may be as much about the impoverished nature of academic theory as it is about academics being distracted by consulting gigs. Managerial zeal to ascribe cultural explanations for organizational phenomena and outcomes may hold research back, but it may also drive demand *because* of culture's intuited importance. Most managers, like the CEO quoted above, get how pervasive culture is.

Managerial intuition, in fact, is often well out in front of practice. But faced with watered-down theories or approaches where any espoused value, behavior, norm, habit, or preference can be operationalized as "culture" on the basis of its apparent effect, managerial interest, fueled by self-enhancement and value engineering, lead us to a *Wild West* of practice. Consultants, managers and internal practitioners can selectively draw from research – if they draw from any at all – in line with their own agendas and worldviews essentially unencumbered by science.[37] They reduce and oversimplify culture in accordance with the 5 Myths for the reasons covered in Chapter 1. The net effect is a dumbing down in order to sell services and books to a pragmatic business audience impatient with complexity but, paradoxically, keen for results.[38] Reductions are of three types: *reduction by conflation*; *reduction by compartmentalization*; and *reduction by coaching*.

Reduction by Conflation: Culture as Employee Engagement and Well-Being

My Google newsfeed powered by AI is too hip to my reading habits. It serves me a daily stream of advice on culture. A recent example from *Forbes*, "Celebrating Each Other to Create an Enjoyable Work Culture" (August 11, 2019), sums up this type of reduction best. It's main point: "make your culture one where people are genuinely happy for each other and want to share in each other's good news". As with all such "how-to" takes, these are innocuous, well-intended, and often common-sense. Similarly, one of the Amazon Top ten books, *How to Build a Thriving Culture at Work* by Rosie Ward and Jon Robison, describes how to create a model for employee well-being on the premise that nurturing autonomy and helping employees master skills and purpose helps companies create the conditions for people to bring their so-called best selves to work. That, the authors claim, is culture. The consultancy Booz and Company makes a similar claim.[39] In *Carrots and Stick Don't Work*, Paul Marciano (2010) makes the case employee engagement based on respect is key to changing culture.

These are all wonderful and worthy goals. And there is no argument against the idea that a happy workplace is a productive workplace. But these moves confuse employee well-being and engagement with culture. The two are not the same: positive attitudes do not add up to culture, as we saw in Chapter 1. Employee engagement has to do with manager quality, a congenial work environment, perceptions of career advancement, and development opportunities and similar measures, all which lead to discretionary effort: employees working extra hours or "going the extra mile" without direct compensation.[40] These outcomes, some suggest, lead to improved financial results.[41] The data here is by no means conclusive, but it is less muddled than the research on values, norms, and other common frames for culture. So by conflating employee engagement with culture and business outcomes, practitioners gain air cover and thereby add a veneer of legitimacy to their argument. Unfortunately, there are real consequences to doing this.

When we conflate engagement with culture we fail to distinguish the signal from the noise. We miss the fact employee attitudes may be a reaction to a prevailing deeper cultural reality, a cultural affordance rather than what generates the attitude to begin with. Employees might report they are happy and engaged because of the free food in the corporate café, but the widespread tendency for passive aggressiveness in the organization goes on. And this has opportunity costs. When a corporate transformation – such as turning an industrial manufacturer into a digital company – masquerades as an employee engagement exercise, little in the way of culture change is likely to occur because better managers and happier employees does not mean the organization fundamentally changes the way it thinks about what business it's in, how it conceptualizes risk, how it defines failure, how it allocates resources, how it defines "good", how it goes to market, how it drives innovation, and on. These practices are the real manifestations of culture. Employee engagement and well-being are something else. By reducing culture to these outcomes, the attention and resources shifts away from what drives culture to begin with.

Tip: When culture change masquerades as employee engagement, the opportunity costs are huge because little in the way of culture change actually occurs. Employees might report they are happy and engaged because of the free food in the café, but the widespread passive-aggressiveness in the organization goes on. Engaged employees doesn't mean the organization fundamentally changes the way it thinks about what business it's in, how to conduct business, or what "good" looks like inside the firm. All of that is culture.

Reduction by Compartmentalization: Culture as Employee Behavior

I wrote in the Introduction about our approach to culture change at Microsoft in the 2000s and how we failed because we reduced culture to employee behavior. Several consultancies, such as Aon and Booz, still claim culture is synonymous with behavior.[42] Boards conflate culture with talent, as mentioned. Several Top ten books make the same claim. A majority of managers and executives tend to think of culture as behavior.[43] Or as a blog featured by the *Economist* recently put it, quoting a culture consultant:

> If, for example, a company selects integrity as one of its core values, it needs to define what integrity looks like when it's done well … The behaviours that designate integrity must be tangible and observable, so that everyone can agree on it when they see it in practice.
>
> **(Rodriguez, 2019)**

Certainly if you want to inculcate values, specifying the behaviors that define those values is important.

Culture does indeed relate to behavior; that is not in question. The question is whether culture can be reduced *exclusively* to employee behavior. When that happens, several problems ensue.

When culture is synonymous with people, the "solution", as we found out at Microsoft, is to focus on HR processes and programs, such as selection, on-boarding, retention, rewards, training, and the like. This makes HR responsible for culture. As put by Gartner:

> Heads of HR have responded to this scrutiny by investing more time and resources in managing culture. These efforts tend to be people-focused: generating buy-in among current employees and bringing in new employees who are good fits for the culture.[44]

Most companies believe this constitutes culture shaping. But when they do this they unwittingly push culture into a black box. They fall into the trap of thinking that getting people to do things differently is a talent problem: hire the "right" people that "fit" our culture, then indoctrinate, train, and manage them to do what we want. Specify some desired input – more accountability, greater collaboration, increased innovation – put it into the HR or talent agenda and, magically, out will come the desired behavior.

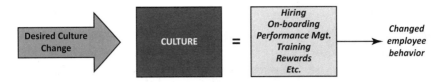

FIGURE 2.1
The "black box" (behavioral) model of culture change.

Not only does this relegate culture to a function that historically has struggled to establish its own credibility, strategic impact and relevance, it also absolves business leaders of responsibility[45] (see Figure 2.1).

And this leaves much of what constitutes culture out of the picture. How people think, how they make sense of their worlds, and what they find meaningful, is unaccounted for. It assumes culture, the stuff in the box, is static and unchanging, a presumption of much academic thinking as well. What is missed is the possibility that with each new hire the shared system of thinking and meaning may change. Culture is never static; it is only in our minds that we make it so.

Another consequence is that by reducing culture to behavior, we don't address sustainability. Hiring to ensure cultural "fit", whatever that means, is important, especially in smaller organizations. But so is making sure new hires have the right skills and competencies to do the job. And so are many other practices – budgeting, strategic planning, management reporting, innovation, go-to-market, and so on. Unless all relevant practices change, changing culture by targeting behavior alone will not produce sustainable change (and see later chapters).

Reduction by Coaching: Culture as What Leaders Should Do

Reducing culture to what leaders should be doing (or not doing) is the most popular reduction in the pop-culture-of-culture. As we saw in the last chapter, this idea is deeply entrenched in the minds of CEOs and senior executives as well as in the wider society, evidenced by the many bestsellers, articles, interviews, and blogs from across the spectrum of business punditry. Most culture bestsellers on Amazon claim culture *is* leadership, in so many words. The assumption, of course, is by role modeling or stating what is desired, the culture will somehow take root, or as put by McKinsey's Randy Cook and Alison Jenkins, "leaders carry the responsibility for modeling" (2014).

Think about it: in this conception, culture, arguably the most complex of human social phenomena, is reduced, essentially, to coaching. Coach the leader to get the culture she wants by helping her "walk the talk". One can begin to see why it's easier to sell books and consulting gigs with this message rather than an inconvenient but honest alternative: culture is complex, messy, contradictory, hard to change, pervasive, deep seated ... Culture-as-leadership is an easy sell, and a billion-dollar industry. The irony is that only about 15 percent of surveyed executives believe their culture is where it needs to be, though when asked why, the most common answer is that leadership needs to invest more time to develop the culture![46]

A major consequence of focusing on coaching for culture change, again, is opportunity cost. By fixating on what the top of the house should do or say (or not) we miss higher-leverage interventions that sustainably impact culture. This doesn't mean leaders get a free pass. But impactful and sustainable interventions have to be targeted at practices – the habits, routines, and processes of the entire organization (see Chapter 5).

> Tip: Imagine being told the key to successfully managing financial performance is to solely focus on EBITDA. Or that every marketing strategy must include a television advertising campaign. For many anthropologists, mainstream approaches to organizational culture shaping and change amount to the same kind of thing: reductive and simplistic approaches masquerading as culture "solutions".

THE MANAGER'S DILEMMA

Managerial intuition about culture, as said, is ahead of mainstream practice and thinking in MBA programs. But this intuition, and the corresponding drive for results, leads inevitably to the false conclusion that an effective culture will improve firm value and profitability. A great culture with the right values will deliver results even with a mediocre strategy, so goes the myth. Managers hold these beliefs even though establishing causal links between culture and business outcomes has never been adequately demonstrated, and even though much of the theory and methodology for doing so is flawed. Call it fear of falling behind the competition, sheer faith, or self-fulfilling prophecy; it is usually enough to put in motion a lot of people and resources in the name of culture change. What keeps the myth-buying cycle going is corporate intolerance for any idea that is not easy to understand and implement, which is especially prevalent in the United States.[47] The cycle is enabled by the many idiosyncratic and reductive ways culture can be defined and operationalized, which makes any "solution" appear plausible if it meets ordinary purchasing criteria, such as trust in the purveyor; cost; fear of what competitors may be doing; ease of implementation; and so on.

Does this mean culture has no bearing on firm performance? Does this mean we give up on the concept altogether (and you stop reading here)? Hardly.

The big tantalizing dilemma is cultures *do* exhibit underlying patterns, tendencies, and orientations that are, at some level, recognizable and exert a deep, if mostly hidden, influence on social systems. It remains an open question as to whether these underlying patterns, tendencies and orientations can be overtly manipulated to produce predictable outcomes. As if this whole topic of culture is not complicated enough, human systems do not easily give up their secrets in order to lend themselves to overt manipulation.

> *Tip: Cultures do exhibit recognizable patterns that influence social systems. The key question is whether these patterns can be engineered to produce predictable outcomes.*

A Better Way

Throughout the last two chapters I have tried to convince you that much of how we study and work with culture today is misguided. I've tried to show you how the culture field, despite decades of interest, is still immature. I have tried to convince you that much of what we think we know about culture is based on myths which are, in turn, rooted in myopic science from business schools and the relentless need to reduce culture to oversimplified bits so it can be easily studied, packaged, and digested by corporate buyers. I've tried to spell out why these myths persist, and why they become fused with other ideas, like employee engagement, in order to make them appear more plausible than they really are. Our wish to believe in these myths given our intuitions as well as our values about business and leadership is very strong.

If you are not convinced, maybe at least what you thought was true about culture now is a bit less solid. Perhaps you might find comfort in knowing that as legacy organizations struggle to transform themselves into relevancy for the Fourth Industrial Revolution, or as tech companies struggle to achieve scale and preserve the magic of their early days, or as national firms try to operate effectively in global markets, many are beginning to realize the need for better theory and frameworks. One example is from Gartner, who call for a more complete approach to culture that involves "changing enterprise-wide systems and processes that differ from the more people-focused approach".[48] Or from McKinsey, admitting "many approaches to assessing and addressing cultural issues are flawed" and that culture is better approached by focusing on management practices.[49] Or from Laszlo Bock, the former SVP of HR at Google, who writes about key practices that sustained culture at Google.[50] Or the so-called "practical" changes made recently at Microsoft to shift aspects of its culture.[51] These ideas are in line with modern cognitive science, though the science laid out in the next chapters goes further still.

I used the pejorative "dumbing down" to over-stress the point that culture is flawed because it is reduced and oversimplified. In seeking to shape and manage it, academics, managers, and practitioners focus on syndromes rather than what generates culture to begin with. Inevitably this produces failed outcomes and missed opportunities. More importantly, as said at the outset, it results in a tinkering at the margins. Until we can better understand *why humans in organizations think and act as they do and how that results in specific outcomes*, we won't be sufficiently equipped for dealing with the challenges ahead.

What we are learning about culture from the last 30 years of cognitive science explains why managers are intuitively correct. Cognitive science has developed major new paradigms for culture, yet much of this work is not yet well known in the business mainstream. Ed Schein (1984, 1992) is one of the few to develop a model for organizational culture that incorporated many of these ideas, and he did so well before the evidence was as robust as it is today.[52] In the following chapters we turn from what's wrong to what the new science of the cultural mind offers, building off Schein and others' ideas as well as those from the last few decades of cognitive science. The new science radically disrupts old myths. It also provides a framework for working with culture in ways that are more sustainable and impactful for true transformation.

NOTES

1. See Harter and Mann (2019).
2. Harter and Mann (2016).
3. From a survey of 2001 U.S. and Canadian employees on loyalty, advancing their own careers, and satisfaction in the workplace. Ceridian's *Pulse of Talent Report* (December 5, 2018).
4. Effectory's *Global Employee Engagement Index*, 2016. Some surveys, such as that conducted by the consultancy Aon, note that job satisfaction globally is at an all-time high, which they attribute to political and economic stability in regions such as Asia and Africa.
5. Steven Greenhouse, *The New York Times* (August 3, 2019).
6. Taffy Brodesser-Akner, *The New York Times* (April 23, 2019).
7. From Pfeffer (2015).
8. For example, between 1980 and 1997 alone, 329 companies engaged in culture change programs of some kind (Helms-Mills, 2003).
9. From "Culture's role in enabling organizational change: Survey ties transformation success to deft handling of cultural issues" (Booz & Company, 2013).
10. See Graham, Harvey, Popadak, and Rajgopal, 2017).
11. I used this same technique to uncover IMCO's primary schemas, detailed in my first book and in Chapter 3.
12. From Gartner, *Creating a Culture that Performs* (2017). This study found that in addition to not understanding their own culture, leaders aren't "driving the culture" and employees can't "operationalize" the culture.
13. Source: Jonathan Bates, Quora.com https://www.quora.com/How-many-employees-are-there-in-the-Fortune-1-000-in-the-US. Average culture spend figures are from Gartner, *Creating a Culture that Performs* (2017). The math: 800 Fortune 1000 firms with an average of 35,000 employees means US $2200 is spent on 28 million employee per annum.
14. I use the term "ontological" to mean an attempt to define the essential nature of corporate culture.
15. This lack of agreement is hardly unique to business scholars. The anthropologists Alfred Kroeber and Clyde Kluckhohn in 1952 famously identified 164 definitions of culture.
16. Some scholars have dubbed this situation the "culture wars" (Martin & Frost, 2011) because of the proliferation of competing theories, each with their own definitions, appeals to authority, epistemologies, and promulgated from within relatively narrow intellectual silos (Martin, 2002). I won't go into a full account of the "wars" here; a complete treatment is in my first book, *Rethinking Culture* (2017). The main combatants form two camps: *objectivists*, who come at culture as something to be rationally and empirically known, measured, and quantified, and therefore treat it as a dependent variable to be leveraged, and a smaller group of *subjectivists* who treat culture as a social construction and therefore as inherently personal and unknowable. Also in the latter camp are *postmodernists*, who equate culture with power and dominance. Objectivists are criticized for being overly reductionist; subjectivists for a lack of pragmatic relevance; and postmodernists for threatening the social order. Another camp, perhaps characterizing the approach in this book, is known as "integrationist".

17. As put by Webster's, ontology is "a particular theory about the nature of being or the kinds of things that have existence".

18. According to Google Scholar, as of August 2019, Corporate Cultures has 11,784 citations; In Search of Excellence has 25,823; Corporate Culture and Organizational Effectiveness has 3547; Corporate Culture and Performance has 6334; Organizational Culture and Leadership, in its 4th edition, has 48,377; Diagnosing and Changing Organizational Culture has 7582; and Good to Great has 11,706. The latter, it should be pointed out, is among the top selling business books of all time. Except for Robert Waterman and Allan Kennedy – who come from the consulting world – all of these authors have spent the bulk of their careers writing and teaching in management and MBA programs. As a point of reference: Joanne Martin's Organizational Culture: Mapping the terrain, a text devoted to analyzing the state of the academic culture field, has 2810 citations.

19. One could argue as the citations leader, *Organizational Culture and Leadership* is the de facto standard for the theory and model of corporate culture. Perhaps, if we are lucky, that will be the case at some point. As a practitioner, however, I can say with some assurance that Schein's work, while known, is not regarded as the consensus view but simply another theory.

20. See Siehl and Martin (1989).

21. This was corroborated in a recent survey by Graham and his colleagues of 933 North American CEOs and CFOs. They quote one of their surveyed executives: "'I don't think you could determine it without the benefit of working there to be quite honest'. A CFO of a large consumer products company stated that they don't discuss culture explicitly in annual reports or conference calls, 'you would not see references to our culture. It was implied, it wasn't direct'" (Graham et al., 2017, p. 20).

22. Remarkably, Kotter and Heskett reported that only 3 out of 600 people said the definition of culture provided was too ambiguous!

23. Denison included multiple layers of culture in his operational definition – assumptions, values, perspectives, artifacts, "practices and behaviors" and "strategies for survival" based on what has "worked well in the past" (p. 2). He attempted to address the causality problem by using more granular measures in the form of practices and policies that reflect core values and beliefs, and the suitability of these to the competitive environment.

24. There was a tradition in anthropology of using dependent variables, such as universal cultural types, for the purposes of cross-cultural comparisons. This is traceable to the work of Franz Boas and E.B. Tylor in the early 20th century, (Jorgensen, 1979). By the second half of the 20th century anthropology had abandoned its universalists notions about culture.

25. Some academics acknowledge such approaches are flawed in their simplicity (for example, see Van den Steen, 2009), but proceed anyway, claiming it is efficient and practical to do so. Others try to finesse the single variable problem by claiming the existence of sub-cultures while still making the case for an overarching culture in which sub cultures reside, like nests in trees. Others punt altogether, admitting their model of corporate culture is problematic when applied globally (for example, see Heskett, 2011). It's as if all of these approaches acknowledge, albeit reluctantly, that there might be a problem with reducing culture to a single unit of measure, but none offer adequate alternatives.

26. To be fair, many of these books were written before the major advances in cognitive science of the last three decades. We know much more now about the social

and cultural mind than we did; from machine learning to neuroscience, many new vistas of research are now available for culture scholars. That said, the goal here was to reveal more about how our myths originated.

27. This in contrast to Gideon Kunda's (1992) thick description, a categorically different way to approach a single case.
28. Graham et al. (2017).
29. For example, see Maturana and Varela (1991).
30. Seen in the work of cross-cultural psychologists such as Schwartz (1994), and Triandis (1996).
31. Schneider (1987); Schneider and Smith (2004).
32. This is one reason why several I/O psychologists have called for a more multidisciplinary stance in I/O work on culture. For example, see Aycan (2000), or Brett, Tinsley, Janssens, Barsness, and Lytle (1997).
33. The differences between the two are subtle. According to Oxford Bibliographies, psychological anthropology "is the study of psychological topics using anthropological concepts and methods. Among the areas of interest are personal identity, selfhood, subjectivity, memory, consciousness, emotion, motivation, cognition, madness, and mental health". Cultural psychology is the study of how people shape and are shaped by their cultures. Topics of study in this field include similarities and differences between cultures in terms of norms, values, attitudes, scripts, patterns of behavior, cultural products (such as laws, myths, symbols, or material artifacts), social structure, practices and rituals, institutions, and ecologies.
34. Cognitive anthropology, however, has well developed methods for empirically studying culture, discussed in Chapter 5.
35. As of August 2019.
36. Charles O'Reilly himself is a well-known consultant on culture.
37. Consultants don't help matters much when they construct "research" as opinion polls asking executives to rate or describe their own "cultures" without any underlying theory of what culture is, where it comes from, or how it is operationalized.
38. I use the pejorative "dumbing down" deliberately. See below, this chapter.
39. See Aguirre, von Post, and Alpern (2013).
40. See the Corporate Leadership Council (2004).
41. The most compelling research was the first to make this link, conducted by Mark Huselid in 1995. For a good discussion of the differences of opinion on the meaning, measurement, and theory of employee engagement, see Saks and Gruman (2014).
42. Aon thinks of culture as how work gets done; Booz operationalizes culture, in part, as behavior (along with pride and commitment. See Fealy, Oshima, Sullivan, and Arian (2013) (Aon); or Aguirre, von Post, and Alpern (2013) (Booz).
43. Graham et al. (2017).
44. See Brooks and Knight (2017, p. 17).
45. The best discussion of this issue that I know of comes from Boudreau (2010).
46. Graham et al. (2017).
47. We have found, in general, a greater tolerance and willingness to entertain more sophisticated ideas about change and culture among European business leaders. Lack of critical thinking also characterizes the discourse of a business fashion on the upswing, while more thoughtfulness characterizes a fashion on the downswing (Abrahamson & Fairchild, 1999).
48. See Brooks and Knight (2017, p. 18).
49. Engert, Gandhi, Schaninger, and So (2010, p. 4).

50. These are "mission", "transparency", and giving employees a "voice". Bock refers to these things as "guiding principles", but they manifest as firmwide practices at Google. From Bock (2015).
51. From *the Economist*, July 6, 2019.
52. A few others have also been working from this perspective, notably Senge (1992), Harris (1994), and Alvesson and Sveningsson (2008).

3

Where Culture Comes From

I got out of law because it was changing my brain.

– Andrew Yang

It was about 5:30 in the afternoon on a hot weekday sometime in September 1993 in the Kendall Square subway station in Cambridge, Massachusetts, the Red Line platform thronged with hundreds of commuters like me. That was the moment I began thinking about *deep structures*. This was the phrase I had in my head for the idea that hundreds of individuals like me on that platform, all going home from work, or to yoga, or the gym, or on a date, or to an evening MBA class, each with their own personalities, preoccupations, dreams, frustrations, and anxieties – all – seemed to be able to abide by a common set of rules, a kind of unspoken logic for how to be on a crowded, smelly subway platform on a hot Indian Summer afternoon. When the train came, people stepped aside in a somewhat orderly fashion to let the other passengers out. No one pushed, shouted insults, elbowed, or looked others in the eye. When the conductor announced that people had to let the doors close or the train wouldn't be able to leave the station, those in the way somewhat grudgingly complied and stepped onto the platform to await the next train. Everyone seemed to know what to do and how to operate, like a school of fish in choreographed motion. Had I waited long enough for the next train, the platform would have refilled with another many hundred commuters and they too would have behaved the same way. What was evident to me that day was a kind of deep structure at work, some unspoken and untaught but no less thoroughly learned set of rules guiding us through the enactment of mass transportation. Had I been aware of it, I would have also realized there were deep structures being enacted at the same time on subway platforms in other cities around the world, and that these would have been similar but slightly different than what I was experiencing in Cambridge that day. For example, in San Francisco I might have observed people standing in a single line to let their fellow BART riders off the train. In Beijing or Frankfurt I might have observed uniformed officials with white gloves pushing riders into trains. Although I didn't know it at the time, what I would have been witnessing in all of these places was the cultural mind, in all its commonality and variability, in action.

DEEP STRUCTURE

Culture is a "deep structure". Up until that moment I had thought of culture as something consciously learned and intentionally engineered, much like the corporate culture mainstream thinks of it today. By then, in my early 30s, I had already been recruited into thinking culture was some kind of blank canvas on which one could paint whatever one wanted. Sure, some of it came from history, but this didn't mean it couldn't be changed. It did not occur to me that culture has a hidden (thus "deep") force that circumscribes a set of rules for every context, and that these rules might not be so easy to change. How easy would it have been for me to lie down in the middle of the platform, or impede others' access into the car? While not necessarily against any law, in most places these actions would simply not be done. What I came to understand much later was that the cognitive science of culture explains my primitive sense of "deep structure". This chapter is a primer on how and why it does.

Before getting to that, a note on intent: the goal here is to give you enough foundation in the cognitive science of culture to appreciate what "deep structure" means in practice. For those who need more, a thorough exploration of the interdisciplinary literature behind the cultural minds thesis is in my first book, *Rethinking Culture*.[1] In it one will find extensive discussion on the core theories and supporting evidence for embodied cognition, analogical transfer, and schemas, or what I call here *shared dominant logics,* that underpin the framework being advanced in this book. One will also find a critical appraisal of the methods used to surface schemas, considerations concerning their identification and labeling, as well as detail of my research at "IMCO", a global industrial conglomerate. This book does not replicate all that. What it does is give you enough of a foundation so you can leverage the science in your own work as a change leader or OD practitioner. What follows therefore is a summary. For those who need less, or who prefer to start from application, I suggest you read the executive summary below and skip to the next chapter. It describes what all this looks like in action at an archetypal company.

WHAT'S IN A NAME?

Cognitive scientists have many terms for schemas. Cognitive anthropologists, for example, also use the term "cultural model" interchangeably. I used "schema" in my first book but favor shared dominant logics (SDL) here because it best conveys to business readers in one expression what schemas are and what they do. They are pervasive – hence dominant – and act as a kind of structuring logic for organizing meaning, ways of thinking, and practices. "Logic" here is not in the sense of formal logic, but as causal reasoning – shared but implicit ways of explaining, justifying, idealizing, as well as systems of rules, scripts, precepts, and standards.

The Cognitive Science of Culture: Executive Summary

Culture comes from the brain. More precisely, it comes from the brain *grounded* – that's the word cognitive scientists use – in experience in the world. This may sound strange if you believe posters and t-shirts and CEO pronouncements are what create culture, but actual lived culture – the stuff we deal with every day at work – originates in shared *grounded* experience.

Saying that culture has to do with experience is a bit like saying the sea is blue. Not very descriptive, and technically as well as experientially not accurate. What does "grounded" mean? What *kind* of experience? And if culture is a mental thing, how do we get from that to culture in organizations? This chapter answers those questions in the form of an argument from first principles – basic theory and science – to application.

Here's the summary:

1. Culture is background knowledge – a ***reference system*** for making sense and successfully operating in a group. Reference systems evolve out of a group's adaptive response to environmental and existential challenges, responses that shape synaptic connections because they require sustained and meaningful collective experience to overcome them.

2. Sustained and meaningful collective experience originates in either ***professional socialization; what you collectively do that is highly successful***; or a shared ***differentiated core purpose***. These are the key shared cognitive "grounding" experiences that give rise to culture in organizations.

3. The reference system has three elements: *shared dominant logics, practices*, and *adaptations.*

   a. **Shared dominant logics** are preconscious and pervasive mental representations for rationalizing, explaining, and idealizing. They take the form of shared assumptions, lived norms, and common standards for what is considered good.

   b. **Practices** are everyday habits, routines, and processes by which the organization runs. They are powered by shared dominant logics.

   c. **Adaptations** are typical behavior or attitudes that are reactions or compensations for dominant logics and practices. Often what is interpreted as "culture", such as employee attitudes, are adaptations to shared dominant logics.

4. Visible culture – what you see and hear in the company, such as stories, myths, symbols, memes, espoused values, corporate tenets, and such – are usually what is *desired*. Highly cohesive or "strong" cultures have reference systems tightly coupled with visible culture.

5. The more successful the organization, the more hardened the dominant logics. This is because reference systems tend to be "overlearned" and reflexively applied in novel situations. This can be good for developing strong and cohesive cultures, especially in smaller organizations, but severely limiting when trying to transform an organization.

6. Change leaders and senior executives should care about all this, for three reasons:

   a. Understanding culture as a reference system can save thousands of hours and millions of dollars on misguided culture intervention strategies. The cognitive science refocuses culture change on what culture is to begin with, and how it actually operates.

  b. By focusing on dominant logics – the "source code" – interventions are targeted at what gives rise to culture to begin with. This allows isolating what is standing in the way of what's desired, or what's undermining strategy or transformation goals.

  c. CEOs and senior leaders play a key role in shaping culture – under two conditions: (1) when their own dominant logics are already widely shared in the organization (as is often the case in start-ups and smaller companies); or (2) when they rigorously align organizational practices to desired logics.

7. The way to change culture, therefore, is to change dominant logic. The way to change dominant logic is to change practices. No matter how well articulated the desired culture may be, only by architecting and instilling practices aligned with the future state can collective neural pathways be altered.

Now to the slightly more expanded explanation.

Culture, as mental phenomena, comes from *meaningful* and *sustained experience* coded in the brain as simplified *mental representations* that make up a body of shared *tacit knowledge*. This knowledge acts as a reference system, a kind of shared mental operating system that helps a community make sense of and structure its world in order to successfully function, just as a crowd does on a subway platform.[2] In organizations this means either:

1. *Where you come from* professionally – the professional socialization and learning of its most powerful occupational group(s), what I call **professionalization**.
2. *What you do* collectively – sustainably *solving* difficult technological or business problems core to the organization, called shared **task solutions**.
3. A highly **differentiating core purpose** – usually a non-commercial, higher purpose that the organization finds deeply meaningful.

These experiences are the primary origins, or "ground", for shared mental representations, what I call *shared dominant logics (SDLs)*. SDLs are the foundation of the reference system that runs in the background of daily organizational life. In addition to SDLs, the reference system consists of *practices*, informal and formal routines, habits, and processes, as well as *adaptations* – reactions to or compensations for SDLs typically seen in behavior or attitudes. Visible culture sits atop the reference system and consists of direct manifestations of logics (such as logos or branding treatments), as well as in expressions of what is espoused or wished for by top management, such as desired norms, values, tenets, beliefs, and such. Like adaptations, these may be direct manifestations of SDLs, compensations for them (as in the organization that wants to value collaboration as a compensation for a widely held craft logic), or completely unrelated, as in the organization that says it values diversity but has no practices or underlying SDLs related to it.

All of this is called *functionally grounded culture*, the core framework for corporate culture depicted in Figure 3.1 and elaborated in the rest of this chapter.

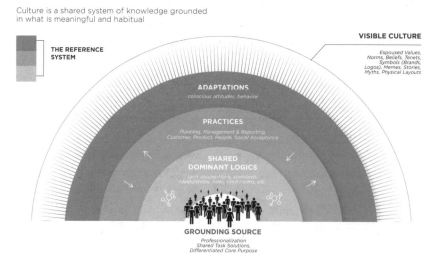

FIGURE 3.1
Functionally grounded organizational culture. *Copyright © David G. White Jr., 2020.*

CULTURE COMES FROM GROUNDED
MEANINGFUL EXPERIENCE

If you have ever spent any length of time mastering a sport, a musical instrument, a craft, or an art form, or devoted yourself to becoming an expert in your chosen field, you will find what follows familiar. This is because our bodies – not just our brains – are integral to how we think. This idea is foundational to the notion of culture grounded in where and how we spend most of our time. Two cases from anthropology and botany help illustrate.

In studying the differences between pastoralists and forager societies, the anthropologist Penn Handwerker (2009) writes that foragers do not lay claim to land, animals, or plants because to do so would mean suicide: foragers need to keep moving to keep eating. Pastoralists, on the other hand, have many animals and each animal needs to have a sufficient amount of land on which to graze. If too many animals live in the same place and consume all the available food, they won't survive for long. For this reason, pastoralist societies created property rights, and organized themselves so they could assemble large numbers of their own to defend their property from others. Sons and brothers were key to the defense of property because they were known and trusted over strangers. Men shielded women from defense and conflict due to the risk of harm and possible extinction. The orientation toward defense based on brothers and sons was maintained by a pattern of patrilocal residence by marriage, whereby sons would live in the same location as their fathers or uncles, and animals were inherited by sons from fathers. From this emerged the idea of joint title to property and animals, a title which could be passed down through generations via patrilineal descent.

Culture, in this case, in the form of property rights and patrilineal descent, thus emerges as a communal adaptation to the demands of pastoral ecology. If we cared to take this example further, linkages between local ecology and culture might be drawn across many other kinds of cultural experience: kinship rules, marriage norms, values, rites of passage, symbols, ways of making sense of the world, standards of good or bad, and so on (Handwerker, 2009).

The anthropologist, botanist, and linguist André-Georges Haudricourt (1962; in Descola, 2013) took this idea further in his account of how Eastern and Western societies evolved cultural practices out of their respective treatment of nature. Asian societies cultivated crops such as rice and yams prevalent in their geographic region by focusing on improving the environment surrounding these organisms so as to favor their growth, a technique he labeled "indirect" control. Western and near-Eastern societies, on the other hand, whose geographies around the ancient Mediterranean favored raising sheep, developed "direct" methods of control and nurturance: a shepherd actively accompanied his flock, guiding it with his crook and dogs, choosing where the flock should find pasture and water and if necessary defend it from predators. This practice of direct control extended to European farmers in the early days of farming as seen in methods for growing grain, whereby herds of cattle trampled seed into the ground and threshed the grain after it had been roughly harvested by scythe. This evolved, or more accurately, was transposed into cultural practice, as seen throughout the history of the Near East and Europe and depicted in the Bible and in Aristotle. In these texts the idea of the leader as one who commands and directs his subjects as a collective body, like a shepherd tending his flock, is widespread and of course extends deeply into Western thought today. In contrast, indirect action as favored by Eastern societies can be traced through centuries in the precepts for good government conveyed by Confucianism in which conciliation and consensus are favored, or as seen in Melanesia where tribal leaders do not issue orders but strive to ensure their actions reflect the general will of the community. Even the treatment of livestock, in contrast with European and Near East societies, is based on indirect action, such as in Indochina where water buffalo were not so much protected by humans as used as a source of protection for children from possible attack by tigers. Indirect action can even be traced in some Asian languages, where plant metaphors are used to represent humans.

It's "Meaningful" Because It Worked

Handwerker and Haudricaurt's point is that these ecological adaptations required specific practices which evolved into widespread cultural patterns. Their evidence, of course, is circumstantial; the opposition between East and West is not convincing on all points. Nonetheless, the main idea is not about East and West or pastoralists and foragers but about culture grounded in adaptations. This is what *grounded* means: culture comes from a community's adaptive responses to its environmental and existential challenges and contingencies, seen in our earlier example about Rossel Islanders. Even mainstream business academics recognize that organizational culture, at some level, is an adaptation to a firm's competitive environment. But as discussed in the preceding, they assume cultural adaptation can be deliberately engineered: supply the right inputs and out comes the right culture. Business schools and consultants have this pernicious habit of wanting us to believe that the dynamics of culture inside organizations is somehow different than what has been happening in human societies through millennia.

How do physical behaviors in response to stressors in the environment become "cultural" deep structures, such as hundreds of people self-organizing on a subway platform?

Physical adaptations become cultural patterns when they work. Because adaptations to the local environment succeed over time they become meaningful. Meaningful experiences, shared by a group, becomes cultural knowledge. This happens because the experience of *doing the things that make adaptation successful*, the behaviors, practices, and social arrangements that lead to the successful experience, are coded in the brain as generalized knowledge. The features of the experience of success and the features of the environment are stored as general patterns and transformed into knowledge to be applied in other domains. This is how "direct" and "indirect" action may become associated with philosophies of leadership and passed on through generations.

How physical adaptations in the world become cognitive structures in the brain is, obviously, highly complex, but the science of the last 30 years has begun to uncover the biological and neurological mechanisms behind these transformations. To understand it, we need to take a short tour through the science of embodied cognition, dominant logics, and the ways in which the mind make sense.

Culture in the Brain, the Body, and the World

What we do shapes how we think. What cognitive science is demonstrating is that *regular* and *sustained* patterns of interaction with *regularities* in our physical and social environments form the basis for *what*, *how*, and *why* we collectively think as we do. Our bodies, along with the experiences we have inhabiting them in space and gravity as well as in technological, social, and cultural contexts, set into place how we learn, reason, and understand our worlds.[3] *Embodied cognition* is the broad term for this idea: cognition is a dynamic between mind and body interacting continually with the physical, social, and cultural worlds of which it is part.[4]

This is much more than saying we learn from experience. The human organism is always in relation to its environment and cannot, of course, exist without it. Humans grow and survive and become who they are not only as the result of a genetic program but as part of an ongoing developmental process in which cognitive development is "scaffolded" by its surroundings (Griffiths & Stotz, 2000, p. 29).[5] This applies to *all* kinds of surroundings beyond simply the family of origin: it includes repeated exposure to the task, technological, social, or pre-existing cultural environment. This is why pastoralist and forager tribes in different corners of the world develop similar cultures, why people on subway platforms, with some variation, behave in similar ways, and why companies in similar industries evolve similar cultures (Chatman & Jehn, 1994). This idea is foundational for corporate culture: to accept that cognition is embodied is to accept that these dynamics *must* be true for people in organizations as they are in any other realm of human life.

Embodiment can be traced down to the lowest levels of human perception and cognition and out to the broadest levels of culture and society. Because the cognitive science of culture is multi-disciplinary, most of the examples that follow are drawn from disciplines beyond business and economics. In addition to cognitive anthropology, the evidence comes from the fields of neuroscience, artificial intelligence, cognitive and developmental psychology, psycholinguistics, cognitive sociology, and even environmental science. A small sample of it is summarized below.[6]

Evidence From Neuroscience

The brain and the body are intimately intertwined in how we experience the world:

- How we see is tied and tuned to our own bodies in relationship to the environment; the brain is in constant concert with our visual system. This is what allows us to maintain an intact image while we move in space, such as how we hold an image of a car constant as we walk around it (Palmer, 1996). And it's what makes the environment visible to begin with: the human eye continually moves while it fixes on an object even though this activity remains below awareness. If eye movements are counteracted, visual perception fades completely as a result of neural adaptation.[7]

- Functional magnetic resonance imaging (fMRI) and ERP (event-related potentials)[8] studies show the brain is actively involved in processing physical as well as abstract and cultural action as well as emotion.[9] When two neurons fire at the same time, such as when we learn something, "spreading activation" along a network of related neurons occurs (Lakoff, 2008, p. 19). The more two neurons fire together, the stronger the link that is formed. This is how experience shapes the brain: new experiences and learning leads to chemical changes among neural networks through which spreading activation occurs. The more of the same kinds of experience that we have – such as those gained through mastery of a profession, or in solving a hard problem over time – the stronger the spreading activation.[10]

- The well-known concept of "mirror neurons" shows that when people think about a physical action or see someone else perform the activity, the same set of neurons fire as when they physically do that activity (Lakoff, 2008). The areas of the brain associated with visual processing are also active when people see pictures depicting both actual and implied motion (Kourtzi & Kanwisher, 2000).

Evidence From Developmental Psychology

As our bodies move through space they are subject to the laws of gravity, the experience of which sets the stage for cognitive development (Gallagher, 2005). Concepts are created and organized from the experience of bodily movement from the moment we are born. For example:

- The way infants perceive space can be negatively impacted by a lack of early crawling experience. Crawling and other physical experiences effect the infant's perception and ability to estimate height.[11] Newborns can imitate gestures such as tongue protrusion, mouth opening and closing, and lip protrusion. At six weeks, infants can imitate gestures even with a 24-hour delay between testing, suggesting that the concept of imitation exists in memory to guide action, put there by the behavior prime (Meltzoff & Moore, 1983).

- 10-month-old infants who follow a gaze and look longer at an object have significantly more rapid vocabulary growth at two years than infants with shorter looks, even when controlling for external factors such as the mother's level of education (Brooks & Meltzoff, 2008).

- There is experimental evidence that physical action, such as moving an unfamiliar shape along a vertical or horizontal path, alters how children conceptualize unfamiliar shapes. Motor actions like these influence what shapes 2-year-olds see as similar and not similar. Action seems to set in place the conditions for object recognition (Smith, 2004).

Physiological and Kinesthetic Evidence

Bodily experience is integral to thinking.[12] I was painfully reminded of this recently when we lost our beloved 14-year-old Australian Shepherd. We travel a lot, and our frequent comings and goings led me to the belief she was ageless. Although I knew her age, she seemed even in her advanced years to always have about the same amount of energy and enthusiasm for life that she had as a puppy; every time we would return from a business trip she seemed just as before. It wasn't until after her relatively sudden demise over a two-week period and we were left in the aftermath of shock and grief that I realized my disbelief was due to the effects of embodied cognition: because we were, literally, the ones coming and going and she was staying home, it seemed as if she wasn't aging at all. We were the ones moving, therefore, the ones aging.

- This same idea was experimentally demonstrated by Boroditsky and Ramscar (2002) at San Francisco airport. Passengers were asked the question *Next Wednesday's meeting has been moved forward two days* and then asked, *What day is the meeting that has been rescheduled?* Passengers getting off a flight were more likely to answer *Friday* significantly more than passengers waiting to depart, who answered *Monday.* People simulate the concept of time in relation to their own bodies moving through space.
- Changes in posture lead to changes in how one perceives space.[13] Work by Andy Yap (2013) and his colleagues showed that individuals who consciously or inadvertently assumed expansive "power" postures on the basis of ergonomics were more likely to steal money, cheat on a test, or commit traffic and parking violations. Environments that allow one's body to feel more expansive can inadvertently lead

to feeling more powerful, and these feelings can cause dishonest behavior.[14]

- Bodily action plays an important role in facilitating short-term recall: memory is enhanced when events are stored and triggered by movement or action rather than solely by abstract features (Mandler, 1983).[15]

Evidence From Cognitive Linguistics and Cognitive Psychology

People create simulations in their heads of physical actions when they communicate, hear stories, or solve problems. For example:

- When a physical action corresponds to a phrase such as *grasp the concept* or *stomp out racism*, people comprehend the phrase more quickly when the physical action of grasping or stomping follows the metaphor rather than a contradictory or unrelated phrase (Gibbs & Matlock, 2008).
- Abstractions like time and space are in part structured by the experience of our own bodies, as shown in cross-cultural studies on direction. Most cultures conceptualize direction in relation to the self, or in absolute terms, such as to points on a compass or a map.[16] But in some cultures such as the Maya, north–south is derived from the mountainous incline of the local environment, and this axis remains constant no matter where a Mayan Tzeltal speaker travels in the world (Levinson, 1996). This shows how in some cultures visual cues based in the local environment can override other physical experience.
- When children learn the "like" construction, as in *x is like y*, they often learn it through gesture, suggesting gesture provides the physical and spatial context for learning abstract concepts (Ozcaliskan & Goldin-Meadow, 2006).
- Gesture grounds concepts such as valence: even though English has many expressions based on "right" (*I am right, do the right thing*, etc.), Daniel Casasanto (2009) found that right- and left-handers associate positive valence with their dominant hands, not necessarily the right hand.
- Gesture and the use of body-based metaphors aid in learning math (Alibali & Nathan, 2012). Everyday bodily experiences ground our ability to draw inferences and organize mathematical concepts well beyond the syntax of formal mathematics. Without it, much of our comprehension of math would be impossible (Nunez, 2008).

Socio-Cultural Evidence

Cultural and social practices and artifacts can shape how we think (Rogoff, 1990). For example:

- In a study of how children memorize spatial arrays, Mayan 9-year-olds were much better than their U.S. counterparts at reconstructing panoramic scenes but performed much worse on list-memory tasks. In contrast, American children seemed to remember lists, most likely because of how they have been socialized to learn, whereas Mayan children relied more on spatial relationships, especially when the spatial relationships involved culturally familiar objects (Rogoff, 1990).
- In work with children between 15 and 30 months of age requiring them to put objects in, on, or under an upright or inverted cup, Mayan children showed a consistent preference for putting objects in inverted cups, in contrast with Danish children. In Mayan culture baskets are used inverted to cover tortillas and other food items, and in children's games such as for catching chickens. In addition, cups are quite uncommon. The Mayan children's experience of interacting with their material and cultural world predisposed them to use comprehension strategies consistent with that world (Sinha & Jensen de Lopez, 2000).
- When people use a tool the neural representation of one's body changes in relation to it (Kirsh, 2013). As mastery over a tool develops, this reshapes perception, altering how the tool user thinks. A good example comes from music. A guitar doesn't sound like a trumpet (unless played through a synthesizer) because it cannot naturally achieve the trumpet's glissando effects. A trumpet cannot replicate the percussive effects of a guitar. The physical shape and materials of each instrument constrain its sound – its timbre, attack, decay, and so on, which delimits not only what can be played but what the musician *hears* and *attempts* to play to begin with. In this way, cognition and material culture make each other up. Interaction with one's material culture – the tools, instruments and artifacts of that culture – shape the cognitive processes of the person using them (Malafouris, 2004).

There are many other everyday examples of this, such as instruments for navigation – compasses, charts, altimeters – as well as clocks and calendars, among others. The key point is *not* simply that tools help people solve problems. The point is that repeatedly and successfully using a tool shapes what and how we think.[17] We cannot mentally perform an operation like fixing the exact position of a ship on the ocean or landing an airplane in fog without critical instruments, and their use helps us mentally simulate what is happening. For example:

- An instrument landing system in aviation uses a combination of ground stations and cockpit-based instruments to create the idea of a "glide slope" to guide the airplane to the runway. The visual metaphor of an actual slope is depicted on navigation charts. Repeated interactions with charts and other navigation artifacts shape how we conceive of landing an airplane, such that when we think about and speak about an approach and landing in low visibility we imagine an actual glide path.[18]

Much of how we learn and think is contingent on the physical and socio-cultural environments in which the learning has occurred and the thinking is put to use.[19] The cognitive linguist and philosopher Mark Johnson (2007) summarizes this best when he states:

> Every aspect of our spatial experience will be defined by recurring patterns and structures (such as up-down, front-back, near-far, in-out, on-under) that constitute the basic contours of our lived world. It should not be surprising, therefore, that we have evolved to take special notice of these recurring shapes, relations, and patterns, and that these patterns exist as topological features of our neural maps…they are one of the primary ways in which we are in touch with our world, understand it, and can act within it.
>
> **(p. 135)**

What we do shapes how we think, down to our basic neural architecture. What this means, then, is if culture is a product of thinking, what a collective *habitually* and *repeatedly* does – the physical, mental, and social acts involved in performing a task, solving a problem, and adapting to the environment – shape what it collectively thinks. Culture in this way follows task. Not just any task, but those habitually and repeatedly undertaken to solve a problem and ecologically adapt. The premise behind this idea – embodied cognition – is central to functionally grounded culture: human brains are "plastic", deeply patterned by the physical and social acts of living and adapting in the world. This partially answers the questions of what constitutes *grounded* and what is meant by *meaningful*. The rest of the answer comes from understanding how key features of experience are coded in the mind, and how this "code" is transformed into culture.

CULTURE IS SHARED KNOWLEDGE

In order for the cultivation of crops in Asia to lead to Confucianism or raising livestock to lead to property rights, there must be some kind of mental processes for storing and transforming these experiences into entire ways of thinking. Indeed, this process consists of two important operations: mental representation, and its application to new experience, including abstract and conceptual experience.

Shared Dominant Logics: Transforming Experience into Basic Units of Culture

Humans are structure-seeking creatures (D'Andrade, 1995). What our minds want most when it comes to organizing and understanding sensory input is efficiency (Rosch, 2002). To achieve this, sensory input is stored in memory as simplified mental representations. Much of the detail of this input is stripped out to leave a schematic image: think a stick figure of a person or an outline of a house. These representations are "schematic" because only the salient features of the input, and the essential features of the relationship between elements of the input, are stored in memory. Together they make up a gestalt of the situation, a holistic representation stripped of details, leaving just the essentials.[20] These representations have been studied under various names, but for our purposes here I call these schemas, or shared dominant logics. (I use the term "schema" when describing basic research, and SDL or logics when referring to schemas related to corporate culture).[21]

Take the concept of a line. As depicted by the picture below, even though each image is quite different the idea of a line can easily be discerned. Before we can consciously name what the images are, the eye and mind have subconsciously extracted a schematic representation of lines and

FIGURE 3.2
Line schemas.

made the connection that the images go together on the basis of linearity. This reflex is automatic and below awareness. This is how dominant logics work: quickly, efficiently, and preconsciously (Figure 3.2).

There is no one location in the brain where memories are stored; memory consists of neuronal connections and changes to those connections based on perception, feeling, language, and movement (Guenther, 2002). Our cognitive system extracts a mental picture of experience and uses it to help us recognize patterns, anticipate events, and visualize particular experiences as instances of situations already encountered (Descola, 2013). Successive and repeated experiences strengthen these associations. Meaningful experiences *especially* strengthen these associations. This is one reason why recall for general patterns is better than for details of an event, or why we can recall events that mean a lot to us over those that do not (Guenther, 2002). This process is key to the concept of professionalization and shared task solutions, as described below.

Evidence for Schemas

Immanuel Kant posited the idea of schemas in the 19th century, but the Cambridge psychologist Frederic Bartlett was the first to empirically study them in his 1932 landmark work on perception and memory. Since then an impressive array of research across disciplines has helped broaden what we know about schemas.[22]

Schemas have been studied extensively in management under different guises mostly focused on managerial cognition and enterprise knowledge. In addition to dominant logic, they have variously been called *knowledge structures; interpretive schemes; interpersonal schemes; implicit theories; frames; strategic archetypes; industry recipes; organizational paradigms;* and *theories in use;* among other synonyms.[23] As stated, only a small handful of researchers have studied SDLs in the context of corporate culture (hence the use of "shared").

Some of the abundant evidence for schemas:

- Studies with amputees suggest feelings in phantom parts of the body involve a body schema (Gallagher, 2001).
- Research with stroke victims shows changes to a patient's visual field through the use of special glasses can help reestablish motor control. This would not be possible unless the patient had a body schema of some kind (Gallagher, 2005).
- Learning *in* and *on* is considered a difficult linguistic achievement, yet these prepositions are learned early by English-speaking children because a schema for *CONTAINMENT* is developed in the first year. Korean has entirely different verb forms depending on whether a verb is transitive or intransitive, yet children are aware of the *in* and *on* distinction as soon as they use these words (Choi & Bowerman, 1991).
- Schemas such as *AGENT, PATH, GOAL, FORCE, COMPLETED ACTION, POSSESSION, CONTAINMENT* (and so on) appear to be essential for learning language (Mandler, 1992). Studies with deaf infants learning sign language draw the same conclusion: without schemas, or if, say, learning verbs was based on grammatical rules, acquiring prepositions and learning the concept of transitivity in general (i.e., if x is true for y it must be true for z because y is like z) would occur at a much later age.
- The existence of polysemy (a word or phrase with multiple meanings) across many languages suggests language is structured and learned through schemas. It is hard to explain polysemy without admitting that a pre-verbal system of representation is running in the background making polysemy possible.[24]
- From artificial intelligence research on neural networks, models show that knowledge is comprised of networks of links and

simple "processing units" (Strauss & Quinn, 1997, p. 51). Thinking does not happen in words but rather via a pattern of interaction among connected units. Cognitive tasks such as learning spatial relationships and word meanings occur through patterns of neural activation. The strength of such interaction varies by the density of the interconnections of the units and the strength of each connection.[25]

- From cognitive psychology we know that certain cognitive illusions may be due to the effects of schemas. For example, the representativeness heuristic – we derive a theory from a single case because it appears to have the same features as the case we are considering – comes from prototype effects. Prototype effects are a feature of learning based on schemas: we learn based on analogically comparing what we already know to what is now before us (Rosch, 2002).

- Research on schemas in business shows their influence on social behavior and business strategy. For example, people experimentally exposed to theories that advocate the benefits and rationality of self-interest will use this to justify how to act in social interactions. They will use schemas (implicit theories) of market logic, namely that people act out of self-interest, to interpret other people's motives or decide which course of action to follow themselves.[26]

- In a study of new product development initiatives at five firms, based on interviews with 80 people across departments in those firms, Dougherty (1992) found schemas (interpretive schemes) inhibited innovation. Departmentally based "thought worlds", or systems of meaning keep innovators from synthesizing their expertise, and routines based on schemas can inhibit learning across a firm.

- Research shows how entire industries, such as pharmaceuticals and mutual funds, have common schemas (mental models; logics) that structure strategic decision-making and performance, and that strategic performance in turn shapes schemas.[27] My research in industrial manufacturing firms (below and Chapter 4) suggests the same.

Shared Dominant Logics

Shared schemas are cultural schemas, or *shared dominant logics* (SDLs), the basic units of culture (Bennardo & De Munck, 2014). SDLs are implicit *shared knowledge*; we know it but don't know we know it until it is brought into our awareness (or we are confronted with a starkly different knowledge system that jars our own or renders it obsolete). We use this knowledge every day in millions of ways trivial and profound, from what to expect when we arrive on a subway platform or walk into a restaurant to how much or how little eye contact to make with someone in an elevator, whether (and where and when) it is OK as a woman to hug a male colleague, whether it is acceptable to have one's laptop open at a meeting, how we define success, to who is considered a real leader, and so on. This kind of knowledge is "known" by the collective, but it is preconscious, which is the crucial point. As we saw with the survey in the Introduction, shared logics reside below awareness until triggered in context or otherwise brought to our attention. This makes SDLs categorically different than belief systems, or any consciously held value, attitude, or norm. Belief systems and such are consciously known – you could summon your own beliefs or attitudes absent a context cue. SDLs are tacit and assumptive, their logic schematic, triggered by situations and contexts, and referenced continually as resources for making sense.

Making Sense: How SDLs Ground Culture

Saying culture is based on SDLs is a bit like describing a car by showing you all its parts on the garage floor. How do these parts become an actual car? How do SDLs comprise culture? For this we turn to two basic cognitive processes that underlie how humans collectively make sense.[28]

Figure 3.3 is taken from my research at "IMCO", a global industrial conglomerate.[29] It depicts IMCO's SDL of "good leadership". The bubbles in the diagram depict individual bits of logic such as *DEEP INSIGHT INTO HOW AND WHY THINGS WORK, PERSONAL EXPERIENCE SOLVES COMPLEXITY, SKILLS HAVE GAPS,* and so on.[30] When we put a label on a SDL it becomes an assumption, much like labeling a photograph. The SDLs in the diagram are shaded by category, such as those that pertain to *personal experience*, or *built structure*, and so forth, which is simply a way to organize these discrete bits of logic. In the next section we will take up where SDLs come from, and later chapters cover how they were identified. For now I simply want to use this example to illustrate two principal ways in which we collectively make sense: the organization of cultural knowledge, and analogy.

IMCO's Cultural Model of Leadership

Based on primary shared schema

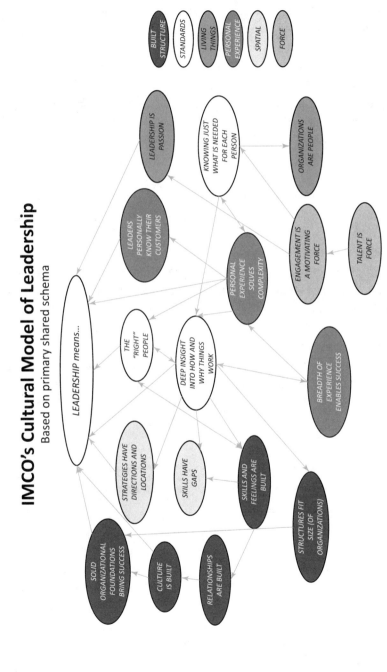

FIGURE 3.3

The implicit logics making up IMCO's cultural model of "good" leadership.

From SDLs to Culture: Models for Making Sense

Some SDLs, like the amount of acceptable eye contact in an elevator versus in a meeting, are more basic and foundational than others. Some, like conceptions of leadership, what constitutes risk, or what is success, are made up of more primitive SDLs that structure more complex or elaborate SDLs, or collections of SDLs. This is not an academic distinction. SDLs are shared mental models *of* or *for* something.

The example in Figure 3.3 is IMCO's implicit model of good leadership. IMCO, like most organizations, has many such implicit models (for good management, how to successfully run the business, how to treat customers, what is innovative, and so on). All are taken-for-granted shared standards of what is "good". The arrows show how each connects with another. For example, in this model leadership success derives, in part, from having a solid organizational foundation, from building a culture, from building (strong) relationships, and from having the right kind of organizational structure for the size of organization.

What might be obvious from this diagram is how unremarkable the individual SDLs are: they sound mundane and familiar. Anyone who has spent time in manufacturing will have a "so what" reaction to them. And that's exactly the point: as individual units of cognition, they are trivial, obvious, and incomplete. Taken together as a network, however, they structure a complex and elaborate shared mental model for leading a successful manufacturing enterprise. By "structure" I mean shaping and characterizing a particular way of making sense, in this case in terms of *built structure, standards, personal experience*, and so forth. This is what makes SDLs unique, distinct and, well, *cultural.*

Pervasive Forms: SDLs for Sense-Making and Structure

Why care about basic versus more elaborate SDLs? After, they're all SDLs. For two reasons. First, like DNA, simple SDLs don't tell us much. What they do is set the parameters and limits for what is possible in how we make sense. *PERSONAL EXPERIENCE SOLVES COMPLEXITY* or *DEEP INSIGHT INTO HOW AND WHY THINGS WORK* (etc.) by themselves could apply to many companies, especially in manufacturing. What tells us more is the network of logic in which they exist. The complexities and nuances of every culture reside in how discrete SDLs come together to structure complex domains, such as shared concepts of leadership.[31] SDLs, thus, are resources for making sense, such as applying standards, rules, or precepts to hundreds of everyday activities and situations.

Second, SDLs supply more than content. They provide a structure for organizing ways of thinking and acting. For example, the cognitive anthropologist Giovanni Bennardo (2011) showed how a foundational SDL (cultural schema) of "radiality" explained a wide range of Tongan cultural behavior, such as conceptions of time, kinship, religious beliefs, navigational practices, and many kinds of social relations. Vern Glaser (2016) and his colleagues demonstrated experimentally how cultural logics – of the market (*people are buyers or sellers; people are self-interested, etc.*) versus the family (*people are related to each other; people operate based on other-interest, etc.*) – drive behavior. My own research in manufacturing shows how these systems have low tolerance for abstract thinking and conceptual models in general (such as Figure 3.3), because the task environment of making tangible things endows these environments with SDLs of *concreteness, seeing is believing,* and *first-hand knowledge* (captured as *PERSONAL EXPERIENCE*). This is a general orientation that manifests in many different ways: standards of good (e.g., *PERSONAL EXPERIENCE SOLVES COMPLEXITY*); how plans are put together and presented (based on first-hand knowledge of the issues); the use of particular metaphors and jargon ("hands-on"); how managers are expected to behave (also "hands-on"); and so forth. The logics of *concreteness, seeing is believing,* and *first-hand knowledge* take many forms. One could say a dominant logic is as much the water in the channel as the channel itself. SDLs not only supply a culture with cultural content, but also with structure that shapes habits, routines, and typical behavior. When an SDL is pervasive in ways of thinking, and widespread in routines and habits, it can be said to be foundational to a culture.

We Think in Analogies

Analogy is arguably *the* major process of human cognition.[32] We create analogies in order to solve problems, make sense of our environments, and learn: we create patterns in order to compare what we know and are familiar with to what we don't know.[33] Cultures form by analogical derivation from the particular to the general (Descola, 2013). Figure 3.3 provides a clear example: the model for leadership shared by IMCO leaders is built up from SDLs that have little to do with leadership (save for those having to do with *living things*). Rather, it is powered by SDLs analogically derived from IMCO's experiential grounding in manufacturing.

When we form an analogy we retrieve the structure of the source of the analogy – the source of our comparison – and to map it to the target, what we are comparing.[34] This is how schemas are learned, or more precisely, *induced* – we don't consciously "learn" them.[35] Think of a primitive schema like CONTAINMENT. This schema has a general structure of an inside, a boundary, and an outside. The parts make no sense without the whole: there is no inside or outside without a boundary, and no boundary without any sides. This is the "structure" of the conceptual source. Primitive schemas like CONTAINMENT thus are induced within the first year of life. Once induced, we impose it analogically many times a day on what we see or hear, such as when we separate out the melody in a piece of music from the rhythm, or the beginning from the end. We impose a container schema on movement, such as when a baseball coach breaks down a batter's swing into its component parts.[36] We impose CONTAINMENT on emotional and psychological states, such as depression: just as an object can be deep in a container and hard to get out, someone can be deep in a depression and hard to get out.[37] And we can use CONTAINMENT in language, such as when we compare our office to a jail. The idea of forced containment is immediate and obvious in the metaphor: the visual imagery provided by the schema is what gives the analogy its descriptive power.[38] The human capacity to analogically extend embodied experience into abstract thought occurs in myriad ways, but it is core to how we think.

Analogical processing, through schemas, is how cultures form. The more interactions we have with the same kinds of sensory input and experience, and the more congruent the experience, the greater the likelihood of schema induction from those experiences (Hutchins, 2010). In cognitive psychology this is called progressive alignment: what is learned early and often becomes more and more generalizable and resembles a wider variety of new contexts.[39] Once induced, schemas are applied analogically to progressively more abstract situations that over time become the basis for new conceptual categories and abstract rules.[40] This is how leadership in a manufacturing company becomes associated with something built. This is why solving hard problems core to a business' means of production tends to induce schemas applied to new situations. And this is one reason why organizational change is so hard: past success induces very durable schemas.

Analogical processing is at the core of professionalization and shared task solutions, two of the three major sources of culture in organizations, to which we now turn.

TECHNOLOGY CHANGES CONCEPTIONS
OF SPACE AND TIME

Our concepts of time and space come from the material and technological world and our ongoing interaction with that world. These interactions shape how we make sense of our experience and how we think. For example, the invention of the steam engine and the railway in the 19th century changed the way time and space were conceptualized. The introduction of the railroad in France in the mid-19th century "annihilated" space and time. A given distance that once took days to travel by horse and carriage could now be covered in a few hours. The perceived space between points was shrunk. Travel guides described the waves of the North Sea breaking on the "doorsteps of Paris" and regaled travelers with the promise of the smell of "German linden trees" in Parisian railway stations.

In England, the railroad forced different ways of keeping time to be standardized, as these efforts were at first uncoordinated: "Each morning an Admiralty messenger carried a watch bearing the correct time to the guard on the down Irish Mail leaving Euston for Holyhead. On arrival at Holyhead the time was passed on to officials on the Kingston boat who carried it to Dublin". The lack of coordination across rail lines forced the various railway companies to cooperate and settle on Greenwich time as valid on all lines.

(Schivelbusch, 1977, pp. 33–43).

WHERE CORPORATE CULTURE COMES FROM

As long as there are humans adapting, storing key experiences in memory, making meaning, and trying to make sense of their environments, cultures will form. While leaders help this process, cultures form just as well without them. And while cognitive science provides a powerful antidote to the myopic and overly simplified ideas about culture in the mainstream, what I've described so far isn't quite enough. Our short tour through embodied cognition, schemas/SDLs, and analogical processing deposit us at the railhead of corporate culture but don't get us all the way into the heart of the city. Our analysis thus far doesn't give us a more fine-tuned understanding of cultural nuance and variation in large, complex organizations, and help us understand why some organizations have easily discernable cultures while others do not. Why do certain SDLs and not others become pervasive and dominant? How are SDLs revised, and what role do leaders play in this? When it comes to *corporate* culture, something more is needed. That something more is *functional grounding*.

Doing Meaningful and Habitual Things: The Ground for Culture

The basic idea is pretty simple: organizations develop cultures by doing meaningful and habitual things. Meaningful and habitual to whom? The CEO? Top leadership? Not necessarily. Meaningful and habitual to a majority in the organization. Cultures originate from the organization's dominant occupational group and their *professionalization* (*who you are* collectively), or the organization's *shared task solutions* (*what you do* that is meaningful, habitual, and successful), or, less often, a *differentiating core purpose*. The experience involved in becoming a professional; the tasks, technologies, practices, and routines people use to accomplish work and solve challenging problems; or a highly motivating higher purpose or mission – all can provide the opportunity and adaptive context for SDLs to be induced. While these may seem like different environments, they share one important feature: they all are meaningful to the people working within them. For the reasons already put forward, SDLs induced in these contexts will tend to be applied widely throughout the organization to form its cultural reference system. These dynamics merit examination.

Professionalization

When the primary work of the organization is closely aligned with one profession, the SDLs from that group will tend to become dominant. This happens because the power and influence of the group will be conveyed through SDLs anchoring the prevailing reference system and serve as the source of its visible culture. The organization may even owe its very existence to the occupational know-how of its founders. Or the unique market, customer or technological (etc.) problems the organization solved in order to be viable will have come about because of the founding team's professional expertise. As the organization evolves, SDLs associated with that influential professional group will proliferate and become the anchors for cultural practices and adaptations, often long after the actual influence of that group has been diluted.

Professionalization therefore refers to the developmental, social, and cultural acts involved in becoming a fully productive member of an occupational group. I use the term more broadly here than doctor, lawyer, engineer, and so forth. Profession is a matter of identity. It consists of a well-defined field of inquiry that has a specific range of problems in its agenda; the required use and mastery of specific tools and techniques; either formal education, apprenticeship or on-the-job exposure where the craft of the field can be learned and practiced; a set of personal beliefs about the sense of mission and social value provided by the field; and a career that is possible to be obtained within it.[41] Thus, under this definition construction work qualifies as a profession. Fast food work does not.[42]

SDLs are induced via professionalization in six ways:

1. *Progressive alignment.* Becoming a professional involves extensive amounts of interaction over time, usually many years, with highly meaningful and congruent inputs and experiences. As discussed above, these inputs and experiences induce schemas that are applied to new situations, thereby generating new inputs and experiences to reinforce existing schemas. The more alike and congruent these experiences, the greater the number of schemas induced. The greater the number of schemas induced, the more durable they will be. Professional orientation, thus, is a reliable predictor of attitudes.[43] This is why engineers think like engineers, lawyers argue like lawyers, surgeons believe they are heroes, and so on. These are stereotypes and clichés, sure, but they reflect schemas that anchor the thinking of these occupational groups.

   One example comes from software. Software engineers at Microsoft use the metaphor *STACK* to characterize phenomena well beyond computer architectures, such as career progression within a discipline (*go up the career stack*), or to calibrate individual performance (*stack rank*). This metaphor was adopted widely across the company by non-engineers. *Career stack* and *stack rank* are not just figures of speech but whole conceptual categories denoting a range of activities, social processes, and emotions (few people like to be "stack ranked"). The *STACK* metaphor, anchored by a *VERTICALITY* schema would not "work" if the structure of the target domain (performance calibration or career progression) did not exhibit the features of the source, in this case the vertical partitioning of disks found in computer hardware architectures. This is *progressive alignment*: the software engineering profession provides a concept used widely across the enterprise that both reinforces and enables the schema (*VERTICALITY*) to be applied to new practices. The more broadly applied, the more *VERTICALITY* is reinforced, and the more durable it becomes (Microsoft, interestingly enough, is quite hierarchical).

2. *Expertise.* Schemas become "dominant" through repetition.[44] The more you do something, the more the embodied effects of that action will strengthen neuronal connections through the effects of spreading activation. This is why "practice makes perfect", and why complex domains from sports to the arts to professional expertise cannot be "learned" or gained without extensive socialization and practice. The literature on expertise is clear on what's entailed: 50,000 examples,[45] thousands of hours,[46] or ten years of dedicated study.[47] The effect of expertise on schemas and cognition has been demonstrated in numerous experiments. For example, experts are able to extract the underlying rules and principles from relevant input in areas where they have expertise far more than novices (Blanchette & Dunbar, 2001).

3. *Indexing and Coding.* Problem-solving requires recognition of what counts as a problem to begin with, as well as strategies for solving it. The way professionals index and code data within their field may be the most important mechanism behind schema induction.[48] For example, how physicists frame problems by deduction from first principles, in contrast with biologists who use induction from trial and error, structures discourse, and practice within those communities and the underlying schemas anchoring them.[49] Through framing, highlighting, and coding data, professionals learn "where and how to see" (Goodwin, 1994, p. 615). Professional cognition is entrained in the minute details and tools, practices, technologies, and modes of production of the profession. The example of pilots understanding an instrument approach as a glide slope is one among many examples of this.

4. *Identity.* Becoming a fully functioning member of a professional or occupational group is obviously meaningful. Part of this meaning comes from the sense of identity that expertise and mastery confer. For example, Bucher and Stelling's (1977) work on professional

identity showed that doing work deemed important to others was the single most meaningful experience for instilling professional identity, defined as the moment when the novice professional labeled herself a professional (e.g., a "biochemist" rather than a "student").[50] Identity is also closely tied to motivation: what one is motivated by relates closely to ones' sense of identity.[51]

5. *Social Evaluation*. Becoming a professional is an experience filled with evaluation – by peers, mentors, teachers, students, clients, and so on – and these experiences are usually emotionally charged. Medical students, for example, receive intensive and lengthy socialization into the beliefs, values, norms, and accepted practices of medicine (Fonne & Myrhe, 1996). Social evaluation aids in determining what groups find meaningful to begin with. And as discussed, schemas themselves can be emotionally motivating (Strauss & Quinn, 1997). Social power, for example, can be experienced as a *FORCE* schema, which motivates thought as well as language and behavior.[52]

6. *Historicity*. Schemas are historically persistent and can be transmitted across generations through norms, practices, language, and other social conventions, a process the cognitive anthropologists Claudia Strauss and Naomi Quinn (1997) call "historicity". SDLs are generally not transmitted as bodies of rules and precepts but are internalized little by little, without any overt teaching or transmission (Descola, 2013). Many professional schemas are "handed down", as it were, over generations, much like the story of the daughter who always cut off both ends of the ham before cooking it. When asked why, she said, "I don't know, my mother always did it this way". When the mother was asked, she said the same thing. When the grandmother was asked, she said, "Oh, we did it that way because we did not have a pan that was big enough to fit the entire ham!" (from Strauss & Quinn, 1997). Similarly, nearly every one of my IMCO "informants" mentioned a key formative experience in their career was learning from a highly respected mentor or boss.[53] Not surprisingly, this group shares a strong SDL associated with first-hand knowing, *THE PRIMACY OF PERSONAL EXPERIENCE*. Historicity is a common inducer of shared logics because the past is often very meaningful for action in the present: *because a set of actions worked in the past, they should work today*.

Tip: One of the main reasons why organizational change is so hard is because firms that have solved hard problems core to their means of production – whether these be market, technology, product, or service problems – induce SDLs that are applied to novel situations. Unfortunately, these new situations may require learning new SDLs for the firm to be successful. This is why change is particularly difficult in firms that have experienced sustained success in one domain, such as manufacturing, to succeed in a new domain, such as digital technology. What got you here won't get you there.

Shared Task Solutions

Organizations develop cultures by doing meaningful and habitual things, like successfully solving a hard problem or meeting a tough challenge deemed important to the collective. They do so with particular tools, technologies, habits, and routines over time. When these actions solve a problem central to the firms' survival or core to its business, they induce dominant logics. The more successful and important the solution, the more durable the SDLs become. This is how *culture follows task*. This simple but profound fact has deep implications for corporate culture.

Many of these dynamics are the same as for professionalization; grounding sources like historicity, for instance, manifest in organizations as much as they do in professions. But task solutions are not confined to dominant professional groups. Rather, they pertain to the organization as a whole. For example, HR has a distinct professional socialization process and a material task environment, but unless it's an HR consultancy it's unlikely any HR task solution will induce SDLs shared by the enterprise (any SDL induced will be localized to the HR function).

Shared task solutions have four distinct grounding contexts: *Shared solutions, technological grounding, regionality,* and *routines*:

1. *Shared Solutions.* When people in organizations solve recurring problems, the successful solutions tend to proliferate. When they do, they tend to induce SDLs associated with the solution. For example, Strauss and Quinn's (1997) showed how shared solutions to the problems inherent in forming lasting marriages created a shared schema of *OVERCOMING OBSTACLES* for U.S. Americans. The schema has added salience because it linked to broader ones in U.S. American

culture of *YANKEE INGENUITY, HARD WORK,* the value of *LASTINGNESS,* and *PRIDE IN ONE'S WORK,* creating a robust model of marriage.

An organizational example of this is illustrated by a technology client of ours that does a significant amount of work in the defense industry. A few years ago it went through a traumatic event. As a consequence of sequestration, the U.S. government's automatic spending cuts that froze all defense spending, the company's customers, major defense contractors, canceled or suspended all their programs. This forced our client to lay off nearly a quarter of its workforce. For a company of its size at the time, approximately 800 people, this was a significant blow. The company survived sequestration and now its stock is trading at an all-time high, but it bears scars from that experience, as seen in its pervasive SDLs of executive *CONTROL, RISK MANAGEMENT, TRACKING DETAILS,* and *DELIVERING RESULTS.* These SDLs are expressed not only in the company's espoused values, but manifest across practices, such as weekly detailed business reviews between the COO and all general managers, and detailed risk management planning. Company executives acknowledge this practice is a direct outgrowth of the sequestration experience. Shared solutions, thus, induce schemas not only by solving hard problems, but also by successfully overcoming difficult events.[54]

HISTORICITY

Pascual Restrepo (2015) provides an intriguing case of historicity in his study of the settlement of the Canadian prairies.

Communities that in the late 1880s were located 100 kilometers or more from former Royal Canadian Mounted Police forts during their settlement period, over a century later – in 2014 – had 45 percent more homicides and 55 percent more violent crimes per capita than communities located closer to former forts. Historical census data shows that settlements removed from the Mounties' reach had unusually high adult male death rates. Even a century later the effects of this legacy can be seen: those living in once more lawless areas are more likely to hold conservative political views. Hockey players born in areas historically outside the historical reach of the Mounties are penalized for their violent behavior more often than those who were not.

These differences, he suggests, may be explained by a culture of honor that emerged in settlements farther from Mountie forts as an adaptation to the lack of a central authority during the settlement period, which has persisted to this day. The code or practice of honor in these communities may have been fueled by schemas that hold violent retribution rather than the rule of law as legitimate redress for offense, and these schemas, embedded in codes and practices, may have been resident for generations.

Restrepo does not draw from schema theory to explain his data, but his research illustrates the interplay between ecology, social adaptation, and culture that persists through generations, and is entirely consistent with the notion of historicity – the historical durability of SDLs.

2. *Technological Grounding.* Culture is closely linked to the material technologies of the enterprise, particularly technologies that give rise to or enable its primary business. For example, the creation of the Windows operating system at Microsoft and the market success that Windows experienced can be seen in the company's primary SDLs (see Table 3.1).

A good example comes from the history of Qwest and U.S. West. Qwest, a much smaller fiber optics company, merged with the much larger and older telephone company, U.S. West, one of the original Baby Bells, and within a matter of months completely absorbed it such that, for all intents and purposes, the larger company ceased to exist. Qwest's fiber-optic business ground the company in values of speed and service captured by the slogan, "Ride the Light" (Leonardi & Jackson, 2009, p. 405). Qwest's entrepreneurial way of operating was justified on the grounds of its technology, along with the perception that U.S. West was old, bureaucratic, and slow. Fiber optics, in essence, provided the grounding context for the shared SDL of speed and technological superiority, which enabled a set of norms, behavior, practices, and values it deemed better than that of its merger partner.[55] Qwest gained cultural control during the post-merger

TABLE 3.1

Examples of How SDLs Manifest in Different Industries and Organizations Based on Dominant Profession, Core Task, or Mission

Type of Organization	Dominant Profession, Core Task, or Mission (source of dominant logic)	Shared Dominant Logics (SDLs)
IRS	• Tax collection, audit	• Careful checking • Suspicion
Airline	• Moving people and bags safely and efficiently from A to B	• Time pressure ("be on time") • Cost • Safety
Consumer Products	• Bringing new products to market quickly and taking market share	• Market intelligence • Secrecy
Law Firm	• Litigation, advocacy	• Argument • Win–lose • Others are adversaries
Social Services Organization	• Serving under-represented constituencies with low-cost psychotherapy • Social work	• Fight for life and justice
Microsoft (mid 2000s)	• Creating software platforms (APIs, tools) for partners to build applications • Success from inventing the Windows OS and dominating in the market	• Platforms • Competence and "intellectual horsepower" (know your stuff and solve hard problems) • Partners and ecosystems
"IMCO" – Global Diversified Manufacturing	• Manufacturing pumps, valves, connectors, elastomers and other products for industrial applications	• Built structure • Personal Experience • Standards

Sources: Steele (1972); White (2017).

integration process by continually referencing its technological superiority to frame the future of the organization, suggesting that dominance over U.S. West was inevitable despite its smaller size and briefer history.[56]

While technology and task have the potential to ground the cognitive orientations of the company, this doesn't mean it will in every case. *How* people perceive the technology is key. This is a function of how central the technology is to a firm's means of production, how the technology is put to use, and what meaning people attach to the solutions it provides. It is also a function in which professional communities are dominant; the deployment of a new HR informa-tion system (HRIS), even one based on the latest technology, likely won't induce new SDLs unless that HRIS is somehow central to the firm's core business.

3. *Regionality.* Local values, practices, and underlying SDLs embedded in the wider history and culture of the region associated with a firm's origins can exert long-lasting influence on its shared task solutions. Regionality can lend ready-made SDLs aligned with or that give rise to a firm's competitive identity. For example, as mentioned, longstanding social interaction norms among manufacturers in the north of Italy endowed firms there with SDLs of trust and artisan craftsmanship. In Baden-Wurttemberg, Germany, engineering excellence and problem-solving SDLs common in the region helped fuel the worldwide competitiveness of *Mittelstand* firms (Gertler, 2004). In the mutual fund business, differing logics of what constitutes successful investing characterized differences between Boston and New York firms. Boston investment firms emphasized wealth preservation underpinned by a *trustee* SDL, which led to passive, low cost approaches characterized by efficiency. The logic of trusteeship had its roots in the history of the "Brahmin elites" of that city, characterized by values of "pedigree" and "propriety". New York investment firms favored growth, characterized by aggressive short-term investing, underpinned by a *performance* logic engendered by that city's ethos of competition, class mobility, and opportunism (Lounsbury, 2007, p. 291–292). No doubt, the very different embodied experience of these two cities evident to this day – Boston gentile versus New York intensity – likely provided grounding sources for these logics.

4. *Routines.* Organizational routines induce shared logics via repetition, as seen with the discussion on neuronal spreading activation. The more we do something, the more automatic the doing becomes, whether it is hitting a tennis ball or playing the piano or building a team or creating a market strategy. Routines are both the product of SDLs as much as agents that structure and change them, and are closely linked to organizational capabilities, as well as to its history, social context, and competitive environment. Hardly ever do managers construct new ways to solve the same problems, though doing so is key to culture change. Routines and shared task solutions make each other up; routines are an integral part of a company's core tasks as those tasks are embedded in its routines.[57]

A clear example of this is at Amazon, where the routines of online retailing have been taken to the extreme in the company's fulfillment centers. The extensive use of routines, rules, and robotics have led to a "steady stripping of human judgment from work", making people "resemble robots", leading to the charge that Amazon treats workers as if they were something less than people.[58] The extreme expression of this is a video game that entices workers to accumulate points and badges for completing routine tasks under a certain amount of time (the so-called "gamification" of work, itself a unique SDL combining schemas of efficiency, technological innovation, and video gaming). The logics of efficiency and optimization, essential in successful retailing and no doubt writ large at Amazon have come together to dehumanize work.[59]

What we see in Amazon's fulfillment centers is the leading edge of the Fourth Industrial Revolution. And while all of that is true, this is also an example of how shared task solutions – borne out of the company's supremely successful business model and strategy – become self-reinforcing, inducing dominant logics of *efficiency, optimization, the supremacy of technology* (and others) that reinforce the task solution ad infinitum.[60] These logics, inculcated through many mundane and innocuous routines at the center of the company's distribution process, make culture appear inexorable. Which is one reason why culture can feel like an unstoppable force. Until the logics underlying the routines are exposed and examined, it will always feel this way.

SHARED *TASK SOLUTIONS IN THE TEXTILE INDUSTRIES OF ENGLAND AND GERMANY*

Richard Biernacki's (1994) study of labor practices in the textile industry in England and Germany extending from the end of the Middle Ages into the 20th century provides a fascinating view of task solutions and how they anchor culture.

In German textile factories, employment was viewed as a service in which workers provided their own capacity for work. German workers considered time itself as what constituted work. In contrast, British managers viewed labor as worker output. Yorkshire weavers could supply substitutes to operate looms. These differences in labor practice structured employment contracts, disciplinary rules, and extended into the way in which workers figured earnings. For example, German workers believed they had a right to payment for the time spent waiting for work. In England, factory owners did not offer workers "waiting money", and "nor did British workers ask for it" (p. 70).

In Germany work was time; in England it was output. These two fundamentally different conceptions, which had historical roots dating further back over centuries, led to different notions of labor capacity and economic ideology. These differences had ramifications well beyond the mills and factory floors. They extended into the design of factories, how workers in the two countries made demands of their employers, and even to the different ways Marxist ideas were adopted in factories in England in the early 20th century.

As Biernacki states, "the schemas encoded in silent practices within the private factory lent workers the concept of labor they used to voice demands in the public sphere ... the cultural definition of labor as a commodity was communicated and reproduced, not through ideal symbols as such, but through the hallowed form of unobtrusive practices".

(Biernacki, 1994, in Swidler, 2001, p. 84).

Differentiated Core Purpose

A differentiated core purpose is a shared goal or organizational mission that is unique and meaningful to a majority in the organization. Typically it is one whose achievement is deemed essential to the betterment of society, humankind, or the planet. Differentiated core purpose usually goes well beyond normal capitalist or commercial ambitions, which is one reason why they are relatively rare in corporate settings (not that commercial organizations are shy to try and enact them). There is also growing evidence that a well-defined sense of purpose beyond financial goals generates shareholder value.[61] The perceived meaningfulness of purpose can induce dominant logics. The idea is similar to Collins' (2001) "core ideology" *in Good to Great*, and others who make the attempt to link purpose, ideology, or so-called "higher ambition" to social value.[62]

One might be tempted to think a differentiated core purpose is the one grounding source directly engineered by founders or the CEO, as Collins and others imply. While leaders are clearly responsible for articulating a core purpose and mission, organizations also need congruent practices for any logic to be fully induced. For example, Southwest Airlines' highly differentiated core purpose as "the airline for the common man" was only the beginning of a cascade of highly aligned activities and strategies that allowed that unique and differentiated purpose to become more than the expressed wish of Fred Kelleher, its founder (Heskett, 2011). It closely aligned all of its strategies and practices over the years to enable this purpose, such as its choice of 737s as the only aircraft type in its fleet; its single class of service; its fast aircraft turnaround times; its managers helping to clean planes; its point-to-point route structure; and so on.[63] These practices enabled the airline to maintain low fares, which in turn enabled purpose to become reality. The tight coupling of core business practices with purpose, and the managerial discipline in maintaining this alignment over the years, served to reinforce the underlying dominant logic of low cost as the key enabler of the "common man" vision (Raynor, 2011).[64]

The Southwest story is not the product of values. As we saw in Chapter 1, just because an espoused value exists doesn't mean employees will act in accordance with it, especially as the organization grows. Practices are the glue. In order for practices to be reinforcing, they have to be structured with a core purpose in mind, which usually doesn't happen simply in accordance with the founder's expressed vision. It comes about because those designing and instilling the practices have a common logic in mind.[65] When practices don't align with the mission, the result is often alienated and cynical employees.

A differentiated core purpose, thus, is a necessary but not sufficient condition for SDLs (Figure 3.4). The key is *thematic consistency*. By aligning all of a firm's practices to enable its core purpose, and by maintaining discipline to preserve this alignment, a firm ensures its dominant logics will be induced in the widest number of contexts with the greatest number of employees. An inspiring goal and mission statement, or a brilliant vision by the CEO, is not enough; were that the case, non-governmental organizations (NGOs) and other mission-driven enterprises would have highly unified cultures, which clearly they do not.

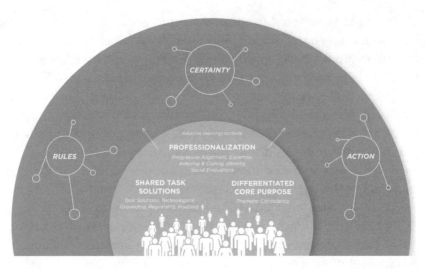

FIGURE 3.4
Sources of culture in organizations: grounding sources for shared dominant logics (SDLs). The SDLs shown ("Rules", etc.) are examples. *Copyright © David G. White Jr., 2020.*

FUNCTIONALLY GROUNDED CULTURES

Functional grounding explains why "engineering cultures" or "sales cultures" or "mission-driven cultures" (etc.) become the dominant metaphors people use to describe their own organizations. It explains why firms in industries have similar cultures: *task constrains how people think*. It explains why retailers like Amazon and Home Depot are characterized by the pervasive use of metrics,[66] or why Google, as the inventor of internet search, is obsessed with data in virtually all aspects of its business. This is also why manufacturing firms have difficulty operating like software firms – no matter how many best-practice cases they adopt. This is why NGOs have trouble implementing professional management techniques from the for-profit world. Functional grounding explains *why* culture is the governor of transformation. Table 3.1 provides some examples of functional grounding. It shows how a dominant profession, core task, or mission gives rise to SDLs in these organizations.

This does not mean cultures can be reduced to dominant logics based on professionalization, task solution, or mission. Functional grounding is not a newer and more clever way of reducing culture.

Managers draw from a wide variety of logics to structure their thinking, many of which are conventionalized in the wider cultural environment. For example, many conventional logics about success in North America and Europe are drawn from sports, entertainment, and mainstream business culture (e.g., *winning*; *capturing hearts and minds*; *shareholder value*). Organizations have hundreds of shared logics based on a myriad of experiential, ecological, technological, and other factors, rendering no two organizational cultures exactly alike. Which logics actually ground a culture is what makes for culture's uniqueness and complexity. While professionalization, task solutions, or differentiated purpose are necessary, they may not be sufficient for a distinct culture to appear. Even though Google and Microsoft employ thousands of software engineers, they do not have identical cultures. But the more that SDLs originate in any of these three grounding environments, the more distinct and coherent the firm's culture will appear, because the logics will be unique to the firm rather than drawn from the wider cultural context.

The Reference System

As products of shared cognition, SDLs are dynamic, continually under stress by market demands, global pandemics, institutional constraints, macro-economic or environmental disjunctions, regulatory issues, and the forces of technological and societal disruption. Dominant logics anchor every culture, but that anchoring can be "loose" – contradictory, not integrated, contested, and weakly bounded. Or it can be "tight" – thematically consistent, durable, sustained by many practices, and highly motivating – the Southwest model. But the idea of a single corporate culture in any organization larger than a small company is a myth. Rather than think of culture as a monolithic whole, cultures are collections of SDLs – some more pervasive than others – that combine to form a unique reference system of taken-for-granted knowledge and socially accepted ways of thinking and acting. Culture, in short, *is a reference system*, an operating system running in the background of our organizational lives.

What about the rest of culture, the other stuff we ordinarily think about when we think of culture – how people behave, values, stories, myths, memes, symbols, brand treatments, office layouts, and such? For this, we need to consider the other elements of the reference system.

Practices and Adaptations

Shared dominant logics are the "source code" of the reference system. The rest of the system is made up of *practices* and *adaptations* (and see Figure 3.1).

- *Practices* are the collection of informal and formal routines, habits, and processes by which every firm runs its business. They are structured by SDLs and can be broken down into six categories: *planning, management and reporting, customer, product, people, and social acceptance*. Practices will be discussed more fully in Chapter 4 when we look at an archetypal company. Practices are key to culture change because only by intervening in the formal and informal habits and routines of the business can collective neural structure be changed.

- *Adaptations* are a firm's reactions or responses to its dominant logic, usually expressed as widespread attitudes and behavior. Adaptations are sometimes exaggerations of dominant logic, sometimes reactions to it, or sometimes compensations for it. Adaptations are often mistaken as *the* culture because they manifest as behavior and attitudes. They are called out separately in this model because they tend to be reflexive, the automatic and sometimes "overlearned" application of dominant logic in ways that can inhibit or preclude change (Steele, 1972). Table 3.1 shows how adaptations manifest in a variety of different firms based on their SDLs. Overlearned reactions to SDLs can be seen in employee attitude surveys, or in widespread patterns of dysfunctional behavior, like passive-aggressiveness. In such cases one might say "our culture is passive-aggressive", and while that would be accurate, it would not necessarily point to what to do about it. As symptoms of underlying dominant logic, adaptations allow the change leader and culture intervener to more clearly separate out symptom from cause.

There is more to culture than the reference system, but the reference system is its essence. Without the operating system and the middleware the applications won't run. So with culture: without SDLs serving as a common foundation, culture will have no organizing principle, nothing to impart the illusion that it is a thinly coherent whole. Which makes the reference system the most important element of culture, because to change a culture requires intervening in ways that alter the reference system.

Visible Culture

Visible culture is what a customer, new hire, visitor, or cultural anthropologist might see upon entering the organization. It consists of things like office layouts and brand treatments or tag lines, as well as what the firm tells itself about what matters – its espoused values, beliefs, and published norms. It consists of memes, such as a video of the founder or founding team on how they established the firm. Visible culture may be the visible manifestation of SDLs, or it might be the espoused wishes of leadership and quite disconnected from the reference system.

Discrete Signatures

By now it might be clear that culture as exemplified by the 5 Myths is quite different from the cognitive science. For one, cognitive science puts most of culture into the background, in the form of taken-for-granted knowledge. It might be disconcerting to think of culture in these terms, especially if, like me, you believed culture was a blank canvas on which you could paint anything. But you might also have the impression that the cognitive science of culture is quite intuitive because it explains lived culture. It explains culture's pervasiveness, as well as its slipperiness and difficulty in changing. Culture is pervasive, slippery, and hard to change precisely *because* it is preconscious, coming from our embodied "deep structure" experience of working and living in the world. Moreover, cultural reference systems are subject to near-infinite variation because they are made up of the cognitions of individuals. In this way cultures don't *cause* us to do anything. At any moment in time any one of us could be operating according to the dictates of a different reference system, as is often the case with people who "don't fit in".

While cognitive science is different than the pop-culture-of-culture, much of the evidence for it as presented above, abundant as it is, is still circumstantial. This does not mean it isn't strongly suggestive, relevant, or compelling, but we are still in the early days of understanding the mind and its relationship to culture. This relationship is complex, and there are many disciplines arriving at the same intersection from different perspectives. This requires triangulation across literatures and disciplines to see the whole picture, which is one reason it takes a few pages to convey the gist. With respect to shared logics, they tend to be so internalized within a community that they seldom surface as products of conscious thought. It's not as if you can ask a person or group, "what are your dominant logics?" This makes working with them challenging. To trace CONTAINMENT or THE PRIMACY OF PERSONAL EXPERIENCE through an organization requires becoming aware and sensitized to these patterns in order to "see" them to begin with. Yet another issue is circularity: how do we know what we are seeing is, in fact, a SDL and not the product of our own projections? And do practices beget SDLs, or SDLs practices? These are all important issues taken up in the next chapter.

But cultures do exhibit discernable patterns and tendencies. Pervasive logics give cultures, as it were, their own signatures. These signatures are always a unique blend of functionally grounded logics with those appropriated from the wider culture (ethnic, national, or popular business). All of this adds up to why culture is the most nuanced and complex domain of organizational life, and also why it presents such a compelling opportunity for the intervener who chooses to put this science to use. So the better question to ask is, what about the possibilities? Is the way we currently approach culture up to the demands of the kinds of transformations being forced upon us by the radical disruptions taking place across industries, and in society at large? The evidence supporting the cognitive science of culture is impressive. Only a small portion of it is here, and more emerges every day, but it poses a direct challenge to mainstream thinking. Culture is now decomposable to its building blocks. This doesn't mean identifying and working with dominant logics will be easy. This does mean it is the first theory and technology available for wholesale and sustainable culture change. You have to decide what this means for you.

The next chapter takes us further into this nuance and complexity by examining a functionally grounded culture up close, in the form of an archetypal Fortune 1000 company. We will look at the ways in which cultural signatures manifest, and what this means for a company trying to transform itself.

NOTES

1. White (2017).
2. The term "reference system" comes from the cognitive anthropologist David Kronenfeld (2018).
3. This idea stands in contrast with classical view of cognition in the cognitive sciences which uses the metaphor of the computer to explain cognitive processes; cognition *is* mental computation. The mind is a processing system that manipulates symbolic representations, and the processing capacity of the brain is modular and impervious to context (de Bruin & Kastner, 2012; Engel, 2010; Fodor, 1975). Thus, abstract and symbolic conceptual knowledge is all that matters for knowledge, and the sensorimotor system is ancillary to or inconsequential in tasks that do not require it (Mahon & Caramazza, 2008). This 'computational' version, needless to say, has been highly criticized by embodied theorists. For more see Hutchins (2010, 1987), Johnson (2007, 1987), Kimmel (2008), Kitayama and Park (2010).
4. The term encompasses a range of related frameworks known as "embedded", "distributed", "situated", "meditated" and "enacted" cognition, all which stem primarily from three sources: from the theory of *enactivism* as posited by Varela, Thompson, and Rosch (1991); from work on metaphor and embodiment by Lakoff and Johnson (1980, 1999); and from Eleanor Rosch's work on prototypes (2002). The organizing principle among all of them is that how we think is dynamically dependent on and structured by our surrounding environment.
5. See also Bolender (2008).
6. As stated, for a much more complete understanding of the evidence, please see White (2017).
7. Martinez-Conde, Macknik, and Hubel (2004).
8. Event-related potentials (ERPs) are very small voltages generated in the brain in response to specific events or stimuli. They are produced when a large number of related or adjacent neurons (in the order of thousands or millions) fire in synchrony while processing information (from Sur & Sinha, 2009).
9. Just because electronic impulses in the brain can be registered in conjunction with some physical stimuli does not mean one caused the other. That said, the evidence is strongly suggestive. For more, see Kitayama and Park (2010), Lakoff (2008), Lieberman and Eisenberger (2010), Lieberman, Eisenberger, Crockett, Tom, Pfeifer, and Way (2007), Pessoa (2008).
10. This is also commonly referred to as synaptic plasticity.
11. Campos, Bertenthal, and Kermoian (1992).
12. Hutchins (2010).
13. Bauermeister (1964), Wapner and Werner (1965).
14. See also Carney, Cuddy, and Yap (2010).
15. This is one reason why experiential learning is so important as leadership and management development pedagogy.
16. Gibbs (2003), Keller (2011), Levinson (1996).
17. Hutchins (1995).
18. For more on this, I recommend Hutchins (1995), and Sinha and Jensen de Lopez (2000). An extreme example of shared cognition changed through tool use is most tragically being witnessed today in aviation, where a growing reliance on automation in cockpits is eroding basic flying skills, leading to catastrophic accidents. The

aviation industry at large (manufacturers, regulators, airlines) may be 'forgetting', as it were, that pilots manipulating computers in cockpits are sitting in machines subject to the laws of gravity where aerodynamics and basic airmanship skills still apply, and where capacities for sensemaking and action are more easily overwhelmed when an emergency or unexpected situation arises because of the over-reliance on automation (Kitroeff, *The New York Times*, September 26, 2019).

19. There remains a debate about how much cognition is actually "embodied", but the idea that cognition is grounded in one's body and surrounding environment is widely accepted. The argument for 'disembodied' cognition basically is that much of the embodiment evidence can be explained by a disembodied view as well. As put by Mahon and Camarazza (2008, p. 59), "One more fMRI experiment demonstrating that the motor cortex is activated during action observation or sentence processing does not make the embodied cognition hypothesis more likely to be correct..." At the same time, they admit the activation of the sensory and motor systems during conceptual processing grounds abstract and symbolic representations in the body. Sensory and motor information constitutes, in part, the "mental stuff" over which concept are realized.

20. Halford, Bain, Mayberry, and Andrews (1998). See also Schank and Abelson (1977).

21. These concepts have slightly different meanings and applications, but for our purposes here they generally refer to the same kind of thing. For a complete discussion of these nuances please see *Rethinking Culture*.

22. For a complete treatment, see Rumelhart and Ortony (1977), Johnson-Laird (1983), or Senge (1992).

23. See Walsh (1995) or Spender (1995, 1996).

24. For example, in Japanese *hon* can refer to long thin things as well as trajectories, like the flight of a baseball (Lakoff, 1987). In the Tarascan language (Michoacan), the suffix *mari* can refer to facial parts, flat surfaces, vertical surfaces, or a flat part of the body (Palmer, 1996).

25. Regier (1996), Strauss and Quinn (1997).

26. Glaser, Fast, Harmon and Green (2016).

27. See Osborne, Stubbart, and Ramaprasad (2000), Lounsbury (2007).

28. Karl Weick's seminal *Sensemaking in Organizations* (1995) covers much of this same ground. However, I have purposefully not used his term, sensemaking, here because I want to differentiate cultural models and analogical transfer, the two dynamics of culture formation in organizations, from his more elaborate theory of how organizations make sense.

29. Not the company's real name.

30. From here forward, all SDLs are denoted by italicized caps, as in *CONTAINMENT*. Categories of SDLs, such as those pertaining to *built structures*, are in lower case italics.

31. Sieck, Rasmussen, and Smart (2010).

32. Gentner and Colhoun (2008), Hummel and Holyoak (1997).

33. For a good primer on this, I suggest Lakoff and Johnson's *Metaphors We Live By* (1980/2003).

34. Hummel and Holyoak (1997), Mandler (1992).

35. See Gick and Holyoak (1983), Hummel and Holyoak (1997), Gentner and Colhoun (2008).

36. Example taken from Lakoff and Johnson (1999).

37. Example from Rohrer (2006).

38. Gentner and Colhoun (2008).

39. Gentner and Colhoun (2008), Strauss and Quinn (1997).
40. Rohrer (2006), Strauss and Quinn (1997).
41. This definition is from Bucher and Stelling (1977).
42. Not included here is fast food restaurant chain or franchise ownership or management. That would qualify as a profession.
43. For example, see Horowitz, Yaworkski, and Kickham (2019).
44. See Mandler (1983), Munby, Versnel, Hutchinson, Chin, and Berg (2003), Rerup and Feldman (2011), Rousseau (2001).
45. Simon and Chase (1973), as cited in Gentner, Loewenstein, and Thompson (2003).
46. Ericsson, Krampe, and Tesch-Roemer (1993).
47. Hayes (1989).
48. Chi, Feltovich, and Glaser (1981), Goodwin (1994).
49. See Abbott (1998), Fleck (1979), Knorr-Cetina (1999), Leonardi (2011).
50. Bucher and Stelling (1977, p. 265).
51. Epstein (1998).
52. Gardenfors (2007), Kovecses (2008).
53. An "informant" is a term from ethnography that refers to a person typically responsible for informing or guiding the ethnographer with information and insight about the culture or society under study. I favor this term over "participant" or "subject", or similar ones that refer to human research subjects. To further differentiate meaning, I will use the term "client" to mean the person or organization receiving services or research findings.
54. Other studies show similar effects. For example, studies of police culture showed that exposure to and successfully navigating danger and death in everyday police work had a unifying effect on police communities, and gave rise to an entire system of meaning (Paoline, 2003). Gordon (1991), as well as Calori (1992) and his colleagues showed how common assumptions (SDLs) develop among managers within the same industries in response to similar customer demands, competition, societal expectations, and regulatory requirements. These in turn lead to common cognitions and values that preclude organizations from developing strategies or structures in conflict with these assumptions.
55. Technological grounding is likely the product of linkages from the technology itself to practices that employ the technology to things like job descriptions. The structure of the task, enabled by the technology, structures the cognitive orientations of the actors using the technology. This idea is closely related to the so-called mirroring hypothesis, the idea, demonstrated empirically, that there is correspondence between organizational structure and technical architecture (Colfer & Baldwin, 2010).
56. Leonardi and Jackson (2009).
57. See Johnson (1990).
58. See Scheiber, *The New York Times* (July 3, 2019).
59. There is nothing surprising in this example. Amazon, like any other retailing giant and the most successful on-line retailer on the planet, is relentless about optimizing throughput. This is what companies like Amazon *do*, perpetually finding ways to reduce costs by increasing efficiency. It is the essence of good business, and of capitalism, which, in the chain of logic justifying the ever more efficient use of machines, capital, and human resources, inevitably leads to machines taking over human work.

60. The positing of these SDLs at Amazon is speculative. I have not conducted any research at Amazon to substantiate the example. The point is to add flesh to the concept of routines and SDLs by using a real example, albeit hypothetical.
61. For example, see Reeves et al. (2018).
62. For example, see Beer, Eisenstat, Norrgren, Foote, and Fredberg, T. (2011).
63. Porter (1996, p. 66), Heskett (2011).
64. Some ascribe Southwest's values as the reason for the airlines success, but values alone do not explain how the tight congruence between mission and practice could have come about to begin with.
65. Of course, this discussion of Southwest is speculative. No research on SDLs has been conducted there that I know of. The point is the SDL of *LOW COST* embedded in multiple practices better explains the Southwest phenomenon more than values.
66. See Charan (2006).

4

Invisible Hands, Invisible Walls

The driving force of conscious agency is hardly supported by ethnological and sociological data … the customs and behavior observable in a collective do not proceed from deliberate agreement but display a consistency and a degree of automatism which its members are generally unable to relate back to a cultural model or a system of explicit rules.

– Phillipe Descola

On Tuesday, October 29, 2019, the interim editor-in-chief of the popular American sports website Deadspin was fired for refusing to obey an order from his boss at G/O Media, the entity that manages several internet properties for the private equity firm Great Hill Partners. His boss at G/O had requested that Deadspin restrict itself to sports content, an order which the editorial team at Deadspin found profoundly meddlesome and an attempt to interfere with its editorial freedom and principles. This position was summed up by the editor's op-ed piece in the *New York Times* where he stated: "reporting sports with integrity requires knowing that there's no way to wall off the games from the world outside".[1] The following day, most of Deadspin's editorial staff resigned in protest. By Friday of that week, the last editor had left, shutting down the site and commenting that no one from G/O or Great Hill had contacted her on her last day. Reached for comment, Jim Spanfeller, the CEO of G/O Media stated that Deadspin was not dead and that "we've got quite a number of recruiters out there pounding the pavement trying to find great people".[2]

Leaving aside your opinion of either party, this is a case of clashing cultures, or more accurately, reference systems. The *editorial* and *content creation* reference system of the Deadspin editors, characterized, if you will, by logics of *freedom-of-the-press*, *editorial integrity*, the *primacy of content*, and that *"sports is life, life is sports"*, clashes with the *primacy of the bottom line, assets are dollars, people are fungible assets and buy-able commodities* logics of private equity.[3] Rarely do we witness the clash of reference systems in such stark relief, played out in the business pages of the New York Times over a few days. And yet, reference systems collide with each other every day in offices, boardrooms, coffee stations, and water coolers of corporations around the world. Most often these clashes are not thought of as conflicts of cultural systems, or systems of meaning, because when they happen they feel personal. We think of them as conflicts of personality. In the Deadspin case we see the product of what otherwise would remain largely invisible. As put by the quote above from the cognitive anthropologist Phillippe Descola, reference systems appear as recurring patterns in practices and behavior but are hard to "see" and "read", let alone attribute to an underlying system of rules. That is, until something happens. That something always involves change. Whether it is conflicts over editorial philosophy or the disruption of an entire industry, in times of change cultural reference systems will always reveal themselves, often in dramatic ways.

In this same way, the story of Industrial Instruments International presented in this chapter is a study of how a cultural reference system works in real life. Because this archetypal company has been transforming itself from the moment of its birth, its transitions give us the opportunity to observe how cultural logics come to be and take shape in times of change.[4] As reference systems and SDLs are the products of pre-conscious knowledge, this chapter also describes the methods by which they are uncovered. Having a working knowledge of these methods is important to help practitioners leverage these ideas and tools in their own work.

THE REFERENCE SYSTEM IN ACTION

"I3" is a Fortune 1000 multinational manufacturer of products and solutions for measurement, weighing, and analysis for use in industrial, laboratory, and retail applications. The company makes precision weighing, analytical and inspection solutions for entire value chains, with products such as industrial and commercial scales, laboratory balances, and other process and analytics equipment. The company has approximately US $3 billion in annual sales and approximately 16,000 employees worldwide, with the majority in North America and Europe. I3 is organized into three divisions by market segment. It's laboratory business focuses on products and solutions for research and development, and quality control. It's industrial division focuses on instruments for optimizing manufacturing operations, from logistics to quality assurance and regulatory compliance. It's retail division focuses on products and solutions for retailers, from receiving to pricing, inventory management, and supply chain management. I3 benefits from a strong portfolio of brands, many of which have existed for decades, and a large installed base. Much of its revenue is recurring as customers tend to replace equipment with products from the same company, which drives a robust aftermarket and services business. The company has also been investing heavily in digital technology, mainly through a number of acquisitions of small and mid-size companies with these capabilities.

New Company, Old Grounding

I3's history and strategy provides a compelling setting for understanding how reference systems work. The company was spun off from a larger, multinational diversified industrial company in 2014, which put all of the company's precision scale and instrumentation assets under a newly formed independent entity. I3 immediately traded under its own stock symbol on the New York Stock Exchange, which meant being subject to the rigors of operating as a public company from its inception. Management often referred to the company during this time as a "100-year-old start-up", a clever saying that belied the tension of satisfying investors while nurturing to life a newly independent company. The multinational parent company had acquired hundreds of companies and brands over the course of its 100-year history (the oldest holding dating to 1848), many with strong reputations, loyal customers, and well-established distribution networks, and operated these companies as independent entities. Therefore, at the time of the spin-off most employees beyond I3's headquarters in Pennsylvania retained psychological and emotional ties to their own brands and offices in locations around the world. The idea of a "I3" for most employees at the time was an abstraction; people would say they worked for the brand, or their own site.

From birth I3 was faced with the challenge of trying to create a company with its own identity amid a task context shaped not only by manufacturing, but by historicity. The conscious effort by management to form a cohesive and integrated new company was met head-on by the realities of SDLs forged in decades of task solutions grounded in historically successful brands, most with roots in family or privately owned businesses in diverse corners of the world, from Finland to South Korea to California, and many points in between. The juxtaposition of management intention with task and historicity is not unusual, but like Deadspin, what makes I3 unique is the time frame. Start-ups usually take years to evolve their grounding contexts based on the make-up of their dominant professional groups, the accumulated success (or near-failure) of the business and the task solutions these experiences forge, or the extent to which the mission of the founders is meaningful. At I3 there was none of this. The new entity sprung up virtually overnight. Which meant that while the business had a new name, logo, color scheme, and tag line, as of the first Monday of its existence nothing in the grounding context of its dominant logics had changed from the previous Friday. Despite what its CEO and management team might have wished for, culturally speaking, it was the same company: a collection of precision scale and instrumentation holdings in a diversified industrial's portfolio. The only difference was the portfolio had shrunk considerably over the weekend.

Even more significant than the metamorphosis from portfolio holding to independent company is the move from legacy industrial to digital disruptor. I3 wants to be the major disruptor in its industry. To that end it has acquired, and continues to acquire, digital technology and data science businesses, adopting what some analysts label an "M&A as R&D" strategy. This has allowed I3 to gain access to technologies and markets and offer digital products and solutions to customers faced with big challenges, such as industrial and institutional laboratories that are used to operating independently and not sharing data, inefficient manufacturing operations, and distributors and retailers in the food business unaccustomed to data science applications.

As an added byproduct, this archetypal company gives us the opportunity to examine the effects of leadership on culture. The company appointed a new CEO in 2017 from outside the firm. Along with the board and one or two lieutenants, the CEO has been overseeing the formulation of the company's digital strategy, making the case for how I3 disrupts the industry. In these ways I3 is ready-made to witness the effects of *value engineering* (Chapter 1) and whether this actually works. We will look at this when we get to what I3 is doing, or could be doing, to culturally transform.

Trailblazing

Culture is grounded in shared mental representations – dominant logics – emerging from the organization's primary professional group, its task solutions, and (or) its differentiated core purpose. Shared dominant logics (SDLs) are the foundation of a reference system running in the background that people, mostly without being aware of it, use to make sense, define success, and orient meaning in their worlds. Reference systems are what comprise culture. There is more to culture – such as its visible manifestations – but they either spring from the reference system or are reactions to it.

This presents yet another dilemma: *how to investigate something that people are largely unaware of that nonetheless patterns collective thought and action?* To trace, say, *RADIALITY*, as dominant logic through all of its manifestations in Tongan culture, how does the researcher or practitioner keep one's bearing in what can fast become an analytic maze? Is *RADIALITY* a feature of how Tongan's think, the product of Bennardo's analysis, or both? How do we make sense of practices that appear to be the product SDLs without imposing our own patterns and configurations of meaning? This matters: if we are not careful we are liable to be chasing phantoms, much like those who measure employee engagement when thinking they are measuring culture.

Such is the challenge of all cognitive science work on culture. It requires looking into "unthought knowns": knowledge below conscious awareness but no less known and utilized.[5] The issue is circularity. For the new science to not wind up as yet another myth in the trash heap of failed ideas and strategies for corporate culture it cannot succumb to the same critiques levied in Chapter 2. That is, it cannot pretend to be empirical by "proving" through statistical methods an oversimplified concept of culture that misses what culture is to begin with. That is pure sleight of hand, the Three Card Monte of culture research.[6] This kind of research winds up establishing the validity of a construct (e.g., values) that is so oversimplified as to be pragmatically useless. On the other hand, it cannot fall into the trap of storytelling. This is the tendency to make universal claims about culture on the basis of a single case study or a series of anecdotes without any theory, as is often the case with the Amazon best sellers. Their message is, "do what we did". This prevents extracting any generalizable knowledge because no theoretical framework exists to allow transfer of learning or account for differing contexts.[7] Culture becomes anecdote: crowd-pleasing, but useless. How to proceed? The answer is *thoughtfully.*

Into the Unthought Known

The way through the interpretive maze of unthought knowns is to use a mix of qualitative and quantitative methods in combination with an analytic technique called *adduction*. This method, used productively in organizational research, is a way of revealing basic patterns and structure from particular cases or instances, and iterating and refining these pattern observations through different methods, ultimately achieving a kind of data saturation from which the patterns and structure can be readily and conclusively discerned. And doing so while being transparent about one's own biases and methodological limitations (Alvesson & Skoldberg, 2009).[8]

Finding Culture in Talk

The first step is to find a reliable way to identify dominant logic. The late cognitive anthropologist Naomi Quinn (1997, 2005) did just that.[9] Her pioneering technique involved analyzing everyday speech to identify how speakers use causal logic (*if x then y*; *a because of b*; etc.), idealization (*we should be doing this*; *it would be great if … etc.*) and metaphor.[10] Her key insight was that people reason and idealize all the time without knowing it; this is one of the most common features of cognition and reveals the schematic structure of how people think. Using this technique Quinn uncovered a robust cultural model of U.S. American conceptions of marriage, mentioned earlier. [11]

"Causal reasoning" here is not in the sense of formal logic. People take it as a given that their own reasoning is rational and logical, missing the fact most of it is based on assumptions rooted in personal experience, all subject to context, culture, cognitive biases, and distortion (e.g., *I went to the store because I was worried we may run out of ice*; *She might think I'm too forward if I say that*; *We went on vacation because it was good for our souls even though we didn't have the money*; and so on). The very idea of the corporate manager as a rational being, as economists and management scholars would have us think, has been debunked in decades of work on social cognition. Managers, like all humans, reason based on their own experience, one by definition subject to limitations.[12] Just try getting a manufacturing executive to think like a software manager. My own research on professionalization bears this out. I discovered HR professionals predominantly conceptualize business problems in terms of people and relationship logics far more than software engineers. Software engineers, conversely, conceptualize business problems using spatial logics far more than HR professionals. While it might not come as much of a surprise that engineers and HR professionals think differently, what is surprising is how often economists, management scholars, and even executives assume everyday managerial decision-making is somehow bias-free. People constantly use causal reasoning to explain, justify, rationalize, and frame, and do so on the basis of their own subjective logics. When these logics are widely shared, they underpin cultural reference systems.

Along with my previous research at IMCO, the work at I3 is the first research of its kind that I know of that uses cognitive anthropological techniques in a business setting.[13] These methods tend to be unfamiliar to practitioners and change agents, so these next few pages describe what we did there, and why. Because we are investigating unthought knowns, it is important to explain how we arrived at our conclusions. Transparency and reflexivity – reflecting on one's choices and biases as a way to qualify and substantiate research – is too often missing in corporate culture work. Those of you wishing to skip discussions of method and get to the punchlines, you might jump to the next section – with the proviso any questions about how we got there will probably lead you back to the section below.

Unthought Knowns

We started our research with I3 with a series of structured interviews based on Quinn's method with its top 12 executives, including the CEO, key general managers, and several other functional, regional, and unit leaders.[14] The interviews were recorded and later transcribed, and were designed to be deliberately open-ended and conversational to draw speakers out and allow free-flowing discourse. Following Quinn, the idea was to get leaders to reason and idealize about something in which they were conversant, in this case their own business strategies, and to generate as much conversation as possible to have many instances of reasoning to draw from in our analysis.[15] We asked several follow up questions to confirm or correct our understanding of what the speaker was saying.

Putting a label on what is unthought but known takes practice. We're not mind readers; we can never know exactly what the speaker in an interview intends when they reason, idealize, or use a particular metaphor. Everyday reasoning tends to be fragmentary; often it's not clear from single phrases or a couple of sentences what the speaker has in mind. More often than not the logic emerges through a paragraph or story where the logic of the narrative is revealed bit by bit, the analyst piecing together fragments like solving a mystery from shards of glass of a broken window. Like flags marking crevasses on an ice field, certain kinds of metaphors can also indicate the presence of dominant logic.[16] But a metaphor might also have nothing to do with a logic and simply be a figure of speech. Sorting all this out took well over a hundred hours of analysis, reading through transcripts and working, reworking, and reworking again our analyses, often with two of us independently looking at an initial list of SDLs to see if we agreed on the coding – the process of assigning a label to the kernel of reasoning expressed by the interviewee. This was the starting point. We developed our initial list of SDLs based on frequency – how often interviewees made reference to the same logic. The more a logic was referenced by different interviewees, the higher the frequency.

Ethnographic Action Research

After the initial list of SDLs was developed, we conducted several iterations to get to the list in Table 4.1. We were able to do this because we were involved in consulting projects at the company that afforded opportunity to observe and engage with informants in different parts of the business all over the world. These projects allowed us to do *ethnographic action research*, the second phase of our study.

Ethnography is the observation and interpretation of a social system by simultaneously participating in and observing the system from the point of view of the actors in it.[17] Action research is a broad term that has evolved since Kurt Lewin's first use of it in the 1930s and 1940s (Adelman, 1993). It is characterized by research with the dual purpose of problem-solving with clients, often in ways where the client is involved in the solution, and where the client's emergent awareness of the problem constitutes part of the intervention (see Figure 4.1).[18]

Under the umbrella of adduction, we used ethnography and action research in combination as part of our collaboration with I3. Over the course of work with various executive groups engaged in a variety of programs focused on change and representing all parts of I3's global business, we refined our list to the 15 SDLs in Table 4.1. We also developed the initial framework for the reference system draft (the final product seen

TABLE 4.1

Initial List of Shared Dominant Logics (From Interviews, Ethnography, Action Research)

Dominant Logic – Label	Grounding Source PRO = Professionalization STS = Shared Task Solutions DCP = Differentiated Core Purpose OTH = Other (Wider Culture)	Brief Description (Labeling of Pre-Verbal Constructs)
1. *EFFICIENCY*	PRO, STS, and OTH Lean, Six Sigma, continuous improvement – always seeking out greater efficiencies; the need to mitigate the high cost of failure in manufacturing. A common manufacturing management SDL.	*Maximize throughput, eliminate waste*
2. *HIERARCHY*	PRO, STS, and OTH The best way to control an organization is through hierarchy. A common manufacturing management SDL.	*Respect and orientation to organizational hierarchy. The boss knows best*
3. *NUMBERS DON'T LIE*	PRO, STS, and OTH Control achieved by precise measurement of inputs and outputs, most of which are numeric. A common manufacturing management SDL.	*Metrics are everything*
4. *STRUCTURE*	PRO, STS and OTH Successfully managing a manufacturing business requires predictability, much which comes from structured ways of doing things, creating repeatable and efficient processes.	*Orientation to things that enable structure and control: e.g., frameworks, project plans, hierarchy, ROI, A3s, etc. Uncomfortable with ambiguity, abstraction, vagueness, visioning …*
5. *CONTROL*	PRO and STS Manufacturing management: controlling all variables to achieve predictable output; the need to mitigate the high cost of failure.	*Direct control of all possible variables; mitigate uncertainty*
6. *RISK MITIGATION*	PRO and STS High cost of failure in manufacturing requires close monitoring and mitigation of risk.	*Doing everything to minimize uncertainty and risk*

(Continued)

TABLE 4.1 (CONTINUED)

Initial List of Shared Dominant Logics (From Interviews, Ethnography, Action Research)

Dominant Logic – Label	Grounding Source PRO = Professionalization STS = Shared Task Solutions DCP = Differentiated Core Purpose OTH = Other (Wider Culture)	Brief Description (Labeling of Pre-Verbal Constructs)
7. FAIRNESS	STS Legacy of many small companies and brands, many of which were originally family-owned, with local loyalties and histories, engendering a sense of fairness and loyalty.	Loyalty; treating people like family
8. FINANCIAL PERFORMANCE FIRST	STS The effects of being a "100-year-old start-up" where continued and predictable performance for "Wall Street" is key to continued success and independence as a firm.	Dominant orientation to financial outcomes (cost, revenue, OI, ROI, etc.)
9. FIRST-HAND KNOWLEDGE	STS Making physical things – manufacturing; knowing things based on actual, first-hand experience, like walking around the shop floor.	Seeing is believing
10. LOCAL ORIENTATION	STS Long and successful legacy of independent brands and subsidiaries which lends an orientation to what is local.	What is local is known and is best (therefore I trust). What is further away is less known and less good (therefore I trust less)
11. MAKING THE ABSTRACT TANGIBLE	STS Making physical, tangible things – manufacturing.	Orientation to concreteness; prefer examples and practical explanations over abstraction and models
12. ACTION	STS Making and moving physical things from manufacturing to the customer; the assembly line.	Bias for action

(Continued)

TABLE 4.1 (CONTINUED)

Initial List of Shared Dominant Logics (From Interviews, Ethnography, Action Research)

Dominant Logic – Label	Grounding Source PRO = Professionalization STS = Shared Task Solutions DCP = Differentiated Core Purpose OTH = Other (Wider Culture)	Brief Description (Labeling of Pre-Verbal Constructs)
13. CERTAINTY	STS The need to mitigate the high cost of failure in manufacturing.	Seek clarity, answers, avoid risk
14. PORTFOLIO	STS Legacy of running holding company with many independent businesses and brands, where losses in one business may be offset by gains in another. Strategy *is* portfolio optimization.	Hedging risk by managing assets, as if part of a financial portfolio
15. PRACTICAL	STS Making things that work and have immediate utility, e.g., a scale is inherently practical and useful.	Pragmatism above all

beginning in Figure 4.4). At that same time we were engaged in several other projects which allowed us to test and refine our draft SDLs and their expressions in the reference system.

The SDLs in Table 4.1 also show the grounding source. While some grounding sources are common to business generally, many are related to the task context of manufacturing and what is entailed in running a successful industrial business. These SDLs are not evident, for example, in software firms (see again Table 3.1). Two SDL types, *FAIRNESS* and *LOCAL ORIENTATION*, have to do with I3's history of a larger enterprise made up of numerous small companies and brands, many of which were originally family-owned.

Quantitative Analysis

Over time we managed to reduce the 15 SDLs in Table 4.1 to 8 on the grounds several were better described under broader categories. For example, it became clear that *LOCAL ORIENTATION* was most often expressed as a kind of *FIRST-HAND KNOWLEDGE*, and that the latter

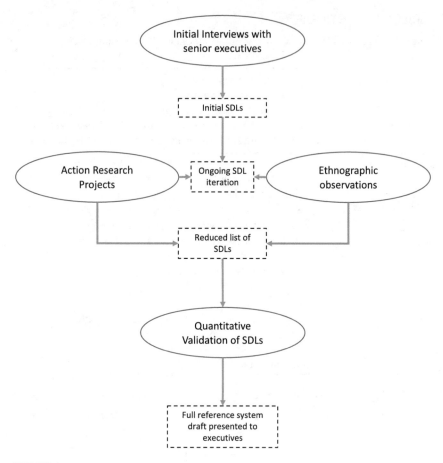

FIGURE 4.1
I3 research process.

was a more accurate description of what we were observing. There were similar issues with the others. This left us with eight:

1. *ACTION*
2. *CERTAINTY*
3. *EFFICIENCY*
4. *FAIRNESS*
5. *FINANCIAL PERFORMANCE FIRST*
6. *FIRST-HAND KNOWLEDGE*
7. *MAKING THE ABSTRACT TANGIBLE*
8. *NUMBERS DONT LIE*

We also concluded that in order to make more definitive assertions, a third phase of work was necessary. Because we were out to show how functional grounding works, we needed more data to convince ourselves what we were seeing through the qualitative research was applicable more broadly across the company, and that these SDLs were, in fact, anchoring a culture. In addition, ethnography and action research is time-consuming; we were only able to derive data within the scope of our consulting projects. And while each project increased our knowledge and confidence that our list was directionally accurate, we were working with a limited number of informants. For these reasons we designed a quantitative study to test the SDLs across organizational levels and geographies. If quantitative analyses could demonstrate what we had come up with through the qualitative research was accurate, this would validate the dominant logics.[19]

Studying schemas through quantitative means is well established in cognitive anthropology.[20] Among several quantitative methodologies, factor analysis (FA) is particularly effective for the simple reason it isolates whatever latent variables may underlie a set of observed data. As put by Bernard (2011), "if the things we observe are correlated with each other, they must have some underlying variable in common" (p. 552). That underlying variable is often a SDL. To capture the content of a collective's unthought knowns, factor analysis is well suited to the task. If the SDLs could be grouped by factors independently determined by FA, this would support the idea these particular SDLs were distinct cognitive orientations, at least for this sample.

We designed a survey to elicit how much of each kernel of cultural knowledge we had identified in the qualitative work was "known" by each respondent. We took our eight SDLs and turned them into 57 survey items, each one a response to the prime "your perception of the degree of importance of each statement to someone who works at I3". Each item was an expression of a single SDL, and we used multiple statements to express the same SDL.[21] As said, it is usually unproductive to ask people directly about their own dominant logics. But because of our knowledge of the firm we had a good sense of how to phrase items in ways that made sense to survey respondents. As with our original interviews, statements were in the form of reasoning or idealizations expressed as a polarity and choice-constraint (e.g., *It is better to be rewarded for achieving goals against one's own P&L rather than work with other groups against a company-wide P&L*; *It is better to be skeptical of new ideas until one can see for oneself whether they are viable or not*). The statements themselves were verbatim from the interviews, ethnography, and action research. Recipients were presented with a short statement, absent additional context, and asked to rate its degree of perceived importance to someone at I3 (5 = Extremely Important; 1 = Extremely Unimportant).

We used mean scores and FA to analyze results. Responses were depicted on a correlation matrix showing the greatest amount of correlation between statements, or variables. Factors were extracted from the matrix in the order of the amount of variance in the matrix they explained. Factors with the highest loadings would account for the most variance – the highest correlations between the factor and variable (all other things equal; see below).

We administered the validation survey in two waves.[22] Participants represented a cross-section of the company comprising all divisions and functions, with the most in general management (17 percent) and manufacturing operations (14 percent) roles, and the rest distributed among 11 other functions. Given this distribution we did not anticipate seeing SDLs with evidence of professionalization, even though a majority of managers in the firm have mechanical engineering, finance, or operations backgrounds. The majority of survey respondents were from North America (53 percent) and Europe (22 percent).

Results

Tables 4.2 and 4.3 contain the results of the surveys. As shown in Table 4.2, we set a threshold for mean scores of 3.5 or greater, confirmed with a t-test with a .95 confidence interval. From this we identified 11 variables (survey statements) out of the 57 deemed of greater importance by our sample, and factor analyzed these to derive six distinct factors representing the greatest amount of variation on which one or more variables loaded. Instances where multiple variables loaded onto a single factor provided the strongest evidence that these variables support a single latent SDL.[23]

The results below show the six SDLs accounting for the majority of the variance, with two clusters in particular, that for *FINANCIAL PERFORMANCE FIRST* and *RULES* showing the highest factor loadings. The *RULES* SDL was not one of the original eight, but through the FA we noticed a cluster of three variables loading together. Although each of these had been coded as a different SDL, we decided to reclassify the cluster as one pertaining to rules because of the presence of the word "always" in the survey statements. Indeed, this factor could be a subset of *CERTAINTY*, but *RULES* described the factor in a more precise that corresponded with our observations.

TABLE 4.2

SDLs with means >3.5

Item	Shared Dominant Logic	Statement
Quest 1	*RULES*	It's always good to build in countermeasures to a plan even when above target
Quest 3	*FIRST HAND KNOWLEDGE*	It's important that different functions (e.g. finance, procurement) have visibility into operational status items such as inventory and budget rather than relying on the word of department heads
Quest 6	*RULES*	New initiatives or projects should always have financial benefits spelled out before they are approved
Quest 8	*CERTAINTY*	New projects or initiatives involving multiple stakeholders across the organization should always allow those stakeholders to have a say in the project before it begins
Quest 9	*CERTAINTY*	It is important that upper management weigh in on new projects or initiatives before they begin
Quest 10	*RULES*	Projects that are successful always have a project management framework for running them
Quest 12	*RULES*	The best strategies always have roadmaps for how to achieve them
Quest 22	*ACTION*	I believe more in leaders whose actions align to their words rather than those whose words are very inspiring
Quest 27	*FINANCIAL PERFORMANCE FIRST*	If we don't task groups to financially perform we will be at risk as an organization
Quest 29	*FINANCIAL PERFORMANCE FIRST*	Despite the effort it takes, making the numbers each quarter is more important than anything else
Quest 42	*FINANCIAL PERFORMANCE FIRST*	Business success in my organization means financial success above all

t-test significant at >.95 n = 87

How These SDLs Make Up the Reference System

The quantitative validation exercise is a good reminder of the need for a robust, multi-method process for studying cultural logics. Because we started with 15 SDLs and ended up with six, one might say this is a modest validation of our qualitative research. On the other hand, we subjected eight SDLs to quantitative validation, of which six loaded as distinct factors, a very solid confirmation. Funneling toward

TABLE 4.3

Factor Loadings on Significant Variables

Item	Factor 1	Factor 2	Factor 3	Factor 4	Factor 5	% Var Accounted by Each Variable	Shared Dominant Logic	Statement
Quest 29	0.87					6.88%	*FINANCIAL PERFORMANCE FIRST*	Despite the effort it takes, making the numbers each quarter is more important than anything else
Quest 42	0.65					3.84%	*FINANCIAL PERFORMANCE FIRST*	Business success in my organization means financial success above all
Quest 27	0.49					2.18%	*FINANCIAL PERFORMANCE FIRST*	If we don't task groups to financially perform we will be at risk as an organization
Quest 10		0.72				4.71%	*RULES*	Projects that are successful always have a project management framework for running them
Quest 12		0.52				2.46%	*RULES*	The best strategies always have roadmaps for how to achieve them
Quest 6		0.49				2.18%	*RULES*	New initiatives or projects should always have financial benefits spelled out before they are approved
Quest 1			0.99			8.91%	*RULES*	It's always good to build in countermeasures to a plan even when above target

(Continued)

TABLE 4.3 (CONTINUED)

Factor Loadings on Significant Variables

Item	Factor 1	Factor 2	Factor 3	Factor 4	Factor 5	% Var Accounted by Each Variable	Shared Dominant Logic	Statement
Quest 3				0.86		6.72%	*FIRST-HAND KNOWLEDGE*	It's important that different functions (e.g. finance, procurement) have visibility into operational status items such as Inventory and bucket rather than relying on the word of department heads
Quest 9					0.53	2.55%	*CERTAINTY*	It is important that upper management weigh in on new projects or initiatives before they begin
Quest 8						<2%	*CERTAINTY*	New projects or initiatives involving multiple stakeholders across the organization should always allow those stakeholders to have a say in the project before it begins
Quest 22						<2%	*ACTION*	I believe more in leaders whose actions align to their words rather than those whose words are very inspiring

*t-test significant at >.95 n = 87

Note: The factor correlation between the two "Rules" factors [factors 2 and 3] is only.15. So those factors are essentially independent of each other and not part of the same SDL conclusiveness is how adduction works: the more you subject the same set of data to different methods of analysis, the more refined the data becomes (and if not, this also provides important information about your data and methods).

This approach is particularly important because these logics could have been misclassified. Our use of two coders, and our winnowing down to eight SDLs were iterative ways to achieve more precise renderings of unthought knowns. That said, we cannot be sure there are not variables out of range of our research. The logics were the ones we observed, but, obviously, we have not been to every office and manufacturing plant in the company nor sat in on every meeting, and so forth. And logics can never be completely represented in words; language is a proxy for preconscious content. Which is why using multiple methods is essential: they enable greater precision and provide confidence that the results are indicative of a shared cultural reference system.

But a major question still remained. How could we be sure these SDLs underpinned the entire reference system? To answer that we had to take one more step.

Patterns in Practice

Although our quantitative study revealed latent factors associated with SDLs, these results were – of necessity – derived through language (codings based on interview data, observations, responses to survey statements, and interpreting latent factors). To observe what Descola calls the "structural subconscious" one must use not only language but practice, how logics take form "among the properties of the institution that reveal it to the observer" (2013, p. 93). Practices, as discussed earlier, are the formal and informal habits, routines, and processes by which a corporation runs. Corporate practices never emerge out of thin air; they are always a product of a shared system of meaning. Practices can be "read" for the SDLs (schemas) they contain (Swidler, 2001). Logics endow practices with particular and often idiosyncratic qualities and features. Because they are structured by dominant logics, practices are key to identifying and changing SDLs, and by extension culture, a process we will get in to in the next chapter.

Adaptations

SDLs also manifest as behaviors and consciously held attitudes. I call these *adaptations*, as stated, because they often take shape as reactions to or compensations for SDLs and practices. Adaptations are often interpreted as a firm's "culture" because they tend to be what people hold as conscious attitudes and beliefs, and are often visible in behavior. The problem is attitudes, beliefs, and behavior can often be as much reactions to cultural practices and logics as expressions of them. Which is why attempts to change culture by targeting employee attitudes, beliefs, or behavior do not lead to culture change. These interventions target symptoms rather than cause, and often the symptoms belie the actual root cause because attitudes or behavior may be collective attempts to emotionally or psychologically deal with deeper cultural phenomena.

The final validation of these data involved showing the reference system in its draft form to 39 I3 executives. In two separate sessions we used these data as part of a "Culture Lab" workshop. These executives represented all parts of the company globally, so the results of these workshops come as close as any to a complete snapshot of a lived culture.[24] The cohorts were asked to validate its contents, or provide alternative SDLs, practices, or adaptations, and then design intervention strategies to challenge the SDLs and intervene in practices they deemed most emblematic of their own culture (more on this in Chapter 5). From these sessions we were able to ratify the contents of Figures 4.2 through 4.7. While people added examples of practices and adaptations, there were no changes to the base logics. All agreed it was an accurate description of the lived cultural experience of I3.

THE I3 REFERENCE SYSTEM

Reference systems are hard to "see" unless presented as intact systems. Which is why the figures depict the six SDLs and how they play out across practices and adaptations (Figures 4.2 through 4.7). Each SDL is depicted as a hub and spoke to emphasize the prototype nature of logics, meaning shared logics have a central primitive concept (e.g., *RULES*) that structure more elaborate logics for setting standards (e.g.,

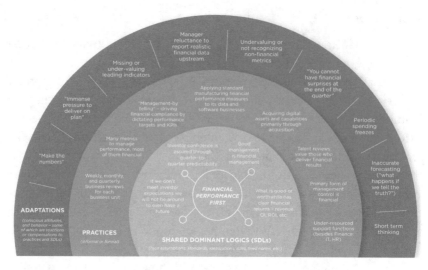

FIGURE 4.2
Shared dominant logic: *FINANCIAL PERFORMANCE FIRST.*

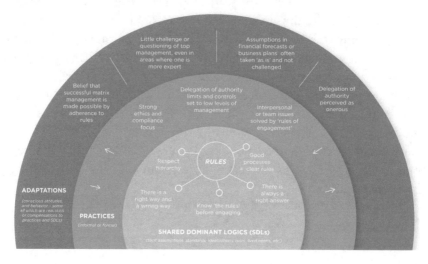

FIGURE 4.3
Shared dominant logic: *RULES.*

good processes have clear rules), idealizing (e.g., *we should never do it unless the rules of engagement are clear*), rationalizing (e.g., *it didn't work because there were no rules of engagement*), norming (e.g., *tell me what's expected here*), and other implicit ways of making sense. For reasons of space, not every practice or adaptation in each SDL is discussed.

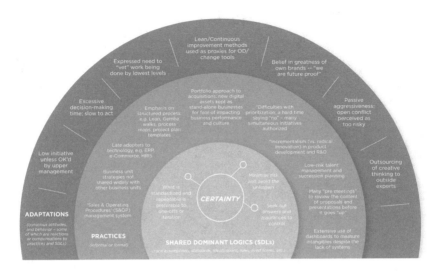

FIGURE 4.4
Shared dominant logic: *CERTAINTY*.

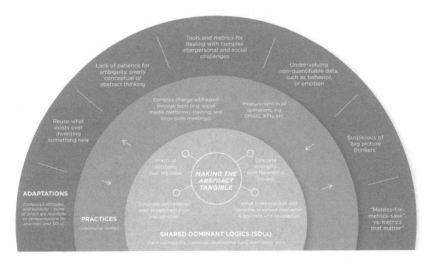

FIGURE 4.5
Shared dominant logic: *MAKING THE ABSTRACT TANGIBLE*.

FINANCIAL PERFORMANCE FIRST

By far the most prominent shared logic at I3 concerns financial performance. All companies monitor their financial performance; sound financial management and reporting is a basic fact of life for all public companies. The question here is not whether financial performance matters; the question is to what degree. *FINANCIAL PERFORMANCE*

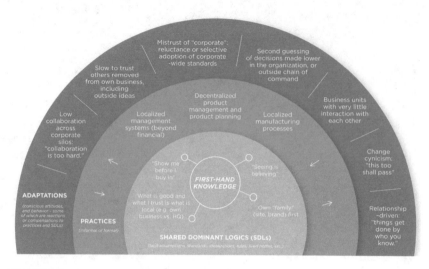

FIGURE 4.6

Shared dominant logic: *FIRST HAND KNOWLEDGE*.

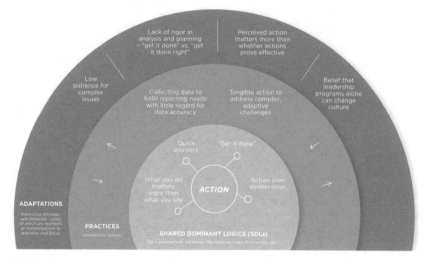

FIGURE 4.7

Shared dominant logic: *ACTION*.

FIRST is a dominant orientation at I3, a way of thinking and a set of practices and priorities that trump most others: it is the logic with the most significant factor loadings in our sample (see Table 4.3); it has a large number of practices associated with it (8; see Figure 4.2); and many commonly shared adaptations (see Figure 4.2). This SDL figured prominently in our observations at all levels and in all geographies.

How Does It Show Up? (Practices and Adaptations)

The primary lever for understanding and assuring business performance at I3 is financial.

Practices associated with tracking or assuring financial performance are numerous, such as monthly business reviews where managers report key financial and performance metrics in their business to senior leaders, a process which often takes twice or three times as long to prepare for than to enact due in part to the absence of effective information systems (see below). This same practice is repeated each quarter with quarterly reviews. In some struggling businesses the practice is weekly. Typically performance targets are not set by individual business units but by corporate headquarters based on commitments made to analysts and shareholders.

Several of the Adaptations in Figure 4.2 come in the form of comments about this logic and its practices. Reactions to the SDL are widespread, especially with regard to the pressure people feel to deliver financial results, and the complex behaviors and attitudes that result (Figure 4.2).

One would think a dominant orientation to financial management would drive precise forecasting habits, but finance leaders and senior executives would often share their frustration over business unit leaders and their struggles to produce more accurate forecasts. This suggests possible issues of trust (discussed below), the influence of another SDL (*FIRST-HAND KNOWLEDGE*), lack of time, or fatigue: many of our informants mentioned how the ongoing weekly and monthly pressure to deliver results and generate the many reports to track revenue and margin activity lead to a kind of indifference and fatigue as to whether the data is accurate or reliable.

When Overlearned …

When a dominant logic is applied automatically without awareness or a consideration of alternatives, this is called *overlearning*. One example of overlearning *FINANCIAL PERFORMANCE FIRST* has to do with how I3 holds its newly acquired data science and software businesses to the same financial reporting and performance standards as its manufacturing businesses. Measuring and valuing digital businesses on a monthly and quarterly basis is problematic, seen most notably in GE's digital business struggles and the problems associated with applying industrial financial performance standards to newer businesses (Govindarajan & Immelt, 2019). The digital businesses at I3 have not met the company's own financial performance expectations in part because the monthly and quarterly financial and reporting standards by which they were being measured did not apply. Interestingly, executives at I3 were aware of this as a potential issue from the time they acquired these assets. They tried to solve it by instituting a "lite" version of the monthly review (in six-week cycles instead of each month) This is laudable. It also shows the pervasive power of SDLs; while the problem was recognized, the well-intended "solution" was drawn from the same well of logic, leading to a lesser version of the same practice. If culture change had been the goal (in this case it wasn't), what would have been needed is a change to the underlying logic itself.

Where Does This SDL Come From?

One might think I3's financial management practices indicate it is in a difficult financial position. It is not. The company is very successful. It has a very strong balance sheet which it has put to work to make its digital acquisitions. It has consistently out-earned its cost of capital, and since its inception has only missed two-quarters of forecast performance. Its stock price has tripled since its initial offering.[25] All this has earned praise on Wall Street. Indeed, the CEO is one of the staunchest promoters of the need for sound and predictable financial performance, often forcefully articulating one of the core elements of the SDL: there is no future if the company does not meet its publicly stated financial obligations. This begs the question, where does this SDL originate? Is this the product of the CEO's avowed commitment to fiscal performance? If so, this would be evidence of a dominant logic directly set from the top, counter to Myth 1 and a refutation of the functional grounding thesis.

I would say not quite. Functional grounding provides a more robust and complete explanation for the dominance of this logic than Myth 1, for three reasons.

First, the "100-year-old start-up" refrain, heard in the early days means senior leadership was aware of their position as a stand-alone public company newly spun-off without a financial backstop. Indeed, this SDL was identified in all our original interviews. Management collectively spoke of the need for predictable and consistent financial performance, with strong guidance from its board. That the company has successfully delivered financial results amid the existential stresses of being a new public company *is* the task solution. This is precisely how task solutions work: the company has survived, thrived, and continues to be rewarded by investors for closely managing its fiscal activities. This conveys an important message: *what we have been doing works*. Because it works, its meaningful. The more practices reinforce the financial performance logic, the more the logic is strengthened.

In addition, recall I3 sprang forth from a holding company. Holding companies, by definition, exist to diversify and produce better financial returns for shareholders with the main goal of growth of earnings.[26] It follows that one of the most important competencies for any holding entity is financial management. The diverse nature of holding company portfolios means they tend to focus primarily on financial management rather than other forms of control. For example, I3's parent at one time required 40 to 50 financial reports each month from its operating units. I3's management team inherited this implicit knowledge and was well-versed in how to run businesses by exercising strong financial control. This is how historicity works: *because it worked in the past, it should work today.*

Third, the existence of another SDL, *RULES* (below), reinforces the *FINANCIAL PERFORMANCE FIRST* logic by making rule-following and adhering to performance mandates normatively important. Despite managerial grumblings, it's simply not an option for a manager to *not* deliver financial results. The normative pressure to deliver financial results may be even greater than any punitive consequences. I3, in fact, is relatively deliberate and cautious in taking action on poor individual performers, for reasons likely having to do with another SDL (*CERTAINTY*). The more typical way of dealing with chronic (financial) under-performance is to reorganize the business. Eliminating roles through restructuring, although not without legal risk, is easier and less risky than going through the extensive process of documenting and counseling the low performer. I3 is in no way unique; this is typical of industrial firms. The logic of risk-avoidance (*CERTAINTY*), strengthens the *FINANCIAL PERFORMANCE FIRST* SDL.

The prevalence of *FINANCIAL PERFORMANCE FIRST* is strong proof of the power of practice over CEO pronouncements. I3's CEO, like most CEOs, is strongly convicted that the company must achieve its short-term financial goals to assure its future, but this conviction had been reinforced in numerous practices that made the logic pervasive and dominant long before she arrived in the company. This is also an example of how dominant logics take hold; reinforcing practices ensure *FINANCIAL PERFORMANCE FIRST* will be induced frequently throughout the enterprise at all levels.

RULES and CERTAINTY

These SDLs are described together because *RULES* is closely related to *CERTAINTY* (see Figures 4.3 and 4.4). *RULES* was identified by the FA and manifests as a respect for process and hierarchy, and a strong belief that there is a right and wrong answer to all problems. The overarching orientation is positivist: rules provide order and clarity and are enacted by authority.

CERTAINTY is common to manufacturing. At the core of the logic is minimizing risk: making things predictable and maintaining order and control, important actions in running a successful manufacturing enterprise. You don't release beta versions of refrigerators. *CERTAINTY* seeks out what is standardized and repeatable, not just in manufacturing processes but in *everything*. Standardization makes things controllable; more control minimizes risk, increases predictability, and makes the world more certain.

How Does It Show Up? (Practices and Adaptations)

One manifestation of *RULES* is in the company's strong ethics, compliance, and audit practices. Another is the widespread formal delegation of authority responsibilities that spell out how much decision-making latitude front line managers can have. This tends to push relatively tactical decisions up the chain of command.

One of the most notable adaptations of this SDL is how little challenging or questioning there is of upper management, even in areas where one is more expert. This stands in stark contrast, for example, to technology companies, where questioning authority is common. As said, this SDL is one reason why the financial logic is so widely adopted.

Much of I3 operates according to the *CERTAINTY* logic (see Figure 4.4). The most obvious manifestation is the adoption of formal sales and operations planning (S&OP) techniques. S&OP is a planning and alignment process where sales, production, inventory, customer lead time, product, and financial plans are all aligned and harmonized with the goal of balancing the supply and demand sides of the business, obviously critical in manufacturing. As such, S&OP is about reducing uncertainties and aiding trade-offs. As in other industrials, at I3 the most important element of S&OP is the monthly business review, the ongoing and primary management listening system and mechanism for business alignment.

S&OP is by no means unique and unusual. What is more unusual is how its underlying logic, with its orientation to minimizing risk, shows up in practices removed from supply and demand management. As one executive put it, "I3 won't move from A to Z unless all the letters of the alphabet can be spelled out beforehand." For example, in its talent practices and succession planning few chances are taken on promoting individuals into executive roles. What little turnover there is among the senior leadership team has been addressed by hiring from outside the firm. One could argue there is a dearth of talent in middle management, but in our observations having worked with middle managers at many industrial companies to form a reasonable basis of comparison, we believe this is not the case. Because the organization tends to primarily notice and reward managers who deliver financial results, many talented and experienced managers remain "unseen" in the organization. For all intents and purposes, people have to be doing the target job already in order to be considered for promotion to that job. And while this by no means is unique to I3 – all organizations prize those who deliver financial performance – this is an example of how two SDLs can underwrite standards of success to such an extent that few other criterion "count", at least when it comes to executive promotions.

Similarly, a low tolerance for risk can be seen in I3's product development practices, which feature incrementalism over radical innovation. For example, the industrial scale business has only one product with a fully integrated software control system for self-monitoring and data reporting to the cloud. This could be considered unusual for a business in the business of measurement, but speaks to the pervasiveness of the industrial logic. Another manifestation of *CERTAINTY* is the excessive focus on obtaining customer input (so called "Voice of Customer" processes) before authorizing any new product design. Other, similar risk-averse practices can be seen in Figure 4.4.

Adaptations to *CERTAINTY* are many (Figure 4.4). One of the more interesting is in how conflict is handled. Open differences of opinion are rare; more typical is polite and deferential agreement in public and inaction or passive resistance in private. Conversations with informants have confirmed this numerous times: open conflict is perceived as too risky. As mentioned, despite the emphasis on financial results, managers in general are reluctant to proactively address performance issues. Other adaptations include the outsourcing of strategy development or the creation of business models for new businesses or markets to outside "expert" consultants rather than rely on internal capabilities, even when the expertise resides in house. Or the need by senior leaders to "vet" work of more junior staff. The typical practice is to have many preparatory meetings before any mid-level or junior staff member presents anything to the executive team, which leads to the humorous saying "we need a pre-meeting to prepare for the pre-meeting for the planning meeting for the meeting with the CEO". The dominance of the risk logic is everywhere.

When Overlearned ...

I3's "M&A as R&D" strategy has made it an aggressive acquirer of digital assets, as stated. These are companies with specialization in predictive analytics, and software for Internet of Things (IoT) platform and data backbones. Yet it does virtually no integration of these new companies – some which have fewer than ten employees – with its legacy weights and measures, idustrial process and retail businesses. Instead, the company employs a portfolio approach to these acquisitions, housing them in a separate business unit, each one still based in the same physical location with largely intact management teams from the time of acquisition. This portfolio approach is rooted in *CERTAINTY* – any non-performing asset can be offset by the relative performance of another, and the overall performance of these new assets can be offset by the performance of the legacy manufacturing and services business. A portfolio approach also helps assuage the fear that integrating these new companies into the legacy business will adversely impact their performance and culture. The logic of low-risk/high-certainty is almost deferential, or in the words of one executive, there is a palpable fear the legacy "way of thinking" will spoil the "magic" of these new tech businesses. This caution may well prove far-sighted in the end. Yet it could also be argued that quick and complete integration in order to seed the legacy businesses with digital know-how is essential to fully realize the value of these assets given the speed at which other potential disruptors, especially from outside the industry, may be able to mobilize. Wider and faster dissemination of digital know-how could be critical for distributing learning across I3's traditional businesses, particularly for its lab and retail markets. This is consistent with many observers who claim speed is the critical competency industrials must adopt to achieve digital transformation. For example, companies like Amazon and Microsoft are already working to disrupt traditional industrial markets with their cloud and analytics platforms. I3 counts on its industry knowledge and deep customer relationships as defensive beachheads while it builds up its digital know-how.

The conscious strategy of portfolio and low/no integration may also be aided by another SDL, *FIRST-HAND KNOWLEDGE*, which privileges what is local over what is centralized, and perpetuates divisional silos (see below). This could also be the product of historicity: I3's holding company legacy never imparted any institutionalized know-how or normative orientation for acquisition integration. It is no surprise that to this day I3 runs as three distinct divisions, each one, with few exceptions, with their own way of doing things. When one gets down to individual business units and sites, these differences are more pronounced yet. Whatever the source of the logic, the net result is the company's lack of know-how in business integration keeps much of the data science, IoT, and software knowledge locked up in its new acquisitions, knowledge that if it was more widely distributed and cross-pollinated might allow it to recognize and capitalize on market opportunities faster than demonstrated to date.

Another overlearned consequence of *CERTAINTY* is prioritization, or its absence. It is widely accepted by managers that the company has "trouble saying no" and "killing projects", much to the chagrin of those asked to meet ambitious financial goals and execute, often with limited resources due to profitability mandates. Being asked to do more with less can be considered a legitimate management and motivation strategy. The difference at I3 is that this is not considered a managerial technique but a normal part of doing business. For example, one division of the company had 20 strategic priorities in a recent fiscal year. This was recognized as unrealistic and unreasonable by the leaders of that division, but more kept being added by corporate headquarters over the course of the year on the grounds cost-containment measures were needed to achieve corporate fiscal targets (e.g., streamlining procurement processes or improving financial reporting). In the next year the team vowed to limit the list to six, a major improvement, but only after extensive discussion as to whether they would be "allowed" to do this by "corporate". Making tough trade-offs is hard for any company. In one where limiting risk and following rules is a dominant assumption behind what it means to succeed, that prioritization is difficult comes as no surprise.

Where Do These SDLs Come From?

CERTAINTY and *RULES* logics are common and essential to successful successful manufacturing management. My research at IMCO identified similar logics (see Chapter 3). The tech logic of "move fast and break things" is horrifying to most manufacturing executives, for good reason: the costs of failure in manufacturing are prohibitive. The high costs and risks associated with the production of industrial scale and measurement terminals, or precision laboratory instruments, not to mention procuring raw materials, managing inventory and global supply chains, overseeing complex distribution networks, and working with labor across many countries, requires close and accurate oversight of processes to ensure productivity and profit.[27] This is one reason why manufacturers were early adopters of industry standards like ISO 9000,[28] and why firms have tried to address operational and cost challenges through flexible manufacturing techniques such as just-in-time production, the focused factory, value stream mapping and lean production.[29] These are highly rational ways to construct and organize complex operating environments to ensure insight and mitigate risk.

MAKING THE ABSTRACT TANGIBLE

Manufacturers make things, obviously. This SDL is one of the clearest examples of functional grounding: the act of making things induces thinking oriented to what is tangible, concrete, and practical. The logic shows up as a marked preference for pragmatic examples over theoretical models and abstraction. Like *RULES*, this logic is foundational for other logics. For example, *MAKING THE ABSTRACT TANGIBLE* goes hand in hand with *CERTAINTY* and *RULES*, enabling these logics to be supported by the prolific use of tools like dashboards – tangible expressions of abstract data (see Figure 4.5).

How Does It Show Up? (Practices and Adaptations)

Thinking in tangible terms is common to manufacturing, such as in the close measurement of manufacturing operations, or in the tendency to address complex organizational issues through the creation of rules and tools rather than through dialog. For example, the need for greater collaboration across divisions was recently addressed by implementing

Slack, the communications and collaboration platform. Whether Slack improves physical human collaboration can be debated, but the point is the reflex: addressing what is fundamentally a social problem (collaboration) in the physical world through a technology tool.

The tangibility logic, however, is most visible through adaptations. One is the tendency to under-value non-quantifiable data. Another is the lack of patience for ambiguity or highly conceptual versus practical ideas, which manifests as suspicion or a lack of trust of those who are too "big picture" or "out there" in their thinking.

When Overlearned ...

I3's interest in metrics and dashboards is by no means unusual in manufacturing, or even business. And of course, I3's primary business *is* measurement.[30] What is unusual is that managers seem more interested in creating dashboards rather than scrutinizing what these measures mean. The idea of "metrics-for-metrics-sake" versus "metrics that matter" is widespread, and suggests the propensity for tangibility may be overlearned. Of course, there could be other reasons. For one, the company has historically under-valued the need for a single standard, corporate-wide enterprise resource planning system (ERP). Instead, the company runs on numerous local ERPs tied to individual business units and geographies, making the collection of reporting data time consuming and complex, which shortchanges analysis time (and may be the product of another SDL. See below). The clearest example of overlearned tangibility was in the company's recent effort to create a "culture dashboard" without any operational definition of what culture is or what would constitute a valid way to measure it. While this is by no means easy (see Chapter 1), that managers would lead with a dashboard before addressing more fundamental questions highlights the way in which the logic of concreteness takes shape: *to know it we must first measure it* pervades thinking well beyond the factory floor.

As said, there is nothing unusual in any of this for industrial manufacturers, or for I3. That is until the logic is confronted by "foreigners", in this case managers new to I3 coming from its digital acquisitions. They report being "overwhelmed" by the amount of information sought each month by corporate functions such as Finance. Their reactions to this and other manufacturing logics are much like someone in the midst of hailing a taxi in a foreign airport after a long flight realizing they don't speak the language and have no idea how to get to where they want to go.

Where Does This SDL Come From?

MAKING THE ABSTRACT TANGIBLE, as mentioned, is common in manufacturing. The task, literally, of making things entrains the mind to favor what is concrete and practical in *all* domains. This *is* functional grounding.

FIRST-HAND KNOWLEDGE

This is the "seeing is believing" logic. It is characterized by an orientation to what is near, local, and "at hand" versus afar, and extends to the concept of "family". One might see it as an extension of *MAKING THE ABSTRACT TANGIBLE* because it is about privileging what can be immediately seen and touched. While correct, the idea of *first-hand* and *local* adds more descriptive color and helps explain why related practices and adaptations are as they are.

How Does It Show Up? (Practices and Adaptations)

One manifestation has to do with decentralization – decentralized product management, operations, IT, and manufacturing practices. Except for financial reporting, continuous improvement, and compliance, most of the company's management, product, and customer practices are still defined according to brand and regional needs, traditions, and preferences. Attempts to instill more unified or common practices across divisions, such as for procurement, product development, or IT have been met with reluctance or outright push-back. For this reason, the company has an espoused leadership behavior focused on collaboration, a desired trait – on paper at least. Like many competency models, this signals a perceived cultural deficit.

FIRST-HAND KNOWLEDGE shows up frequently in push-backs from local business units and divisions to corporate initiatives. One typical argument is that only local business owners can ever "know" what the customer really wants (whether the "customer" is external or internal), an argument that often goes unchallenged by the corporate group driving the initiative. Local managers are adept at co-opting such arguments on financial performance grounds – that local knowledge and practice is what is needed to produce financial results.

There are exceptions, of course. One is a common review and performance management system. Another is the aforementioned continuous improvement focus with Lean and Six Sigma standards and methods deployed across most manufacturing sites. But these and similar practices have been adopted for compliance reasons – read risk mitigation (*RULES, CERTAINTY*) – or because there is a direct impact on financial performance. The farther away the practice is from direct financial impact or compliance, the more likely it will vary according to local business needs and history.

Interestingly, there is a widespread belief that the company is "relationship driven" and that "the way you get things done is to know the right people". Of course, this is not unique. What makes this stand out here is the belief that because of the lack of standardized processes, or on account of inefficiency or bureaucracy related to *CERTAINTY* and *RULES*, people are forced into "workarounds" – improvised ways to solve problems or find information – to get things done. Workarounds require knowing and building relationships with the "right" people. The know-how for "how to get things done" is a belief of the importance of creating and maintaining good relationships, particularly within one's own business. Executives deemed most successful are those who are able to work effectively within and across divisional silos, and especially between business units and corporate.

This may seem contradictory to an SDL that privileges what is "at hand" and local, (see Figure 4.6), but is actually a great example of reference system adaptation. Collaboration is not a well-developed muscle at I3. There is little logic in the reference system for how to do this given the company's history of smaller independent companies working in discrete and diverse markets around the world. Those individuals that *do* collaborate, that *do* build relationships across functional and divisional silos, are deemed exceptional.

This is also one reason why people characterize I3 as "friendly" and "familial". The company, notably, is populated by well-meaning and friendly people across all divisions and levels. The logics of family and friendliness extend into discourse and group membership norms. For example, managers often reframe "problems" as "opportunities." And people who are more assertive and aggressive tend to stick out and perceived as not "fitting in". These norms are an extension of valuing what is local, familiar, and first-hand.

When Overlearned …

To many people, "friendliness" is a hallmark of I3 culture. But to characterize the culture in this way, while not inaccurate, white-washes the more complicated cultural phenomenon of low collaboration, and misses one of the most important byproducts of overlearned *FIRST HAND KNOWLEDGE*: lack of trust. One would think a dominant local and family logic would engender trust, but actually the opposite is the case. The farther away one gets from one's own site and business, the less one trusts, even when the object of trust (a person or an idea) is within one's same division but geographically or functionally distinct. As with individual strengths that get overplayed into developmental blind spots, I3's historicity of small companies and distinct brands with loyal and proud employees makes trusting others beyond one's own local boundaries not intuitive, even to this day, years after divestiture. Low trust manifests across all functions and global sites, from HR to IT to marketing to product development, and shows up as second-guessing and passive resistance of decisions outside of one's direct reporting chain. Even some vice presidents who report directly to the senior team cite lower levels of interpersonal trust with their own bosses than with others, even though they report high degrees of trust in the overall direction of the company. One reason may have to do the financial performance logic and the continual sense of pressure it creates each quarter.

Where Does This SDL Come From?

I3's legacy as a collection of brands and companies, many with storied histories, which for years existed under the auspices of a holding company that did virtually no integration beyond basic email and financial systems, is no doubt the major inducer of this logic. Many of these companies were originally family-owned businesses, some dating back over 150 years. The logic of local and family runs deep.

And because *FIRST-HAND KNOWLEDGE* privileges relationships, this inhibits standardization on practices, processes and technologies like ERP. It inhibits standardizing on common product management methods, or integrating new businesses. Combined with *RULES* and *CERTAINTY*, this makes for a perfect storm of logics: *of course* the company has difficulty driving standard practices beyond basic financial conformance or compliance: there are no available mental models to draw from that would guide thinking on how to do so. Absent awareness of these pervasive logics, the reference system pulls people back into default ways of thinking and acting that can become self-fulfilling and difficult to overcome.

ACTION

The *ACTION* logic only loaded on one variable in our FA, but figured prominently in our qualitative research and consulting. Action is about deeds over words, action over deliberation, a kind of "just get it done" bias. It may be a close cousin to *MAKING THE ABSTRACT TANGIBLE* since an emphasis on the concrete and physical implies action. Or it may be an enabler of other dominant logics, namely *FINANCIAL PERFORMANCE FIRST, RULES*, and *CERTAINTY*. *ACTION* may be a reaction or compensation for these SDLs; not just an adaptation but as something more fundamental. It is a reflex logic, a kind of *fire-ready-aim* orientation that has the effect of precluding analysis while giving the sense that something is being done.

How Does It Show Up? (Practices and Adaptations)

Its major manifestation in practice is in data collection (see Figure 4.7): the organization spends inordinate amounts of time and resources "chasing down" information – financial data, order status, parts availability, product quotations, and so on – largely because of its organizational structure disconnected information systems. Getting the basics of one's job done is hard; doing so takes *action*.

One adaptation to *ACTION* is the preference for expediency over efficacy. For example, several senior finance executives often tell us that when countermeasures to business challenges are reported in monthly reviews, they are often acts of "hand waving" rather than seriously considered measures to close performance gaps. In such cases, saying "I don't know", or "I need to study this issue and get back to you" is rarely heard. The norm is to promise action, even if those doing the promising are not clear on what to do. These gestures are rarely challenged by senior managers, for the conflict norms already stated (*CERTAINTY*).

When Overlearned ...

As stated, a common example of overlearned *ACTION* is a preference for action over analysis. This is not to say I3 managers are not analytical. It's simply that action is a general default orientation. These judgments, of course, are relative. For example, in my experience, the degree of scrutiny on a typical business case presentation at Microsoft was more intense and onerous than at I3. At Microsoft it was not uncommon to be interrupted early in one's presentation to be asked a question about a minor detail buried deep in the appendix, a detail, no doubt, that the audience member had picked out as foundational to the premise of the presentation and if falsified could show the entire argument lacked merit. In contrast, at I3 generalizations or assumptions in presentations often go unquestioned, and if they are the challengers are often perceived as "difficult" or "all about themselves". Presenters are routinely given the benefit of the doubt. The family and local orientation underwritten by the *FIRST HAND KNOWLEDGE* SDL undoubtedly contributes to the collegial and polite presentation norms. Teams have vowed to try and change this by encouraging "calling each other out" and "challenging one another", but these aspirations prove difficult to sustain in practice, especially beyond the confines of the team. There are exceptions, of course. The corporate M&A team, comprised of lawyers, finance professionals, and business strategists, often with the help of an outside strategy consultant, display a high degree of analytical rigor befitting their professionalization and, to be expected in a firm whose primary engine for market disruption and R&D is M&A. Many R&D teams exhibit the same. But these are functional exceptions, not the norm.

Where Does This SDL Come From?

This logic originates in the amount of time and energy it takes to make the business of I3 run, and especially according to finance, rules, and certainty logics. Managers report they lack time, and complaints about long hours and work–life balance are common. The amount of financial data generated each month to help senior management monitor business performance is a source of anxiety and frustration. Monthly reviews consume significant amounts of preparation time collecting data from multiple sources on metrics, many of which are not referenced in the review. The problem is exacerbated because much important information is locked on spreadsheets on local computers, and in people's heads distributed across divisional silos. Simply obtaining answers to basic questions can take days, which leads to workarounds and engenders the action reflex. If you don't take action, you will run out of time.

───────

THE REFERENCE SYSTEM SUPPORTS ...
UNTIL IT DOESN'T

After reading through the preceding, one might be tempted to say these SDLs are not tacit logics at all but simply conscious beliefs and attitudes, deliberately chosen actions and practices to successfully run a company. This reaction would not be a surprise, for two reasons. First, as with SDLs in any company, taken individually none are particularly earth-shattering or radical; most people who have worked in manufacturing are likely to have a "so what" reaction in reading them. Moreover, many, if not all of the practices and adaptations are rational and reasonable ways to run a complex, global and successful manufacturing enterprise. And that is precisely the point. As basic cognitive orientations the product of the task environment and the ecological challenges the company has navigated to get to where it is today, they are necessary and successful adaptations. Like all adaptations, in retrospect they have a way of making us believe they were what we intended all along. We want to believe all we do in life, and in business, is conscious. What is missed is the recognition that more fundamental cognitive orientations, as logics or mental models anchoring our collective reference system, are the source and structure of our conscious agency *to begin with*. Put more basically: cultural free will exists. But it runs on already lain tracks. To change it requires laying down new tracks.

These SDLs, regardless of the exact label put on them, are the contours of I3's collective preconscious, the reference system habitually drawn from to justify, organize, account for, idealize, set standards, and chart the future. The logics themselves and the pervasive ways in which they manifest in practice and adaptation – taken together – all reveal a distinct pattern and structure that can be thought of as I3 culture. Except "culture" here is not in the sense of a monolithic whole, but as a collection of discrete logics that, like DNA or source code, give rise to an entire integrated system of meaning.

I3, by all accounts, is a very successful company. It has been rewarding investors with consistent financial performance over many years. It has loyal customers, and a significant portion of its revenue is recurring. It's employee engagement scores, rank about average for global industrials. In other words, what I3 has been doing as a major manufacturer is working.

Cultures Are "Perfect" …

I3's cultural reference system is a byproduct of its core task focus and history. A dominant, finance-first orientation, supported by rules, certainty, tangibility, local knowledge, and action logics, work together in additive and consistent ways to make the company feel culturally distinct. These logics may manifest in ways not detectable by employee engagement surveys, but they are for the most part successful adaptations to the demands of the operating environment, especially given the company's sudden birth as a stand-alone entity beholden from day one to shareholder interests.

In this way, cultures are always *perfect for their environments*. "Perfect" because, of necessity, they are fine-tuned as systems of knowledge and meaning for the demands of their current worlds. If they weren't, the social systems that bear them wouldn't survive. Subway blockers would go to jail, pastoralist societies would die out, Rossel islanders wouldn't be able to rebuild after a major typhoon, and companies would disappear (as they do). Culture in this way is an evolutionary adaptive response to basic functioning and survival: reference systems come to be because of meaningful and sustained adaptations to existential challenges. They run in the background, that is, until you try to block access to a subway car, stare at someone in an elevator, try to triple the size of your company in two years, or try to turn an industrial manufacturer into a digital enterprise. Then our attention is suddenly drawn to our reference systems much like a notice from the bank saying our account is overdrawn. The systems we draw from are so habituated they are invisible – until they no longer serve us.

… Until They're Not

And so here. The problem with the I3 reference system is that what it is today is not what it needs to be given the company's ambitions for tomorrow. Only in endeavoring to transform does the reference system become visible. Or partially so. Its aspired digital transformation goals bring its reference system into relief in a major way, because what it takes to be a successful legacy industrial and what it takes to be a digital disruptor are two very different things. Zoom out to consider why.

Companies "born digital", that is, born in the middle of the 20th century or later have experienced social, technology, and market ecologies vastly different than that of companies born prior to that time. So-called "digital natives" are far more comfortable with experimentation, risk taking, reinvention, and different modes of public expression (YouTube, Facebook, Instagram, blogging, avatars, and so forth), to name but a few obvious differences (Palfrey & Gasser, 2008). I would add to this list differences owing to fundamentally different task environments: "move fast and break things" might be cliché, but is pretty far out of the comfort zone of most industrial managers, for the reasons already discussed.

Digital Values and Practices

Not surprisingly, many management consultancies and business schools have developed models to describe what it takes for legacy companies to "go digital" and compete in the world of sensors, AI, and ubiquitous computing. One such model, developed by George Westerman and his colleagues at the Sloan School at MIT, describes a set of digital "values" and "practices" legacy companies should adopt to become more "agile" and "innovative" to compete as digital transformers.[31] This model, and others like it, provide a target for industrial companies to aim at. Based on a review of published frameworks and "stories" of digital cultures, and analysis of a survey administered to over 500 traditional and digital companies, they identified key values and practices legacy companies need to drive digital transformation (2019, p. 61). These values are *impact* (defined as constant innovation); *speed* (moving fast and "not having all the answers"); *openness* (engaging broadly with "diverse sources of information"); and *autonomy* (allowing high levels of discretion). The key practices identified are *rapid experimentation* (including learning from results and applying new insights quickly); *self-organizing* (fluid collaboration across boundaries); and *driving decisions with data* (using accurate data for decision-making).

From the foregoing it might be obvious that enacting these practices and values at I3 will not be straightforward. The reference system explains why.

Figures 4.8 and 4.9 show Westerman and colleagues' digital values and practices against the company's SDLs. The juxtaposition of existing logics with putative best-practice values (Figure 4.8) and practices (Figure 4.9) illuminates some of the challenges lying ahead for I3 and other industrials endeavoring similar transformation.

Take Impact (Figure 4.8). The idea of constant innovation, while attractive and espoused by many companies, is more of an ideal at I3 than reality. Innovation practices are, as mentioned, relatively localized and variable according to brand and product needs, markets, and legacy. Nonetheless, most R&D teams follow a stage-gate review process and complete "A3" project plan templates that lay out a structured and serialized planning approach before beginning any initiative, no matter how small (see Figure 4.10).[32] Most innovation is incremental – predictable and contained upgrades to products either on a set schedule or according to the preferences of the particular product's R&D team. In an environment where what is considered implicitly good or worthwhile has clear financial returns (*FINANCIAL PERFORMANCE FIRST*), where minimizing risk and avoiding unknowns is prized, and where what is standardized and repeatable is preferable to iteration (*CERTAINTY*) – these and similar orientations are unwitting detractors to constant innovation. How do you drive constant innovation in an environment where there is an implicit right and wrong way of doing things, and where one needs to know the rules before embarking on any initiative? Imagine trying to drive constant innovation amid prevailing beliefs that measurability and tangibility are preferred over abstraction and conceptualization, and that experimentation and iteration are to be avoided because they are too risky, too impractical, and too costly (*MAKING THE ABSTRACT TANGIBLE*)?

The same kinds of challenges apply to the rest of Westerman and colleagues' digital values. For example, autonomy will be hampered by the need for management to control what and how junior staff communicate with upper management (*CERTAINTY*), and where delegation of authority rules (*RULES*) constrain how much latitude managers have in decision-making. Speed will be constrained by the impulse to want to have all the risks spelled out before beginning a new initiative (*CERTAINTY*). Openness, defined as a broad engagement with diverse sets of information, on the one hand could be thought of as a company strength given its propensity for data and metrics (*MAKING THE ABSTRACT TANGIBLE*). But *RULES* and *CERTAINTY* may conspire against it, and prevailing

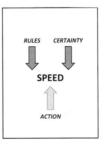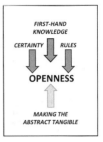

FIGURE 4.8

How dominant logics support or subvert digital values.

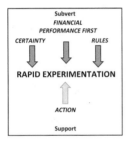

FIGURE 4.9

How dominant logics support or subvert digital practices.

assumptions based on *seeing is believing, show me before I buy-in,* and *what is good and what I trust is what is local (FIRST-HAND KNOWLEDGE)* will tend to preclude wide engagement with new information.

Practices associated with digital transformation (see Figure 4.9) will also be met head-on by prevailing logics. Rapid experimentation, potentially enabled by *ACTION,* will be met by the dominant orientation to financial performance, particularly as regards the notion that what is good has clear short-term financial returns. Despite beliefs that it is possible, it is very hard for managers to incubate digital skunkworks or innovation projects amid quarterly and monthly financial pressures and an ongoing pull on resources to maximize profitability. Self-organizing will be constrained by pressures to minimize risk and avoid the unknown (*CERTAINTY*), and particularly by the concomitant needs for managerial control and the tendency for managers to wait for the chain of command to make the call on hard issues or bless new initiatives. Data-based decisions, with their emphasis on breadth and accuracy, will be precluded by *FINANCIAL PERFORMANCE FIRST* and *ACTION,* which privilege financial data often at the expense of other kinds of data, and, as said, lead to inaccuracies in

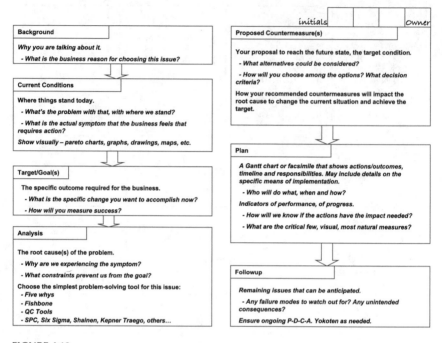

FIGURE 4.10
Example of an "A3" project plan template.

forecasting. An emphasis on financial returns above all keeps managers chasing down information to comply with the many metrics I3's controllers employ to track performance, an activity that precludes forethought on what the metrics are trying to achieve, or why. The company is habituated to action, but too often that means *reaction*.

Figures 4.8 and 4.9 also show how certain SDLs, particularly *ACTION*, might function in service *of* transformation. In the next chapter we will explore how I3 might go about culture change in a way that leverages its SDLs. Certainly the company's orientation to quick answers, and action over deliberation will predispose it to speed and impact. For now, suffice to say the action logic needs to be re-oriented away from a bias for motion – action for action's sake – to one purposefully directed at transformation.

In short, from the above, and from what else has not been explicitly mentioned but implied in Figure 4.8 and 4.9, I3 faces obstacles in achieving its digital ambitions. The company has begun to acknowledge this when it recently adopted a different set of financial metrics to value the performance of its digital businesses. An argument could be made that I3 will only realize the true value of its digital investments when it can fully leverage and deploy these capabilities with its existing customers. This is what the founders and managers of these digital companies, in fact, hoped for when they were acquired. The question is whether I3 is moving with sufficient speed and nimbleness to seize the market opportunity being afforded. We may soon start to see players from outside the industry move to bring digital solutions and AI to the lab, industrial, and retail weight and measurement spaces. I3 tends to believe its deep customer relationships and distribution networks are the bulwark against such threats, but the market only needs choice for doubts to be cast and buying indecision to be introduced. Many of I3's industrial and retail customers are risk-averse, so there may be time still for industrial players like I3 to get their digital acts together. Domain expertise tends to be highly valued, which may also be a barrier for new entrants. On the other hand, the speed at which business models are disrupted and paradigms inverted in this time of massive technological and social upheaval is seemingly overnight, and shouldn't be underestimated (look at Amazon in logistics, Microsoft in health care). New, deep-pocketed, digital-ready entrants from far beyond might momentarily confuse and splinter the market, at which point I3 will have lost any first-mover advantage it might have sought.

But the point here is not to debate I3's digital strategy. The point is to underscore how and why "going digital" is, culturally speaking, exceedingly difficult. It is difficult precisely because the company's cultural reference system is not suited to the digital world. The reference system was born as an adaptive response to industrial era contingencies and challenges, and, to bend the metaphor a bit further, like antibodies attacking a virus it will naturally try to stymie cultural moves in the digital direction. The logics for doing so are obvious: constant innovation, moving fast, not having all the answers before commencing, engaging broadly, using high levels of discretion in decision-making well down the chain of command, rapid experimentation, self-organizing, and using accurate data while employing measures of success beyond short-term financial returns – all of these values and practices will be undermined by I3's unassailable industrial logics of financial assurance, rules, certainty, risk-aversion, concreteness, practicality, local knowledge, and reflexive action. The company's natural and habituated way of making sense may not be able to make collective sense of what it is now being asked to do. And not for lack of *conscious* knowledge – its senior leadership, led by their CEO and their board of directors are well aware of what's required *strategically*. Like most executive teams, they have read all the articles and been steeped in best-practice advice. Their extensive investments in digital capabilities is proof. They believe they are on their way to digital transformation. And why not? Nothing in their reference system would lead them to believe otherwise.

The problem is the blind spot: their reference system is keeping the company mired in the industrial age by undermining its digital ambitions with well-designed, irrefutable, and implicitly held logics for *why* running the company in this way is perfectly justified. Not only justified: highly successful. That's exactly what cultural reference systems are designed to do: keep you believing in the inevitability of your own success.

Leaders one or two levels below the senior executive team are a bit more skeptical. But owing to the pervasive logics concerning respect for authority (hierarchy), local orientation (optimized for one's own business and brand interest), and a pronounced inertia owing to quarterly financial pressures, few managers can muster the willpower to convince the executive team that they have a bigger problem than they think they do. If they did, they would have to do this collectively to overcome their own potential job security.

From all this, one begins to see why culture change is so hard. The challenge for leaders in any organization steeped in its own logics (as all are) is to find ways to break out of their existing paradigms to seek logics far from their own professional grounding, industry and strategic task orientations. This is not easy (see Chapter 5). It requires a willingness to engage in an honest examination of prevailing assumptions, implicit standards, beliefs and norms, and current practices – the core of the reference system. It requires admitting that the very attributes that have made the company successful may be its greatest weakness. It requires acknowledging strengths while surfacing gaps. It requires a bracing look into unthought knowns. All of this, as said, takes significant reserves of curiosity and courage, not to mention humility. And so, while culture doesn't come from the top, *transforming* organizations requires changing cultural logics in ways that force leaders into thinking and acting differently, well outside their comfort zones. This is another part of culture change the myth-makers miss: culture change leadership requires hard *learning*, including hard *personal learning*. In the next chapter, as we explore how to intervene in cultural reference systems, we will cover what I3 is trying to do to transform, and what it might do instead.

NOTES

1. *The New York Times* (November 11, 2019).
2. *The New York Times* (November 2, 2019).
3. Of course, these are speculative logics intended to illustrate the point. I have not done any empirical work on dominant logics in publishing, media, or private equity.
4. Not the company's real name or identity. While the research presented in this chapter was conducted at a Fortune 1000 company and the results and implications presented are relevant to it, several facts about the firm have been changed and blended with those of other organizations to preserve anonymity. The company profiled here is an archetype created solely for the purposes of illustrating how functionally grounded culture takes shape and operates in practice. It is not a case study of an actual company.
5. I borrow the term *"the unthought known"* from the psychoanalyst Christopher Bollas (1987, p. 4). In psychoanalysis, the unthought known casts a shadow on all aspects of that individual's existence without the individual being aware of it until it is brought into consciousness.
6. Quantitative research in the social sciences usually involves surveys and statistical analysis of survey data. Qualitative research usually involves interview, observational, or action research methods and the inference and interpretation of data from these methods. Of course, qualitative methods involve an extensive amount interpretation and coding of data, a process prone to bias. Quantitative methods, however, are equally prone to bias: who the researchers chooses to survey and what she surveys, whether the survey items are imposed by the researcher from external sources (external to the social system) or derived from within – these are all judgment calls prone to bias. For more on this, I recommend Alvesson and Skoldberg's excellent *Reflexive Methodology* (2009).
7. Obviously there is much more to this discussion on methods that I am omitting for space and general interest. For example, we could get into a discussion of what actually constitutes knowledge. Or we could reflect on the fact problems are constitutive features of the questions that frame them, the situatedness of the observer, and the observed features of the investigation. Readers interested should refer to my *Rethinking Culture* and its entire chapter devoted to methodology. Organizational scholars may also be interested in Alvesson and Skoldberg's *Reflexive Methodology: New Vistas for Qualitative Research* (2009), highly relevant for qualitative research in organizations.
8. For examples of this method in use, see Dougherty (1992), or Lounsbury (2007).
9. Quinn's technique is described in her 2005 book of the same title as this section.
10. With respect to analogy and metaphor, reasoning typically occurs by reference to prototypes: schemas are usually fragmentary bits of generic knowledge that have a central, prototypical core, much like a house schema is a mental stand-in for a yurt, igloo, teepee, high rise apartment, or a suburban mansion (Descola, 2013).
11. I used this same technique to uncover IMCO's primary schemas, detailed in my first book and in Chapter 3.
12. See Calori, Johnson, and Sarni (1992).

13. One of the others is the work of Sieck (2010) and his colleagues on Cultural Network Analysis.
14. The "we" here is my colleagues at Ontos Global that formed the research team, Lisa Koss and Chris Fagan. All interviewees were male except for two. All were white except for one (Asian). Five were non-native English speakers fluent in English. All had engineering, finance, or manufacturing operations backgrounds.
15. This technique is similar to the Critical Incident Technique developed for candidate assessment and selection (see Edvardsson & Roos, 2001). There is a significant body of research establishing its validity as a method for eliciting patterns denoting how someone reasons in a particular domain.
16. This class of metaphors are known as metonymies. For a complete discussion please see *Rethinking Culture*.
17. Although this comes with epistemological problems alluded to earlier and discussed later in this chapter.
18. Chris Argyris and Donald Schon refine this definition with greater precision in their essay, *Participatory Action Research and Action Science Compared* (1989).
19. This additional step is one most managerial studies of culture do not undertake; they typically limit themselves to single methods. These are either qualitative studies (interviews, text analysis of annual reports and 10K filings, and such), or quantitative studies based on externally imposed (etic) constructs.
20. For a thorough review, see Bernard (2011).
21. The number of statements on the survey corresponded to the frequency of schemas adduced in the qualitative studies – there were more *CERTAINTY* schemas because *CERTAINTY* appeared more frequently in our interviews and observations. This means some "under-represented" schemas, like *FAIRNESS*, may not have been captured as factors because there were fewer questions pertaining to those variables.
22. Employees voluntarily participated based on attending a management or leadership development course.
23. We also ran a Confirmatory Factor Analysis (CFA) to evaluate fit which indicated a Tucker-Lewis Index (TLI) of .85. CFA was then used to eliminate weaker variables to create a new factor model of 15 variables on five factors accounting for 61 percent of the sample variation with a TLI of .95.
24. To such an extent this is even possible. No one person can ever hold all the cultural knowledge of a system in one's head.
25. For purposes of preserving anonymity of the company, actual financial performance figures are omitted. They are not relevant to the thesis of functional grounding or cultural reference systems.
26. Smith and Schreiner (1969), Weston (1969).
27. See Clinton and Chen (1998), Schmenner and Vollmann (1994, in Gomes, Yasin, and Lisboa, 2004).
28. Singh, Feng, and Smith (2006).
29. Newman, Hanna, and Maffei (1993).
30. One might go further and say it is unusual for a company with a primary business in weights and measures to value the act of measurement, per se, over accuracy. I would speculate there are two reasons for this. First, this is evidence of the logic

of measurement being overlearned. Second, the prevalence of other SDLs, namely *FINANCIAL PERFORMANCE FIRST,* serves to subordinate this SDL. Another way of saying this is that some SDLs are more primary and foundational than others.
31. Westerman, Soule, and Eswaran (2019).
32. The term "A3" refers to the 11″ × 17″ ledger size piece of paper on which the template is produced (goleansixsigma.com).

5

Change the Practice, Change the Culture

Rather than fulfilling the expectation that they will provide answers, leaders have to ask tough questions...Instead of orienting people to their current roles, leaders must disorient them so that new relationships can develop... Instead of maintaining norms, leaders have to challenge "the way we do business" and help others distinguish immutable values from historical practices that must go.

– Ron Heifetz and Donald Laurie

"No CEO will ever get fired for being ignorant about their own culture", my friend and colleague Paul provocatively likes to say. CEOs do get fired for lots of things, including dodgy ethical practices attributable to culture, but rarely is culture directly one of those things. This is because by the time they and their boards realize their strategies may be failing on account of something (usually unspecified) having to do with culture, it's too late. The invisible wall of the reference system will have already inhibited or sabotaged the desired changed to such a degree that the company will have no chance of delivering on its hoped-for results or promised ambitions. This is because reference systems optimize for the status quo, for maintaining equilibrium at all costs. This is another reason why leaders are so easily misled by culture: they tinker at the margins thinking they are making something happen – through the great speeches, the values training, or that new competency model – when in fact nothing in people's lived experience of the cultural reference system is changing at all. Exceptional CEOs – those with enough self-awareness, psychological flexibility, curiosity, and courage – will realize developing an unflinching understanding of their organization's cultural reference system is key to avoiding this fate. They realize their own reference systems hold the secrets to successful transformation.

REFERENCE SYSTEMS HOLD YOUR SECRETS

This is because contained within your company's cultural reference system is all the information you will ever need on whether what you desire for your organization is possible, and if so, how so. Reference systems contain all of this information because they are the repositories of your organization's accumulated knowledge, the sum total of all of the cognitions, assumptions, beliefs, heuristics, rules-of-thumb, folk wisdoms, and other lore about what it has taken for your organization to get to its current place in its evolutionary arc of history. Reference systems are the product of successful adaptations – "successful" because your company exists today in large part because of them. If the adaptations weren't successful the organization wouldn't be here. And because they are this huge tacit repository of accumulated wisdom, they also contain all the information about what will keep your organization from becoming the one you desire it to be. In this way reference systems are proverbial canaries in a coal mine, the early warning sign that something may be amiss and inhibiting the desired change. Understanding the contents of your reference system, as such, becomes one of the most important things a CEO and change leader can do.

And yet, as you might have gleaned from the last two chapters, doing so is not exactly straightforward. Most of the time our reference systems are invisible, unthought knowns, as it were. We use cultural reference systems (multiple ones) daily in our lives and yet are unaware we are doing so because we don't need to be aware of them. We don't need to be consciously thinking about what to do or how to be with others when we catch a subway or ride in an elevator with strangers, or how to act in a meeting, or how to talk to our teams. Our brains have the infinite ability to filter out what is already known to free capacity for more important tasks, the sense-making at hand. It is only when we are confronted with stark differences – catching that taxi in the airport of a foreign city; having a dispute over editorial content with a private equity executive; dealing with the Swedish engineering team as a non-Swede; or trying to turn your decades-old industrial into a digital company – that it dawns upon us that some other system is governing the situation. So the (literally) million-dollar question is, how do we begin to understand the contents of our own reference system so as to make better use of them in service of corporate transformation?

Exploring One's Reference System Is an Adaptive Challenge

As Yuval Harari reminds us in the Introduction, culture doesn't give discounts. Understanding your reference system is not a linear process of asking yourself and your organization questions like, *what are our dominant logics?* And yet, while not straightforward, exploring and changing one's reference system is entirely possible. This chapter lays out a framework for doing so. Or rather, two frameworks. One is a Process Framework – the steps leaders can take to leverage and alter their own reference systems for sustainable transformation. At the core is a focus on practices, the key to culture change.

The other is a Leadership Framework – what leaders must do to create environments where investigating unthought knowns is even possible, let alone productive. My partner, Lisa Koss and I have been developing this framework over the last few years with several different clients. At the core of that is the concept of *holding environments*, contexts where groups can feel psychologically safe enough to take risks in surfacing and interrogating the content of their collective unthought knowns. Challenging and changing reference systems will always be perceived as risky and controversial, because doing so invariably challenges the status quo (cultures are perfectly adapted to preserving it). To create holding environments where reference systems can be understood and challenged leaders and change agents must also personally possess enough of four key personal orientations, in roughly equal measure: *self-awareness*, *psychological flexibility*, *curiosity*, and *courage*. We will return to them again at the end of this chapter.

With that in mind, an important caveat: these are not recipes or playbooks. There are no formulas in culture change (run for the hills when any are presented), because any attempt to intervene in a cultural reference system is inherently an *adaptive* challenge.

Ron Heifetz and his colleagues at Harvard a few years ago introduced into the change lexicon the concept of *adaptive leadership*.[1] Adaptive leadership is what is necessary to overcome adaptive challenges, challenges where the organization itself needs to develop fundamentally new ways of learning and seeing, new capacities to adapt and change in order to survive and thrive amid far greater ambiguity and far less predictability in a dynamic and changing world. Adaptive challenges are to be distinguished from technical challenges. In the latter the problem space is generally known and the solution path generally clear. Technical challenges – how to design a product, how to go to market, how to engage customers, how to set strategy, how to develop people, and so on – are the stuff we deal with every day at work. These are the challenges we get paid to solve, and they usually draw upon our expertise and experience as professionals. Adaptive challenges are categorically different. In adaptive challenges the problem space is the nature of our own assumptions about the world we live in. The change is defined not as the path to solution but by how we frame issues, what questions we ask, and how good our diagnoses and interpretations are of what is going on in our systems, whether those be personal, interpersonal, or whole-organizational. Adaptive challenges are what the world increasingly presents to us with the advent of the Fourth Industrial Revolution, or via global pandemics like Covid-19. Digital transformation is an adaptive challenge; most organizational transformation of any consequence are adaptive challenges. The problem is most organizations try to deal with adaptive challenges through technical solutions. The approaches to culture change outlined in Chapter 1 fall squarely into that category.

So don't mistake what is presented below as a technical approach to an adaptive problem. What may appear to be a linear, step-wise method for intervening in a cultural reference system is simply an artifact of needing to explain something sophisticated in as clear a manner as possible. In reality, intervening in reference systems will always be adaptive, iterative, and dynamic, as much a process as a frame of mind that entails careful scanning and diagnosis while being simultaneously reflexive, open-minded, and curious. Which is why the Leadership Framework presented below is a crucial component, a parallel process that must accompany any intervention.

Throughout we will continue to use I3 as our archetypal example, examining these two frameworks in the context of the company's SDLs, practices, and adaptations. We will be coming back to two questions: what is I3 doing, and what could it be doing to intervene in its own reference system in order to successfully transform into a digital company?

CHANGING REFERENCE SYSTEMS: THE PROCESS FRAMEWORK

At a high level, intervening in cultural reference systems appears straightforward. Figure 5.1, depicts this process as three steps:

1. Define your **Principles** by articulating what is most important to enable your vision. What values must be kept in mind as you do this?
2. Gain **Perspective** by making the preconscious conscious: become aware of your own dominant logics and how they manifest in the reference system.
3. Prioritize **Practices** by identifying where you have high-leverage opportunities to shape logics through redesigned or new practices.

As you read through these, again, keep in mind what is being presented as a linear process is in fact a highly dynamic and emergent one, with Step 3, for example, helping inform Step 1, and so on.

1: Define Principles (Values That Enable the Future)

As with any change, articulating the design principles to actualize your desired future state is the key first step in intervening in a reference system. This usually happens against an already-articulated strategy, vision, or plan vetted by the board or key stakeholders, which is why "Vision" and "Strategy" is depicted as the leftmost element of Figure 5.1. However, this can also happen without a formally defined strategy. One of our clients, a $800 million defense company, for example, merely has a "growth and

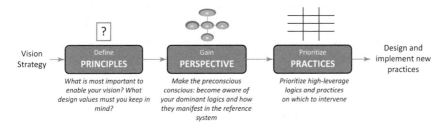

FIGURE 5.1
Reference system intervention process framework: how to understand and change references systems.

scale" ambition to triple in size within five years. The ambition to scale provides enough of a future direction from which principles, in the form of design values, can be articulated. In their case, one principle is to preserve as much of the current culture as possible, which of course will not be easy.

The importance of defining principles in this first step is twofold. First, proceeding directly from a vision or strategy to practices that alter dominant logics is not easy. Several layers of translation must be gone through to determine which SDLs and practices to target, and why. Second, reference system intervention by definition involves trade-offs. Knowing what matters as you go is important; principles and design values provide that.

The best way to define principles is to brainstorm answers to two questions: *what would it take for us to achieve our transformation ambitions?* And, *what design values must we adhere to as we do?*

I3 has partial answers to these questions. What they don't have is a digital strategy per se. They have embedded their digital ambitions into various strategic initiatives under a broad strategy focused on – no surprise – growth through profitability. These initiatives include items related to technology and innovation, product quality and excellence, M&A, and customer focus.[2] Within the technology and innovation initiative, for example, one finds items related to data analytics and IoT. The technology and innovation initiative is also about the "efficient use of capital", showing once again how *FINANCIAL PERFORMANCE FIRST* permeates every facet of strategy, even those that are most forward-looking. The M&A initiative, as mentioned in Chapter 4, is about using M&A as a competitive advantage for acquiring or enhancing "IoT platforms and AI" capabilities. Again, pervasive logics of *FINANCIAL PERFORMANCE FIRST* and *CERTAINTY* inform the approach to R&D, a strategy that at its core is about mitigating risk by offsetting potential losses in some assets with potential gains, and reducing the number of variables and risks involved in the innovation process by acquiring ready-made assets and capabilities. And there is nothing unusual about any of this. Every company exists to ensure profitability and smartly manage risk. The point here is how dominant logics are visible even in the way I3 formulates strategy.

I3's approach to digital transformation is rooted in financial and certainty-driven strategies. Logics of financial assurance, rules, certainty, risk-aversion, concreteness, practicality, local knowledge, and reflexive action are, as said in Chapter 4, unassailable, based on the tacit knowledge of its industrial era reference system and corporate success. I3 leadership believes it can get to its digital future by doing exactly what it's been doing, that is, by working the problem in a risk-managed, certainty-driven, predictability-oriented, industrial-logics-based way (with a portfolio of digital assets as proof). In other words, it believes its digital future is assured based on what it has been doing in the past. And why not? Nothing in its own cultural reference system would suggest otherwise.

Interestingly, I3 has defined a list of digital enablers, a close proxy to the idea of Principles in Step 1. These come in the form of leadership competencies such as *Takes Intelligent Risks, Drives Results*, and *Brings New Ideas to Life* among others. This list, of course, is not simply about digital transformation. And like most companies, these behaviors are not formally integrated into any of the company's talent management practices such as selection, performance management, or succession planning. They are available to be used by managers in these activities, but, not surprisingly, their use is not mandated or driven by any process (see *FIRST-HAND KNOWLEDGE; ACTION*). As with many companies, I3 management believes simply publishing desired behaviors is enough to change how people think and behave.

Absent anything else, leadership competencies, or generic leadership traits or values when posited against a desired future state can be sufficient for articulating a desired culture in Step 1. In Step 3 we will return to look at which leadership behaviors in particular are most allied with digital transformation, what the embedded logic is within them, and how these can be drawn forward to inform specific practices.

2: Gain Perspective (Seeing Dominant Logics and the Whole Reference System)

This next step is about exposing the contents of one's reference system. The goal is to get the organization, in particular, the strata of key leaders who control resources and wield significant influence, to understand "who they are", culturally speaking.[3] For most this step will feel deeply familiar. In fact, you know your data is "correct" when it is met with collective head nods and a kind of shrugging, *tell us something we don't already know* response. Unthought knowns, once revealed, seem almost trivial or obvious.

What is most important in this step, however, is revealing how dominant logics show up as patterns across practices and adaptations. For it is here the organization begins to understand how pervasive, and potentially inhibiting and constraining to transformation their own logics are. Understanding "who we are" is really about understanding *implications: because our dominant logics are as they are, this means our practices, behaviors and attitudes are also as they are. And this has big implications for what we want to be.* Getting a leadership group to this insight is the goal.

The artifact that enables this is depicted in Table 5.1. This, again, is the view of I3's reference system, but this time in table format. How you get to this output, of course, will vary depending on your specific transformation goals and stakeholders. As the late organizational researcher David Nadler so rightfully pointed out many years ago, data collection and presentation *is* intervention.[4] What data we choose to collect and present will guide and influence the organization's behavior. Nowhere is this more the case than revealing the contents of a reference system, for it is the picture of the cognitive underpinnings of everything the organization does, a kind of MRI, or more accurately, an fMRI of the organization's collective neural network. How the change leader chooses to reveal, or have the organization reveal onto itself the contents of its reference system is a design decision that very much has to take into account the prevailing logics of the system.

At I3 we had the benefit of observation and action research to be able to present to various leadership groups a complete picture of the I3 reference system (Table 5.1). But we also chose to do it in this way because of the prevalence of two logics, *ACTION* and *MAKING THE ABSTRACT TANGIBLE*. We knew these SDLs biased the organization to want to work with tangible versus abstract data, and to spend more time wanting to "fix" and "solve" the problems suggested by these data rather than debate how they were derived. This exercise at a different firm, such as a technology company, would in all likelihood look very different. There we might only present the SDLs, and show in much greater detail how they were derived. We would design a highly facilitated process to allow leadership groups the ability to generate their own list of practices and adaptations based on the SDLs. The process would take longer, but groups would feel as if the content was "their own", consistent with the logics of a typical tech company. Every organization should design and manage this step in a way that takes into account its own shared logics.

Below are three options. Readers not interested in the specifics of intervention methods should skip to the discussion on practices.

TABLE 5.1

The 13 Reference System, with Practices and Adaptations (Table Version)

	The Reference System	
Shared Dominant Logics *Tacit assumptions, standards, beliefs, idealizations, rules, lived norms, etc.*	**Practices** *Habits, routines, informal or formal processes*	**Adaptations** *Conscious attitudes, and behavior – some of which are reactions or compensations to practices and SDLs*
FINANCIAL PERFORMANCE FIRST Dominant orientation to financial outcomes (cost, revenue, OI, ROI, etc.)	• What is good or worthwhile has clear financial returns – revenue, OI, ROI, etc. • Investor confidence is assured through quarter-to-quarter predictability • Good management is financial management • If we don't meet investor expectations we will not be around to even have a future	1. Weekly, monthly, and quarterly business reviews for each business unit 2. Many metrics to manage performance, most of them financial 3. Primary form of management control is financial 4. "Management-by telling" – driving financial compliance by dictating performance targets and KPIs 5. "R&D as M&A": Acquiring digital assets and new capabilities primarily through acquisition 6. Talent reviews value those who deliver financial results 7. Under-resourced support functions (besides Finance: IT, HR) 8. Applying standard manufacturing financial performance measures to its data and software businesses	• Short-term thinking • "Immense pressure to deliver on plan" • Missing or undervaluing leading indicators • Undervaluing or not recognizing non-financial metrics • Spending freezes • "You cannot have financial surprises at the end of the quarter" • Manager reluctance to report realistic financial data upstream • Inaccurate forecasting by managers

(Continued)

TABLE 5.1 (CONTINUED)

The 13 Reference System, with Practices and Adaptations (Table Version)

	The Reference System	
Shared Dominant Logics *Tacit assumptions, standards, beliefs, idealizations, rules, lived norms, etc.*	**Practices** *Habits, routines, informal or formal processes*	**Adaptations** *Conscious attitudes, and behavior – some of which are reactions or compensations to practices and SDLs*
RULES There is a right way and a wrong way; assumes there is always a "right answer"	• Need to know "the rules" before engaging • Process orientation; good processes have clear rules (process owners, rules of engagement, milestones) • Strong belief and respect for hierarchy	1. Strong compliance focus (cost of non-compliance is significant) 2. Interpersonal or team issues solved by having "rules of engagement" 3. Delegation of authority limits and controls at low levels of management	• Belief that successful matrix management is made possible by adherence to rules • Assumptions in financial forecasts or business plans are often taken "as is" and not challenged • Little challenge or questioning of top management decision-making • Delegation rules perceived as onerous and initiative-sapping
CERTAINTY Seek out answers and assurances to control	• What is standardized and repeatable is preferable to one-offs or iteration • Minimize risk and avoid the unknown	1. "Standard work" 2. Emphasis on structured process: e.g., Lean, Gemba walks, process maps, project plan templates 3. Difficulties with prioritization; a hard time saying "no" – many simultaneous initiatives authorized	• Low initiative unless OK'd by upper management • Excessive decision-making time; slow to act • Risk-averse • Passive aggressiveness: open conflict perceived as too risky

(Continued)

TABLE 5.1 (CONTINUED)

The 13 Reference System, with Practices and Adaptations (Table Version)

	The Reference System	
Shared Dominant Logics *Tacit assumptions, standards, beliefs, idealizations, rules, lived norms, etc.*	**Practices** *Habits, routines, informal or formal processes*	**Adaptations** *Conscious attitudes, and behavior – some of which are reactions or compensations to practices and SDLs*
	4. Portfolio approach to acquisitions: new digital assets kept as stand-alone businesses for fear of impacting business performance and culture	• Belief in greatness of own brands – "we are future proof" – little sense of the need for change
	5. Low-risk talent management and succession planning	• Lean/CI used as OD/change tool
	6. Incrementalism (vs. radical innovation) in product development and R&D	• Outsourcing of creative thinking, e.g., strategy development, new business models to outside consultants ("experts")
	7. Late adopters to technology, e.g., ERP, e-Commerce, HRIS	• Expressed need by leadership to "vet" work being done by lowest levels
	8. Business unit strategies not shared widely with other business units	
	9. Many "pre-meetings" to review the content of proposals and presentations before it goes "up"	
	10. Extensive use of dashboards to measure intangibles, even despite the lack of systems	

(Continued)

TABLE 5.1 (CONTINUED)

The 13 Reference System, with Practices and Adaptations (Table Version)

	The Reference System		
Shared Dominant Logics *Tacit assumptions, standards, beliefs, idealizations, rules, lived norms, etc.*	**Practices** *Habits, routines, informal or formal processes*	**Adaptations** *Conscious attitudes, and behavior – some of which are reactions or compensations to practices and SDLs*
MAKING THE ABSTRACT TANGIBLE Orientation to concreteness; examples and practical explanations over abstraction and models	• Learning through concrete examples over theoretical models • What is measurable and tangible is valued over what is abstract and conceptual • Practical solutions over big ideas • Concrete deliverables over experimentation and iteration	1. Measurement in all operations, e.g., DMAIC, KPIs, etc. 2. Complex organizational/culture change addressed through tools (e.g. Slack), training, and large scale meetings	• Lack of patience for ambiguity or overly conceptual or abstract thinking • Suspicious of "big picture thinkers" • Undervaluing non-quantifiable data, such as behavior or emotion • Reuse what exists over inventing something new • Tools, structural solutions and metrics for dealing with complex interpersonal and social challenges such as trust, collaboration, conflict • A propensity toward metrics-for-metrics-sake, rather than measuring variables that are truly meaningful and actionable

(Continued)

TABLE 5.1 (CONTINUED)

The 13 Reference System, with Practices and Adaptations (Table Version)

	The Reference System	
Shared Dominant Logics *Tacit assumptions, standards, beliefs, idealizations, rules, lived norms, etc.*	**Practices** *Habits, routines, informal or formal processes*	**Adaptations** *Conscious attitudes, and behavior – some of which are reactions or compensations to practices and SDLs*
FIRST-HAND KNOWLEDGE "Seeing is believing"	1. Decentralized product management and product planning	• Business units with very little interaction with each other
• What is good and what I trust is local	2. Localized management systems (beyond financial)	• Low collaboration across corporate silos: "collaboration is too hard"
• "You need to show me before I can buy in"	3. Localized manufacturing processes	• Mistrust of "corporate": Reluctance, push-back, or highly selective adoption of corporate-wide standards
• Own "family" (site, brand) first		• Slow to trust others removed from own business; includes mistrust of outside ideas ("outside" can be own unit/site, division, or the company
		• Change cynicism: "this too shall pass"
		• Second-guessing of decisions made lower in the organization, or outside chain of command
		• Relationship – driven: "things get done by who you know"

(Continued)

TABLE 5.1 (CONTINUED)

The 13 Reference System, with Practices and Adaptations (Table Version)

	The Reference System	
Shared Dominant Logics *Tacit assumptions, standards, beliefs, idealizations, rules, lived norms, etc.*	**Practices** *Habits, routines, informal or formal processes*	**Adaptations** *Conscious attitudes, and behavior – some of which are reactions or compensations to practices and SDLs*
ACTION Bias for action	1. Tangible action to address complex, adaptive challenges 2. Collecting data to fulfill reporting needs with less concern for data accuracy	• "Get it done" vs. "get it done right" • Low patience for complex issues • Process over impact, e.g., reporting of countermeasures in business reviews are more about perceived action rather than whether countermeasures are actually proving effective • Leadership programs change culture

(Shared Dominant Logics cell content:)
- What you do matters more than what you say
- Value quick answers
- Action matters more than deliberation
- "Get it done"

Option 1: Full Research

One option is to employ the same basic approach we used to derive the I3 reference system, but on a shorter timescale. The overall approach was laid out in the previous chapter. The full research option omits the ethnographic and action-research component to streamline the process, and consists of the following steps:

A. **Structured interviews** with key leaders, including the C-Suite and other key executives. The sample here should be between 8 and 20 people depending on the size of your organization; more than 20 and you will start to find redundant themes in the data.

DOMINANT LOGIC INTERVIEW QUESTIONS

Use follow up questions to ensure clarity. The overall goal is to generate ample conversation in order to elicit as many instances of causal reasoning as possible.

1. *Please describe your business strategy.* (Question asked at the level appropriate to the interview subject, i.e., corporate level for C-Suite; divisional, regional or functional level for others, as appropriate).
2. *Please describe your top three challenges in executing that strategy.*
3. *Please describe what you are doing, or plan on doing, to overcome or mitigate these challenges.*
4. *What is the one thing you could do to change the way your organization operates that would make the biggest difference to where you think it needs to be in the future?**

*This is a variant on our original research question. It is designed to elicit a set of idealizations about the future. Idealizations usually reveal dominant logics.

Interviews should be recorded (with permission) and transcribed.

B. **Analysis of the interview data.** This is the critical step to derive SDLs. The analysis consists of deriving patterns of logic expressed in the narratives from all instances of *if-then, a because of b,* and *idealization* (e.g., *we should be doing this; it would be great if ...*), as well as the use of *unconventional metaphors*, and coding these instances based on the theme being expressed. The greater the number of speakers expressing the same theme (e.g., *RULES; ACTION*), the higher the frequency of the theme. The greater the frequency, the higher likelihood that what is being expressed is a dominant logic.

Obviously, this step takes practice and involves some training. But it does not require any specialized expertise beyond solid analytical skills and the ability to listen closely. Using two or more analysts to review each other's work and develop the SDL codings is important. The process of coding itself is highly iterative and requires some practice and discussion in order to arrive at codings that make sense to people within that system.

HOW GOOD DOES THE LABEL NEED TO BE?

One of the many fascinating things about working with unthought knowns is that the codings of SDLs could be slightly different and yet the contents of the reference system would be largely the same.

How can that be? Would not accurate SDL labels make a big difference in modeling a reference system?

Not really. The reason why is that the goal is to expose patterns. Causal reasoning analysis will reveal distinct patterns characterized primarily (though not exclusively) by SDLs. More important than how you code SDLs is how they reveal themselves in pervasive assumptions, beliefs, standards, and lived norms, as well as in practices and adaptations. In this way you are always iteratively and inductively moving backward and forward with these data. By asking yourself how every SDL reveals itself in practice, or in a set of observed beliefs or norms, you test the accuracy – and of necessity refine – the label. The ultimate goal is not perfection in labeling but fidelity of alignment and understanding among stakeholders: you know your codings are correct when there is a high degree of fidelity between the logic as labeled and how it shows up across practices and adaptations.

In this way obtaining face validity from a leadership team is critically important to intervention.

C. **Validation.** The next step is to validate the interview data through quantitative analysis. SDLs developed out of the analysis are turned into survey statements. These statements, ideally, are verbatims of the logics expressed in the interviews. The SDL survey is administered to a target population based on the size of the organization, and results are analyzed using factor analysis (FA) as described in Chapter 4. SDLs with the highest factor loadings are extracted from the results and used to form the final draft (see Table 5.1, first two columns). Results are then presented to a leadership team in order to develop the rest of the reference system, per step D.

D. **Reference System Development and Validation**. A final draft of SDLs is presented to a leadership team in a day and a half-long workshop. The goal of the workshop is to develop a final draft of the reference system that looks like Table 5.1. The "leadership team" here is the C-Suite (CEO and direct reports), as well as leadership groups one level below the C-Suite, and other key influential stakeholders. Ideally this session puts all stakeholders in the same room at the same time, though for practical reasons meetings can also be staggered with the proviso subsequent meetings will be needed to consolidate data from all the different meetings into a final draft. The Practices and Adaptations columns (see Table 5.1) may be filled in prior to the meeting, or partially filled in, based on the research team's knowledge and observations of the system, but this should only be done if the team believes discussion will be quickly advanced with more up-front content. While additional content may allow the group to move more quickly through the data, it may preclude buy-in or understanding.

Once the SDLs are validated by the leadership group, development of the Practices and Adaptations can proceed, with the participants in the workshops generating these lists. Once these lists are complete, the rest of the workshop is devoted to identifying high-leverage practices in which to intervene, discussed below.

Option 2: Partial Research

Another option is to do all of Option 1 but omit the quantitative validation. The advantage of this is it speeds up the process, and the quantitative analysis may not be necessary if there is a high degree of willingness to embrace findings and a readiness to engage in intervention. Including the FA results, however, may be important when there is resistance or reluctance to accept findings, or when the prevailing logics in the system favor the use of quantitative data.

Option 3: Co-Creation (Reference System Reverse Engineering)

Another option is to co-create the reference system with a leadership group in real time using a method called *reference system reverse engineering*. In essence, what is developed is the contents of Table 5.1 in real time in a facilitated workshop without any pre-populated content. This extends the original day and a half session to three and a half days, but has the advantage of ultimate process transparency and high involvement of all leaders in coming to "know" their cultural foundations (not to mention often generating significant team-building benefit).

REFERENCE SYSTEM "CO-CREATION" WORKSHOP DESIGN

The session begins by asking leaders to collectively document their own practices and adaptations against the practice areas listed in Step 3 of the Process Framework, and then document how they collectively behave and how they feel enacting them. As an optional step, participants are also asked to brainstorm what assumptions motivate each practice. From this a set of working practices, adaptations, and assumptions (i.e., preliminary SDLs) are derived, which completes the first day of the workshop. Working overnight without the participants, the facilitators consolidate the derived content to create draft SDLs, which they present the following morning. The group then ratifies or edits what has been presented, after which the final reference system is refined and agreed upon in the same way as in the other options.

The limitations of this approach, as with any action-research content elicitation technique, is that it is empirically difficult to separate antecedent cognition from group influence, particularly when there are asymmetrical power dynamics in the room, such as with the CEO or other highly influential stakeholders. If the facilitators are not familiar with these dynamics and cannot control or account for them, the output will be skewed. The facilitators may also not know what represents a pre-existing SDL from one rendered as the result of groupthink (Janis, 1971), or some other social desirability effect. This is why facilitators and leaders doing this kind of work need to be well-versed in the Leadership Process Framework and all it entails. In cases where leaders are unaware of their own influence or power and its impact on the group, the other options are preferred. One of the best ways to control power dynamics and groupthink is to bring independent data to the table.

That said, this approach productively demonstrates it is possible to evoke collective unthought knowns in a structured and facilitated manner without prework. This exercise also demonstrates the *dialogic* nature of SDL investigations; that is, the "reverse engineering" process generates language describing the nature of the group's own reference system as a semiotic artifact. Once identified as *our reference system* – the *essence of our culture* – the process of changing is accelerated and takes on a life of its own. Diagnostics of this kind, thus, are interventions themselves, and are highly effective ways to jump-start work in the next step of the process.

3: Prioritize Practices

The only way to change a reference system – the underpinnings of culture – is to change practices. This is because culture is first and foremost a cognitive phenomenon, a function of shared tacit logics with a neurochemical basis. To change brain chemistry requires forming new neural pathways. Per the theory and research substantiating embodied cognition (Chapter 3), new neural pathways can only be changed through new *physical* habits – new and sustained ways of doing things. It's not enough to want to do new things. It's not enough to talk about it, or evangelize or preach it. You can't even inspire people to do things differently – unless you instill a supporting set of practices to allow their inspiration to be enacted in sustained ways over time. Put another way, your organizational culture got to where it is because specific practices allowed it to successfully adapt to its environment. These practices, recall, come from the organizations' professionalization, shared task solutions, or its differentiated core purpose. Therefore to change culture requires changing the very practices that may be accounting for your success to begin with. As you might surmise, this is much easier said than done.

Practice Areas

Practices, as said, are the *informal and formal* routines, habits, and processes by which every firm runs its business. They are structured by SDLs. Some of this structuring can be quite overt, such as in I3's use of delegation of authority. Practices are the most visible form of culture, because they are the expressions of dominant logics. Often it is practices that managers, especially those new to the organization, first bump up against that cause them to voice dissatisfaction with a prevailing culture. Learning to "read" one's own organizational practices for the logic and patterns they evidence, therefore, is the single most important diagnostic tool a change leader can use to instigate change.

"Practices", however, is a broad term. To work with the concept in reference system change, they are best broken down into six categories:

1. **Planning.** How you plan, forecast, and set strategy.
2. **Management and Reporting.** The ways in which you monitor and track what is going on in the business.
3. **Customer.** How you engage and deliver value to customers, partners, etc.
4. **Product.** How you define, develop and produce products and services (includes operations as well as research and development).
5. **People.** How you hire, manage, promote, and develop people. Includes the standards by which you evaluate and promote.
6. **Social Acceptance.** The ways in which you determine social acceptability, such as how you deal with conflict, how you tolerate difference, how and whom you include, or not include, and so forth.

Gaining Leverage: The Practice Prioritization Matrix

As you might expect, changing a firm's practices in all six areas is daunting, not to mention highly destabilizing, and would likely put any business at risk. I know of no CEO or management team who would venture to do this, nor would I recommend this except in the most dire turnaround scenarios. Thus, intervening in one's own reference system requires identifying both the logics and the practices that represent the *highest leverage* opportunities to drive change.

By "high leverage" I mean opportunities where if change could be enacted, clear benefits would be seen to help the organization learn, adapt, and move faster in the direction of transformation. This usually means addressing practices and logics deemed fundamental barriers to transformation. Intervening in practices and logics is about creating effective experiments – interventions that generate new data to help the organization learn new logics and adapt to new ways of operating. High leverage doesn't mean making only cosmetic or peripheral changes, such as changes in parts of the business deemed too small or too remote from the core. Changes that do not impact many people will be deemed trivial or inconsequential and only reinforce skepticism that the change is not working. In risk-averse organizations such as I3, this is a very real possibility. High leverage does mean enough people will be impacted by the change such that their own logics, seen in collective assumptions, beliefs, and standards of success start to shift. When enough people start to think and act differently based on enacting new practices, the reference system shifts.

Thus, high leverage means two things: *efficacy* – the SDLs impacted are directionally critical to the desired change; and *quantity* – a sufficient number of people are impacted by the change so as to make a discernible difference in their own SDLs. By demonstrating it is possible to change SDLs, momentum and confidence are generated in the direction of the change.

Table 5.2 contains the *Practice Prioritization Matrix*, a tool designed to help identify which logics and practices, and in which combination, represent the highest leverage opportunities. Deployed in the second or third day of the workshop described above, the matrix is designed to help facilitate discussion among a leadership team on where the high-leverage opportunities exist, and help identify which SDLs should be addressed first.

Changing the I3s Reference System

In the case of I3, the most obvious place to start is to target the most dominant SDLs, as measured by FA results, interviews, and observation, and redesign the practices where these SDLs cause the most "pain" and most inhibit transformation. At I3 these are *FINANCIAL PERFORMANCE FIRST, RULES*, and *CERTAINTY*. However, recall that financial logic is deeply rooted and reinforced by I3's success, and that rules-certainty-risk logics are endemic to manufacturing. By targeting these SDLs one would be going after logics at the existential core of the company. Fierce resistance at all levels is to be expected. On the other hand, if the leadership team chooses not to address these logics in any

TABLE 5.2

Practices Prioritization Matrix (I3 Example)

	Practice area	Planning	Management and Reporting	Customer	Product	People	Social Acceptance
S	FINANCIAL PERFORMANCE FIRST	Δ	↓1	Δ	Δ		
D			⊗8				
L	RULES		⊗3				Δ2
	CERTAINTY	⊗3 Δ8	⊗9			Δ5	
	MAKING THE ABSTRACT TANGIBLE		↓2				
	FIRST-HAND KNOWLEDGE			Δ1	Δ1		
	ACTION		⊗3				↑
	DESIRED SDLS:						
	Takes Intelligent Risks		↑		↑	↑	↑
	Brings New Ideas to Life.	↑	↑	↑	↑	↑	↑

↑ ENHANCE Δ FUNDAMENTAL CHANGE ↓ REDUCE ⊗ STOP.
Numbers refer to items in Table 5.1. Blanks means no action yet.

way, the perception could be that leadership is dithering and not serious about transformation.

What to do? The optimal answer ultimately pivots on the emotional and psychological capacities of the leadership team and the extent to which they believe their digital transformation agenda is at risk. Is there a sense of a "burning platform?".

With this in mind, the exercise that I3 leaders could engage in is laid out below. It takes into account the need for efficacy and quantity in the SDL-practice intervention matrix while acknowledging that industrials like I3 are by definition risk-constrained. It takes into account the fact the company continues to be rewarded by investors for what it is doing today, which makes change difficult. To change the I3 reference system the change leader needs to find a balance between impact and caution. He or she needs to think in terms of design principles that can balance the risk and success with I3's capacity for transformational change. Such design principles might be labeled *strategic precision* and *targeted boldness* (and could have been identified in Step 1). The former refers to the need for very targeted interventions that achieve transformational impact without unduly disrupting the core business. The latter refers to the need to be bold and aggressive in a contained way so as to leverage I3's certainty needs in a way that is purposeful and directed.

Table 5.2 depicts which logics and which practices could be targeted, with explanations for each. The matrix shows the specific practices numbered from Table 5.1 in terms of whether they would be *enhanced* (up arrow), *fundamentally changed* (delta symbol for change), *reduced* (down arrow), or *stopped* altogether (circle with an "X").[5]

The interventions depicted in the matrix are meant to be applied enterprise-wide. This is why not every practice has an associated intervention. In cases where a number does not appear next to the delta symbol, these are ideas for wholesale changes to practices. At the same time, what is depicted in the matrix may not be enough. In addition to these firm-wide changes, I3 could also consider incubating SDL and practice changes in a new, firewalled business targeted at a specific disruptive market opportunity. By doing so I3 will be demonstrating it can take more radical and rapid steps toward defining its digital future. This idea is discussed below.

SDLs Targeted through Practices

- *FINANCIAL PERFORMANCE FIRST* – Reading across Table 5.2 there are several critical intervention points noted: reducing the monthly reporting burden (#1, 2), stopping altogether the application of standard manufacturing financial performance measures to its digital businesses (#8), and fundamental change across several practices. The former two are relatively obvious and have been touched on in the previous chapter; the latter merits discussion.

- I3 would arguably go a long way toward accelerating its disruption objectives while leveraging its financially-oriented logics by fundamentally rethinking the costs that its burdensome reporting structures impose – its monthly and quarterly reviews, its matrix reporting, its excess layers of management in decision-making, its suppliers burdened with non-value added procurement processes, and many other practices slavishly driven by financial, *RULES* and *CERTAINTY* logics. If the company took steps to cost-out the productivity impacts its financial reporting and compliance activities exert on managers and employees, it might begin to realize these costs are a significant drag on speed, risk taking, collaboration, customer focus, and innovation.[6] By shifting its financial logics away from hard dollars (attainment of monthly revenue and margin targets) to the indirect time and consequent dollar impacts these burdens place on employee productivity, it could begin to see that its own bureaucracy has real costs, and puts the company at a competitive disadvantage against any digital competitor. Ironically, this exercise would leverage *FINANCIAL PERFORMANCE FIRST*, but in a wholly new and innovative way.

- The company's very cost structure is product of an earlier industrial age. Simply eliminating the excessive number of practices and processes it overlays on itself to try and achieve the illusion of control and managerial certainty would help nudge the company, cost-structure wise, into the digital age rather than what it does today to rein in costs – which is to lay people off, curtail investments, or squeeze supply chains. This is the reactive legacy of industrial logic.[7]

- *RULES* – The highest leverage practice change would involve eliminating decision authority rules across the board (#3) and empowering managers to make financial and human resource decisions in accordance with broad guidelines, and holding them accountable for adherence to those guidelines. Less emphasis on *RULES* forces managers to have more rigor (*ACTION*) in how they manage their own businesses and how much discretion they allow in their own organizations in decision-making.

- Another change would be to enable more direct challenge and questioning of authority (Social Acceptance). This is less a practice than a behavior (under Adaptations), and requires senior leaders to be open to this (see the Leadership Framework). Focused leadership development work at all levels of senior management helps to set in place a foundation for this, a practice that is already happening.

- *CERTAINTY* – Shifting I3's orientation away from certainty and risk logics will be difficult to achieve given the company's task grounding. But several practices present low-hanging fruit opportunities. In Planning, leadership teams can begin to adopt stricter practices on how many priorities they are willing to take on in a given year (#3). In addition, sharing business unit priorities and strategies broadly with other business groups (#8) through any and all means available (social media platforms, town halls, etc.) is relatively easy to enact and starts to shift a prevailing mindset that transparent goals somehow risks their attainment. *Under management* and *reporting*, stopping altogether the practice of closely vetting all presentations to senior management (#9) by junior staff will introduce the prospects of risk and failure, a welcome learning. And under People, HR could take a more active talent management stance (#5) in deliberately promoting high-potentials into new jobs, deliberately moving talent from legacy businesses into digital ones, and vice versa, and taking more risks across the board on people. These practices could be enhanced by comprehensive tools and frameworks for evaluating and developing people. Many companies lack infrastructure in this area; the point here is that in the realm of people, it is practices, not just talent, that shifts culture.

- *MAKING THE ABSTRACT TANGIBLE* – This is another deep-seated manufacturing logic that will be hard to change. One practice I3 could enact would be to simply reduce the emphasis on trying to measure complex organizational phenomena such as culture or change through a tools-based approach (#2). For example, collaboration at I3 may not be completely addressed simply through the use of a tool such as Slack. More might be needed.

- *FIRST-HAND KNOWLEDGE* – Changing product/service planning and management practices by trying to standardize on common frameworks and standards for product/service success (#1) is a high-leverage way to reduce the adverse impact of this SDL (an initiative the company has recently embarked upon). The challenge, of course, is not to add more bureaucratic burden to product management and market-definition work but to rationalize efforts across product lines to drive faster innovation, collaboration, and product synergy. The company's local-first logic precludes digital transformation by prioritizing local variation and not-invented-here thinking over common standards and methods, which leads to product line bloat and overlaps, and more importantly, siphons off energy and resources that could otherwise be deployed on higher-visibility, cross-product line digital initiatives.
- *ACTION* – Stopping the reporting of unecessary metrics (#2), which relates to the practice changes under *FINANCIAL PERFORMANCE FIRST*, would reduce the impact of this logic.

These actions, of course, are meant to be illustrative. Nonetheless, from the above it is obvious how different these kinds of interventions are from the traditional approaches to culture change focused on leadership, values, or employee well-being. For one, recognize how tangible these interventions are: most involve routine practices such as reporting or product management rather than on slippery things like norms and values. Only one intervention is directly focused on people practices (*CERTAINTY*). While not denying talent management practices are important in culture change, reference system interventions go well beyond HR. In some cases the intervention leverages existing logic, such as the recommendation to critically consider cost structure by examining bureaucratic drags on productivity.

Getting More Radical: New Logics for a New Business

The practice-logic interventions proposed above will change I3's reference system, nudging it away from legacy toward something resembling a post-industrial enterprise. And, yet, it may not be enough. These targeted interventions may be necessary but not sufficient to help I3 achieve its digital transformation ambitions, especially given the compressed timescales of digital disruption.

A more radical step could be taken in parallel to architect wholly new practices and logics in a newly constituted business unit. The idea would be to create – incubate – a new reference system that could ultimately be transferred back to the core business. This entails creating what Schein calls a parallel learning system (1992), a structure that allows some part of the organization to learn an alternative way of doing something important – like how to transform itself. As Schein says, "it is too painful to give up a shared assumption in favor of an unknown substitute" (p. 317). Incubating new logics in an environment that does not threaten the core could be very attractive for enterprises like I3.

The advantages are obvious: without the constraints of existing practices, I3 would be free to experiment with what a radical shift in culture looks like without taking on much risk. And if this business somehow speeds up the overall digital transformation of the company, all the better. As said, the company believes it is already doing all the right things: experimenting with a new model can only be seen as additive.

One candidate might be to do this within one of I3's digital businesses. The problem with that idea is digital businesses already possess – and readily induce – new logics. These businesses aren't the problem; they already operate according to vastly different reference systems, ones which I3 could benefit from if they possessed the logic and practice experience to integrate them. But they do not. Therefore, a better candidate is a business that can span legacy and digital domains.

I3 has such a business. More precisely, it has a constellation of businesses that if consolidated under one focused strategy would be a prime candidate for inculcating new logics. This is I3's collection of service-related businesses. As stated in the previous chapter, a large portion of its revenue is recurring, driven in part by a robust aftermarket business in parts and services for existing products. When combined with opportunities afforded by digital platforms for incorporating sensor data with predictive analytics (such as predicting optimal throughput in an industrial process, or analyzing cost and weight variables in retail applications to make optimal pricing recommendations), I3 would have under one roof an array of resources that are potentially transformative in its industry – if leveraged at sufficient scale to impact the market. The problem today is these offerings are scattered within different business units in small or regionalized markets, beset at times by competing strategies and demands, and all disconnected from a comprehensive and integrated services strategy that spans the traditional-digital divide (services are usually the first businesses in industrials to integrate traditional and digital assets for this very reason). By consolidating service offerings in one global unit, including relevant digital assets and capabilities, I3 would afford itself the opportunity to accelerate its digital ambitions while incubating a new culture.

Cultures Aren't Blank Canvasses

No business exists in a vacuum; all cultures spring from their own unique grounding sources. This hypothetical new business would have to contend with pre-set logics born by the adaptive contexts in which the various service businesses in I3 "grew up". These legacy logics would have to be carefully considered in any new practice-logic design, taking into account task context and historicity. But this new unit would not have to contend with the burden of architecting new practices amid the risk of destabilizing a successful multi-billion dollar enterprise. The new services unit would have the opportunity to deliberately engineer its own practices with the overt goal of inculcating SDLs and enabling market disruption.

What Does Radical Inculcation Look Like? (It Looks Deliberately Developmental)

How this would be accomplished would require a careful and deliberate architecting of SDLs and practices, using the methodology provided above. Leadership would have to start with design principles, stomach gaining a clear-eyed perspective on its existing logics, practices, and adaptations, and then decide which aspired values and behaviors it deliberately wanted to inculcate as new logics, all the while understanding how these logics play out in the new strategic construct of services.

For example, leaders might want to inculcate into new SDLs some of the I3 leadership competencies such as *Takes Intelligent Risks and Brings New Ideas to Life*. They may want to deliberately inculcate the so-called digital values described in the last chapter of not having all the answers before commencing, adopting high levels of discretion in decision-making at all levels, and self-organizing (among others). To do this would require each of these competencies and values to be translated into assumptions and standards, for these are the linguistic manifestations of SDLs. For assumptions, the key translation question would be *what are our beliefs about this competency or value?* This would generate a list of attributes on which the leadership team would build consensus. For standards, the translation question would be *what does excellence look like when demonstrating this value or competency?* From this combined list, practices could be designed that embody and reinforce these attributes across all six practice areas.

This exercise alone would go a long way toward enabling a new reference system to take shape, one uniquely the product of old and new. But there would be one thing missing: a way to ensure these new practices and logics could grow in the incubated environment. This requires new learning, fostering what is known as a *deliberately developmental* environment.

What Is "Deliberately Developmental"?

My friend and mentor Bob Kegan, along with his co-conspirator Lisa Lahey coined the term *deliberately developmental organizations* (DDOs) in their book of the same name (2016).[8] In it they document their experiences with companies that epitomize employee development not as a matter of human resource policy or strategy but as integral to business success. Developing human potential in DDOs is a business imperative, not a nice-to-have or an afterthought. In DDOs, business success and employee development are strategically fused and critical to surmounting the challenges of business in the 21st century. As they put it, "the relationship between realizing human potential and organizational potential in these companies is a dialectic, not a trade-off" (p. 6).

The connection between deliberately developmental (DD) practices and reference system change is that it is exceedingly difficult for new cultures to take shape without experimentation and learning. This is because doing new things in new ways requires new learning. Without a supportive environment, well-designed logics and practices may not live to see the light of day as people inexorably get pulled back into working in old ways, especially under stress. Learning is integral to culture change. Putting in place deliberately developmental practices as nutrients to support a changing reference system therefore becomes key to ensuring the success of this incubation.

Deliberately Developmental Practices

Key DD learning practices, adapted from Kegan and Lahey's book, appear below. They would accompany the "radical inculcation" approach to ensure the success of the incubation, not to mention the new venture, because inculcating a new reference system requires deep learning at all levels of the organization. Leaders of the new service organization would have to decide which, and how many of these practices they could realistically incorporate, knowing that instilling at least some is essential.

1. *Development is an asset; error is an opportunity.* Coming from the risk-averse reference system of I3, this would be a fundamental shift. In the DD conception, developmental gaps in people are opportunities. Making mistakes, no matter how profound, means an opportunity for learning. This is critical to allow the new services organization to succeed in the rapidly-evolving digital marketplace it would operate within.

2. *Business success is not the ultimate goal; learning is.* Given the dominant financial logic of the parent, this too would be a radical shift. But as the entity puts in place new practices to inculcate new SDLs, the focus would be on learning how these practices serve the development of its new reference system while supporting individual growth.

3. *"Destabilization" is constructive.* To achieve learning, people need to be "destabilized". This can mean everything from continuous feedback to putting people in roles where they may get "usefully" in trouble. It means giving people assignments that might be considered "over their heads" and providing them with just enough support, but not completely stressing people out. It does mean creating an overall environment (see the Leadership Framework) where there is enough trust and goodwill to foster learning.

4. *Devalue expertise.* Environments where learning is prioritized, being the "expert" in a domain does not mean having all the answers. In fact, in a dynamic and disruptive environment, sources of insight come from anywhere and everywhere in the organization.

5. *Prioritize speaking the truth.* In this new organization passive resistance/aggressiveness would not be tolerated. The *CERTAINTY* logic would be challenged by encouraging honest and direct

feedback, and by equipping people with the skills to have productive conflict (and see the Leadership Framework), allowing learning to trump preservation of the status quo.

6. *Always looking to close learning gaps.* This is accomplished not through training but by constant feedback and dialog (with peers, peer coaches, mentors, managers, etc.), encouraging practices of self-reflection, group fishbowls, face-to-face 360 feedback, project post-mortems, and similar structures where the cycle between experience and learning is continually shortened.

DD practices are important in the inculcation of any new reference system. Incorporating these practices into the larger system (I3's existing business units) would pose its own adaptive challenges, which is why it is suggested they be implemented in a more confined context such as the services incubator.

So far we have taken it as a given that leaders would be willing participants in all the steps above. They would openly embrace coming to understand their own reference system and how it conspires to undermine their transformation goals, and they would willingly establish a new entity to incubate a new culture knowing it may represent a direct challenge to all of their most sacred assumptions about their own business. These are leaps of faith. Reference system interventions by definition require significant leadership. This kind of change will push emotional and psychological limits and tap reserves many leaders did not realize they had. Thus, the next section explores the crucial role of leadership in culture change.

CHANGING REFERENCE SYSTEMS: THE LEADERSHIP FRAMEWORK

Culture does not come from the top, but culture change is impossible without courageous, curious, and skilled adaptive leaders. This is because changing a culture in the modern, cognitive science conception is a vastly different enterprise – a much more psychologically and emotionally demanding one – than thought of in the mainstream. In the mainstream conception leaders set culture through what they say and how they behave, and these actions somehow magically produce a desired outcome. This is mythology, of course, but adheres neatly to what I call the "gumball machine model": the leader pops a coin into the culture machine and out comes a gumball – culture. All the leader needs to do is pay attention to the machine by continuing to feed it with compelling pronouncements and model behavior. This is an inherently "positivist" model – logical, technical, rational, built on clear inputs that produce predictable outcomes. And it's I3's model: to the extent the company has done any intentional culture-shaping it consists of leadership competencies, as well as the CEO eloquently expressing her views on how people should behave in order to transform the company. Other companies take this one or two steps further with published manifestos and well-articulated "cultures and values" statements, but the logic is basically the same.

In the cognitive science world, the role of the leader in culture change is vastly different. Because unthought knowns shape the systems of knowledge running in the background of our daily lives of which we are mostly unaware, leaders cannot be positivist about culture change: there is no "there" there. Culture is not a thing, not a dependent variable. It is much more how you see the world, along with what you actually see. Therefore changing reference systems requires starting where power resides. The role of any culture change leader, whether CEO, divisional executive, board member, or other change agent, by definition must proceed along two dimensions. In the first dimension the leader is not "setting" the culture as much as judiciously using her power to frame the need for change, marshal energy in its direction, set the appropriate agenda, and allocate resources to allow practices that indelibly shape logics to take shape, flourish, or be changed or eliminated. Her main task is to use her role and personal power to put in motion the resources and momentum for what must change, and how, and then hold others accountable for it. Her role is two parts architect and one part evangelist: knowing which walls need to be demolished and which parts of the house to expose to the light of day, and laying out the blueprint for how this should happen, and why. Her architectural focus is on practices, knowing which practices best shape logics. These activities almost always involve working through a leadership team, or many leadership teams below the executive level, for these are the practice "owners" and influencers distributed across the organization. Integrated groups of "middles" – middle managers and business unit leaders – in fact, are the true "owners" of culture because they control the practices by which the enterprise runs.[9] The Process Framework laid out above (Figure 5.1) provides the blueprint for how to do this.

While approaching culture change through logics and practices may be novel, any executive who has a led major change initiative for the most part will find these activities familiar: framing issues, setting agendas, allocating resources, and driving accountability are all mostly standard fare for practiced change leaders. Only the change targets – practices and underlying logics – is novel.

The second dimension is more complex and less familiar.

Holding Environments

This dimension of culture change leadership is about creating a *holding environment*. This is a term developed by the British child psychologist and psychoanalyst D.W. Winnicott (1971) that refers to what mothers do as they hold their children in their arms with focused attention and concern, when their children are calm. The child's ability to develop a functioning adult ego is founded on the original and subsequent experiences of being securely held by a so-called "good enough" mother.[10] The term has been broadened in psychotherapeutic contexts to mean a therapeutic "space" where someone fragile or insecure is capable of dealing with emotional issues.[11] In more recent years the term has also found its way into the leadership literature to refer to the feeling evoked by capable leaders who provide a sense of security and trust in order for their teams to become fully self-reliant.[12] When people or groups are too anxious, they are incapable of focusing rationally and optimally on problems and solutions. They create psychological defenses (fight-flight, pairing, leader dependence) that preclude seeking out or being receptive to the full range of others, or functioning interdependently with their "true" selves on display and fully available.[13] In conditions of organizational stress and scarcity, such as during times of significant change, outcomes may be ambiguous, role definitions may be in flux, and competing priorities may abound, conditions all conducive to anxiety. The propensity for a leader to provide support in such circumstances may also be greatly compromised. This dynamic tends to create a downward psychological spiral: when people need support most, they are least likely to get it.

The connection to culture change is obvious: intervening in cultural reference systems is exceedingly stressful. Think about it: the most basic assumptions – about the business, about markets, about competitors, about the organization, about what constitutes success, about the competence of others, even about what you thought you knew and could take for granted – all – are liable to be called into question when exposing and attempting to change dominant logics. If the scope of transformation is significant enough, such as a mid-20th century industrial trying to morph into a digital company, it is highly likely all of these assumptions will be challenged. This is highly disorienting and destabilizing for even the most high-functioning group.

Therefore, how the leader shows up in terms of this second dimension becomes *the* difference-maker in reference system change. Leaders that can "hold" their teams and organizations – in the same way a mother holds her baby – to engender enough trust and security so the inherent anxieties can be successfully mitigated and navigated, will go a long way toward ensuring the overall success of the transformation.

What does it look like for a leader to do that?

Creating Holding Environments

In many ways, the leader's role in reference system change is not unlike any other in the formation of a high-functioning team. Those familiar with the many approaches to team-building will find some of what is below familiar. But there are two key differences. The first is that when an organization is confronting itself existentially, as in any reference system change, the leader's role in creating a holding environment is even more acute. Which means her actions must be that much more deliberate and timely, with little left to chance. Second, psychological holding is inherently dependent on the leaders' own emotional and psychological capacity to hold (see below). Leaders who do not have this capacity will suffer, and make others suffer greatly, further destabilizing an already volatile situation. In this way, culture change is not for the psychologically weak leader, or one with a lot of repressed anger or anxiety.

Figure 5.2 shows how leaders create holding environments. They do this by the provision of what we call "The 3 C's": *Contract, Clarity,* and *Contact.*

Contracting is about doing many of the things laid out in the Process Framework: setting boundaries, framing the need for change, and defining what the group and organization is doing and not doing through the change. It means establishing what is to be valued and cared about (Step 1), and defining who does what, by when, and why. While these activities may seem like basic team formation hygiene, they cannot be underestimated in status-quo challenges such as changing reference systems.

Clarity is a bit harder, but mostly within bounds of ordinary executive experience, especially for those who have led large scale change. It's about consistency – in word and deed – and about striving to continually clarify communications at all levels. I've heard many a senior executive fall into the trap of complaining that their teams "just don't listen". The worst thing an executive here can do is assume all his communication (about the change) is received in the same way by all. The key is to *not* assume, but to listen and strive for understanding. And it's about transparency – of motive, intent, and aspiration. Usually this means the change executive "goes first" in exposing his own wishes, needs, and fears about the transformation.

Contact tends to be more difficult. This is about encouraging all individuals on the team involved to share concerns and anxieties *about the change*, as well as to share more of who they are personally and as leaders (if not already known). It's about surfacing concerns, especially over past actions or inactions for which individuals may be harboring frustration or resentment. It is about wants and needs being openly discussed and negotiated. Importantly, it's about *not* denying any individual concern, motivation, or experience. Nor is it about defending one's own authority, turf, or past actions. Instead, it's about encouraging team members to take risks. This in particular tends to be hard for many CEOs: many defend their actions in subtle ways by saying things like "we're a lot better than we used to be …" in the face of concerned or frustrated staff. These

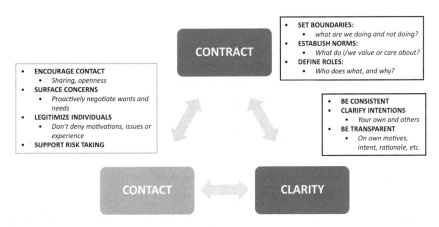

FIGURE 5.2
How leaders create holding environments. (Adapted from Kepner, 1980. © 2018, Ontos Global LLC.)

kinds of expressions, while well intended, are subtle forms of denial. They unwittingly delegitimize the experience of their own teams, which precludes further dialog and ultimately shuts down emotional and psychological *contact*.

Personal Leadership Orientations

I began this chapter (and book) by suggesting self-awareness, psychological flexibility, curiosity, and courage were key orientations, or stances, for leaders leading culture change. From the above it should be abundantly clear why. Two of these four seem like prerequisites: curiosity, because without it how can one possibly be open to investigating unthought knowns? Psychological flexibility, which the historian Yuval Harari defines as the critical competency for the 21st century, means developing the emotional intelligence, resilience, mental flexibility, and capacity to deal with the bio-hacked, algorithmic, machine-driven world of the Fourth Industrial Revolution. In the case of reference system interveners, if we remain rooted in our own paradigms as leaders, changing reference systems will not only be extremely stressful, it may mean the ultimate demise of the enterprise we lead – despite our abundant good intentions.

The other two are more elusive. Why self-awareness? As leaders, of course, we cannot have enough of it. But in this case specifically, self-awareness is critical because the experience of changing a reference system will be much like Alice entering the Hall of Mirrors. What is mine and not-mine? What is the product of my own executive ambition, my yearning to self-enhance and value-engineer (Chapter 1), versus what is being afforded by the reference system through functional grounding? If culture is all task, professionalization, and mission, where do I make my mark as a CEO or change leader? If the executive does not know herself well enough to at least formulate provisional awareness to these questions, the change experience will be rough.

Lastly, courage, for which we must now return to the opening of this book. The new science changes most of what we know about organizational culture, yet it doesn't guarantee anything. It only points to these opaque unthought knowns, logics that show up in a myriad of practices and behavior. But until we develop the ability to "see" them they will remain as invisible and elusive as DNA. Opening our eyes, allowing ourselves the ability to track and notice how these logics manifest across the organization in ways that until now may have been invisible or less obvious – that – takes courage. You may not like what you see. You may even be personally to blame for some of what's there. And intervening will inevitably require you to take on your own assumptions about things you hold most dear, things that you likely have been trained in or experienced your entire career to believe, such as: predictably delivering financial results will assure the future success of the business; or, if we can't create a dashboard for something we can't change it; or, we can't tell each other what we really feel because it is too risky; or, the only way to change culture is to hire new people; and on and on. Altering these kinds of beliefs, or at least suspending them, is very challenging.

I fully recognize developing self-awareness, psychological flexibility, curiosity, and courage is not easy. These are ongoing quests that require personal commitment as well as experimentation and practice, not to mention forbearance – not judging yourself or others when things don't go exactly as you would have liked. That is why they are called "orientations": stances toward one's life and world, a never-ending set of opportunities to develop and grow and become the best versions of ourselves that we can be as leaders, and as humans. The stakes have never been higher. Many companies that today are trying to rapidly scale, become digital players in legacy industries, turn themselves around, or otherwise execute on some significant transformation, will fail because they will not have leveraged more sophisticated approaches to culture and change, approaches that make use of the latest science. Which means not only do leaders bear the burden of this responsibility; they bear the burden for those in their organizations whose livelihoods in some way depend on them being able to lead complex and sustainable transformation in the most self-actualized way possible.

NOTES

1. Heifetz, Grashow, and Linsky (2009).
2. This information is culled from investor and industry analyst material. Facts have been anonymized and blended with that of other organizations.
3. This "strata" is usually the top of the house. But not always. In many technology companies, for example, key influencers will include key technologists such as senior software engineers or data scientists, or influential researchers in biotech firms, and so forth.
4. See *Feedback and Organizational Development* (1977).

5. The symbols are used because they may be more evocative in capturing a sense of urgency for these changes.
6. *Harvard Business Review* (August 10, 2017).
7. This entire intervention idea I owe to Paul Kinsinger.
8. *An Everyone Culture: Becoming a Deliberately Developmental Organization* (2016).
9. The term "middles" is taken from the work of Barry Oshry.
10. Kohut (1977), Winnicott (1965).
11. *Source*: American Psychological Association.
12. Bowlby (1998), Kahn (2001).
13. W.R. Bion (1961).

Epilogue: The Way Forward

As I write these words to close what is essentially the first of many chapters on the cognitive science of culture and all it promises leaders, change agents, and practitioners, I am reminded yet again of the latest "culture" scandal. This one involves Boeing and the 737 Max tragedies and the damning revelations by employees that the airplane was "designed by clowns who are in turn supervised by monkeys", and that "a presentation the company gave to the F.A.A. was so complicated that, for the agency officials … 'it was like dogs watching TV'".[1] Here again is another in an almost daily stream of news laying blame for employee malfeasance and poor judgment at the altar of culture. As said at the beginning, we assume culture is the explanation for everything from exalted corporate success to abject failure. And whether that success or failure is of an entire enterprise (Enron? Uber? GM?) or a few bad apples (Kay Jewelers? Wells Fargo?), we usually point the finger at culture as the villain.

So I wonder after reading the preceding whether you are now more likely, or less, to blame culture for the statements made by these Boeing employees? Recall that according to cognitive science, culture *doesn't make us do anything*. It is a reference system, capable of *being made use of* but not causal in behavior. Or put another way, it may be only causal when we are unaware of the reference systems by which we lead our lives. On the other hand, by now you also appreciate that reference systems are mighty pervasive, powering the many practices and adaptations residing at the core of how a company operates. Culture is far more systemic and invasive in human systems than thought by those who believe free soda or ping pong tables, or the recognition that employees love their CEO but loathe their boss, is culture. By this standard, the reference system powering Boeing is surely culpable, or at least capable, of enabling these statements. So which is it?

If you have arrived at this point more enlightened about culture but still unable to answer this question, *welcome to the new era of culture in organizations*. In understanding organizational culture through the lens of the modern science of the mind, you likely have a greater appreciation of the interplay between ecology, human experience, task, and meaning. Which makes answers to this kind of question always "it depends" – it depends on which of these variables is most salient in the reference system used by the individuals making these statements. This recognition will not satisfy those wanting easy, step-by-step guidance for untangling culture's many mysteries. But if at this point you feel a bit more enlightened *and* a bit more unsettled, I would say you are in a state of heightened awareness, perfect for taking the next step in your journey on how to be a more effective and impactful change leader.

You may feel enlightened, because much of your intuition about culture – that it is pervasive, that it shows up as patterns across entire ways of making sense as well as in practices and behavior – perhaps has been validated. You knew culture mattered; you just weren't aware of how deep and wide that influence was. You have been given a blueprint for how to investigate the logics that tie all of those tacit beliefs, practices and behaviors together. That blueprint doesn't reduce or over-simply culture. It deconstructs it so that it can be worked in more fundamental, and effective ways.

But you may be a bit unsettled because cognitive science shatters many of the conventional myths about culture, leaving you instead with a framework for addressing unthought knowns, the contents of the collective preconscious. When you illuminate this content you begin to see how and why it functions as the governor of change, the invisible wall holding back transformation. But that raises new questions and concerns. The process of illumination will be transformative for your enterprise, and for you, but will require curiosity and courage to take the crucial steps many in your company may not even realize they need to take. Viewing culture as a reference system anchored by dominant logics visible in everyday business practices takes culture well beyond the confines of HR and employee attitudes. It puts culture squarely into everyday activities, like budgeting, management reporting, or how you engage your customers or suppliers. It may feel daunting to try and alter these practices; they tend to be the sacred structures of your enterprise.

Moreover, if we think about culture change as attempts to intervene in specific behaviors, like our CEO in Chapter 1 who wants to make his company more collaborative, or the executive team that wants to improve trust, how does the functionally grounded framework help one do that? The answer is, quite powerfully and effectively. The key, again, is practices.

USING REFERENCE SYSTEMS TO TARGET BEHAVIOR

Take collaboration. The traditional ways most companies target desired behavioral improvements like collaboration is through training and coaching, teaching employees important communication skills like active listening, framing, contracting, negotiation, as well as through personal competencies like adaptability, and so forth. While these are necessary endeavors, culturally speaking they are not sufficient because they target symptoms rather than cause.

In the cognitive science conception, the focus is on the antecedents of low collaboration found in the reference system. Using I3 as our example, if we were going to improve collaboration we would first look at the SDLs inhibiting it. From Chapter 4 we know *CERTAINTY* and *FIRST-HAND KNOWLEDGE* are barriers to collaboration. The former drives risk-averse behavior (*minimize risk; avoid the unknown*) that can make collaboration not a natural reflex. The latter privileges what is local and immediate and engenders a natural mistrust of that which is further removed from what is known and familiar. From there we would target a handful of high-leverage practices in which these SDLs manifest, such as localized manufacturing or product planning (*FIRST-HAND KNOWLEDGE*), or the practice of not sharing business strategies across business units (*CERTAINTY*). We would then change those practices to drive collaboration. For example, we might promote local product owners into global change leadership roles tasked with instituting common product planning standards and practices across the company. We might change product planning practices to force product reviews across divisional silos or product lines, activities which would naturally force collaboration. We might try to increase inter-business dependencies by forming cross-product line mobile teams that rotate across businesses units every six months, tasked with coming up with market studies and localized product plans for particular businesses or markets. And we might look to do the same across other high-leverage practice areas, using the Practices Prioritization Matrix (Chapter 5). Of course, we would have to ensure we are not creating more bureaucracy (*RULES*) and risk avoidant behavior (*CERTAINTY*) with these practices.

But the point is clear: the path to behavior change in the cognitive science of culture is vastly different than in the traditional one. Using the functionally grounded culture framework to target specific behaviors in culture change is not only very do-able; it is the only way to ensure the new behaviors are sustained.

So how does the change leader sum up the framework in this book to lead her own change initiative? And what is one thing she could start doing amid all the things made possible by this approach to help her do this?

Four NEW Laws of Culture & One Takeaway

1. **Culture is *preconscious*** (unthought but known). Culture is background knowledge that we use reflexively, without being aware of it. The more we become aware of our own reference systems the more choice we have in how to leverage or change them. This is key to unlocking the power of culture in organizational transformation.
2. **Culture is *persistent*.** Culture is a system of shared implicit logics designed to organize meaning across a wide range of practices, behaviors, attitudes, and visible forms of culture. It is visible as pervasive patterns across the enterprise, but difficult to change – until you intervene in the shared logics that underpin the practices.
3. **Culture is *perfect*** – perfectly adapted to its current environment because reference systems are adaptations to that environment. Therefore, they pose a major barrier to transformation. The more successful your organization, the more likely your culture will be a barrier.
4. **Culture is only changed** through ***practices***. Because culture is a cognitive phenomenon with a neurochemical basis, the only way to change culture is to change practices – the informal and formal habits, routines, and processes – through which you run your organization and sustains the reference system.

These "laws" may be good summary points for understanding the cognitive science of culture, but in recognition of the fact we live in a world where so much competes for our attention, and where our tolerance for complexity in business is so low, what can we say to the leader in need of one key takeaway, the single thing she could start doing tomorrow to get closer to the framework provided in this book?

Spot the patterns and surface the assumptions.

Begin by noticing patterns. In what people say and how they say it, in what they do or don't do, in how they collectively behave, and most of all, in the habituated formal and informal patterns embedded in the routines that run your business. There is tremendous power available for the change agent who simply *notices:* notices patterns in practice and in adaptations across all parts of her company, from the way it plans to how it deals with customers to how it hires to how it deals with conflict. This is why organizational newcomers and outsiders are so often more adept at "seeing" culture than insiders, those who have been in the company for a long time. Spot the patterns across practices and surface the assumptions behind them, the shared logics that provide their fuel, and you will be well on your way to changing dominant logics. To notice is to have power.

DISRUPTING CULTURE TO DISRUPT YOURSELF

I began this book by speaking of dilemmas, so it is only fitting to end the same way.

When you remember that by some estimates companies spend on average $2200 per employee per year on managing culture, with an annual spend in the billions, and when you remember many enterprises existing today will not exist in ten years for failing to understand the limitations and possibilities afforded by their own cultural reference systems, you begin to see why the stakes are higher now for change leaders than at any point in their careers. The dilemma is that while this is true, the cultural minds approach will not magically fix culture or ensure corporate success. It does not automatically mean you will have unlocked the secrets of employee happiness or made your company a better place to work.

But I suggest in the next 20 years the new science outlined in this book will revolutionize how we work with culture. There are small signs it is happening already as more and more organizations think about culture and change in terms of practices rather than values, attitudes, or leadership pronouncements. This is a small beginning. The disruption of culture is still in the early stages.

What this book hopefully has done is provide greater *insight* into the questions posed at the outset: *why humans in organizations think and act as they do, and how that leads to specific outcomes.*

The answer is that as humans we are structure and meaning-seeking creatures. Our minds seek structure and create meaning in all we do. To accomplish this our minds extract key features and structures in our environments in order to adapt to them, and we use the knowledge that results to make sense of and organize our worlds. This process of adaptation results in culture. When we understand culture on these terms, we begin to see how this can lead to specific outcomes. Culture doesn't drive behavior. But it does delimit the range of options of what is possible. The more we understand and are aware of these limits, including what they mean to us personally, the more choice we have in shaping culture in organizations to the future we want. In the face of the dramatic existential environmental, technological, and social challenges before us, ensuring that future will be the most important thing that we as leaders and change agents can do.

NOTE

1. The *New York Times* (January 9, 2020).

References

(no author) Chips with everything. (September 14, 2019). *The Economist*, p. 13.

(no author) Learning the lingo. (January 11, 2014). *The Economist*, p. 72.

(no author) Send in the clouds. (July 6, 2019). *The Economist*, p. 51.

Abbott, A. (1998). *The System of professions: An Essay on the division of expert labor*. Chicago, IL: University of Chicago Press.

Abrahamson, E. (1996). Management fashion. *Academy of Management Review, 21*(1), 254–285.

Abrahamson, E., & Fairchild, G. (1999). Management fashion: Lifecycles, triggers, and collective learning processes. *Administrative Science Quarterly, 44*(4), 708–740.

Abrahamson, E., & Fombrun, C. J. (1994). Macrocultures: Determinants and consequences. *Academy of Management Review, 19*(4), 728–755. doi:10.5465/AMR.1994.9412190217.

Adelman, C. (1993). Kurt Lewin and the origins of action research. *Educational Action Research, 1*(1), 7–24. doi:10.1080/0965079930010102.

Aguirre, D., von Post, R., & Alpern, M. (2013). Culture's role in enabling organizational change: Survey ties transformation success to deft handling of cultural issues. Booz & Company. Retrieved from: http://www.booz.com/global/home/what-we-think/reports-white-papers/article-display/cultures-role-organizational-changehttp://linkinghub.elsevier.com/retrieve/pii/S088394170400022.

Alibali, M. W., & Nathan, M. J. (2012). Embodiment in mathematics teaching and learning: Evidence from learners' and teachers' gestures. *Journal of the Learning Sciences, 21*(2), 247–286.

Alvesson, M., & Skoldberg, K. (2009). *Reflexive methodology: New vistas for qualitative research*. Los Angeles, CA: Sage Publications.

Alvesson, M., & Sveningsson, S. (2008). *Changing organizational culture: Cultural change work in progress*. Abingdon: Routledge.

Anderson, D. R., Sweeney, D. J., Williams, T. A., Camm, J. D., & Cochran, J. J. (2015). *An introduction to management science: Quantitative approaches to decision making*. Cengage learning. Retrieved from: http://citeseerx.ist.psu.edu/viewdoc/download?doi=10.1.1.464.8929&rep=rep1&type=pdf.

Applebaum, H. A. (1981). *Royal blue: The culture of construction workers*. New York, NY: Holt Rinehart & Winston.

Argyris, C. (1995). Action science and organizational learning. *Journal of managerial psychology, 10*(6), 20–26.

Argyris, C., & Schön, D. A. (1989). Participatory action research and action science compared: A commentary. *American Behavioral Scientist, 32*(5), 612–623.

Argyris, C. S., & Schön, D. (1996). *Organizational learning II: Theory, method and practice*. Reading, PA: Addison-Wesley.

Aycan, Z. (2000). Cross-cultural industrial and organizational psychology: Contributions, past developments, and future directions. *Journal of Cross-Cultural Psychology, 31*(1), 110–128.

Barber, B. M., & Odean, T. (2001). Boys will be boys: Gender, overconfidence, and common stock investment. *The quarterly journal of economics, 116*(1), 261–292.

Bartlett, F. C., & Kintsch, W. (1995). *Remembering: A study in experimental and social psychology*, vol. 14. Cambridge University Press. (Original work published in 1932).

Baskerville, R. F. (2003). Hofstede never studied culture. *Accounting, Organizations and Society, 28*(1), 1–14.

Bauermeister, M. (1964). Effect of body tilt on apparent verticality, apparent body position, and their relation. *Journal of Experimental Psychology, 67*(2), 142.

Baumeister, R. F., Vohs, K. D., & Funder, D. C. (2007). Psychology as the science of self-reports and finger movements: Whatever happened to actual behavior? *Perspectives on psychological science, 2*(4), 396–403.

Beer, M., Eisenstat, R. A., Norrgren, F., Foote, N., & Fredberg, T. (2011). *Higher ambition: How great leaders create economic and social value*. Cambridge: Harvard Business Press.

Bennardo, G., & De Munck, V. C. (2014). *Cultural models: Genesis, methods, and experiences*. Oxford University Press.

Bernard, H. R. (2011). *Research methods in anthropology*. Lanham: Rowman Altamira.

Bernard, H. R., Kilworth, P., Kronenfeld, D., & Salier, L. (1984) The problem of informant accuracy: The validity of retrospective data. *Annual Review of Anthropology, 13*, 495–517. Retrieved from: http://social.cs.uiuc.edu/class/cs598kgk-04/papers/informant_accuracy.pdf.

Beuckelaer, A., Lievens, F., & Swinnen, G. (2007). Measurement equivalence in the conduct of a global organizational survey across countries in six cultural regions. *Journal of Occupational and Organizational Psychology, 80*(4), 575–600.

Biernacki, R. (1994). Time cents: The monetization of the workday in comparative perspective. In: R. Friedland, & D. Boden (Eds.), *Now Here: Space, time, and modernity*. Berkeley, CA: University of California Press.

Bion, W. R. *Experiences in groups*. London: Tavistock/Routledge.

Bock, L. (2015). *Work rules: Insights from inside Google that will transform how you live and lead*. New York, NY: Hachette Book Group.

Bolender, J. (2008). Hints of beauty in social cognition: Broken symmetries in mental dynamics. *New Ideas in Psychology, 26*(1), 1–22.

Bollas, C. (1987). *The shadow of the object: Psychoanalysis of the unthought known*. New York, NY: Columbia University Press.

Boroditsky, L., & Ramscar, M. (2002). The roles of body and mind in abstract thought. *Psychological Science, 13*(2), 185–189.

Boudreau, J. (2010). *Retooling HR: Using better business tools and methods to make better decisions about talent*. Boston, MA: Harvard Business Press.

Boudreau, J., & Ramstad, P. (2007). *Beyond HR: The new science of human capital*. Boston, MA: Harvard Business School Press.

Bowlby, J. (1988). *The secure base*. New York, NY: Basic Books.

Brett, J. M., Tinsley, C. H., Janssens, M., Barsness, Z. I., & Lytle, A. L. (1997). New approaches to the study of culture in industrial/organizational psychology. In: P. C. Earley, & M. Erez (Eds.), *The New Lexington Press management and organization sciences series and New Lexington Press social and behavioral sciences series. New perspectives on international industrial/ organizational psychology* (pp. 75–129). San Francisco, CA: The New Lexington Press/Jossey-Bass Publishers.

Brodesser-Akner, T. (April 23, 2019). The company that sells love to America had a dark secret. *The New York Times*. https://www.nytimes.com/2019/04/23/magazine/kay-jewelry-sexual-harassment.html.

Brooks, M., & Knight, J. (2017). Creating a culture that performs: Results from our 2017 study on organizational culture. Gartner CHRO Quarterly Forum, 4th Quarter *2017*. https://www.cebglobal.com/human-resources/culture.html.

Brooks, R., & Meltzoff, A. N. (2008). Infant gaze following and pointing predict accelerated vocabulary growth through two years of age: A longitudinal, growth curve modeling study. *Journal of Child Language, 35*(01), 207–220.

Bryant, A. (2009–2015). The corner office. *The New York Times.* Retrieved from: http://projects.nytimes.com/corner-office.

Bucher, R., & Stelling, J. G. (1977). *Becoming professional*, vol. 46. Beverly Hills, CA: Sage Library of Social Research.

Bughin, J., Catlin T., & LaBerge, L. (June 2019). The drumbeat of digital: How winning teams play. *McKinsey Quarterly.*

Caballero, R. (2006). *Re-viewing space: Figurative language in architects' assessment of built space*, vol. 2. Berlin: Walter de Gruyter.

Cable, D. M., Aiman-Smith, L., Mulvey, P. W., & Edwards, J. R. (2000). The sources and accuracy of job applicants' beliefs about organizational culture. *Academy of Management Journal, 43*(6), 1076–1085.

Calori, R., Johnson, G., & Sarnin, P. (1992). French and British top managers understanding of the structure and the dynamics of their industries: A cognitive analysis and comparison. *British Journal of Management, 3*, 61–78. doi:1045-3172/92/020061-18.

Camerer, C., & Lovallo, D. (1999). Overconfidence and excess entry: An experimental approach. *American Economic Review, 89*(1), 306–318.

Cameron, K., & Quinn, R. (1999). *Diagnosing and changing organizational culture based on the Competing Values Framework.* Reading, MA: Addison-Wesley.

Campos, J. J., Bertenthal, B. I., & Kermoian, R. (1992). Early experience and emotional development: The emergence of wariness of heights. *Psychological Science, 3*(1), 61–64.

Carney, D. R., Cuddy, A. J., & Yap, A. J. (2010). Power posing brief nonverbal displays affect neuroendocrine levels and risk tolerance. *Psychological Science, 21*(10), 1363–1368.

Casasanto, D. (2009). Embodiment of abstract concepts: Good and bad in right-and left-handers. *Journal of Experimental Psychology: General, 138*(3), 351.

Centola, D. (2015). The social origins of networks and diffusion. *American Journal of Sociology, 120*(5), 1295–1338.

Centola, D. (2018). The truth about behavioral change. *Sloan Management Review.* Retrieved from: https://mitsmr.com/2Owt7rS.

Ceridian Corporation (December 5, 2018). *Ceridian's pulse of talent report: Career growth and purpose crucial for retention.* https://www.ceridian.com/ca/company/newsroom/2018/ceridian-pulse-of-talent-report-career-growth-and-purpose-crucial-for-retention.

Chanchani, S. (1998). An empirical validation of Hofstede's dimensions of value. *Working Paper, School of Accounting and Commercial Law*, Victoria University, Wellington, New Zealand.

Chang, A., & Bordia, P. (2001). A multidimensional approach to the group cohesion-group performance relationship. *Small Group Research, 32*(4), 379–405.

Charan, R. (April 2006). Home Depot's blueprint for culture change. *Harvard Business Review.* Retrieved from: https://hbr.org/2006/04/home-depots-blueprint-for-culture-change.

Chatman, J., & Jehn, K. (1994). Assessing the relationship between industry characteristics and organizational culture: How different can you be? *Academy of Management Journal, 37,* 522–553. Retrieved from: http://scholar.google.com/.

Chatman, J. A., & O'Reilly, C. A. (2016). Paradigm lost: Reinvigorating the study of organizational culture. *Research in Organizational Behavior, 36,* 199–224.

Chi, M., Feltovich, P., & Glaser, R. (1981). Categorization and representation of physics problems by experts and novices. *Cognitive Science, 5,* 121–152.

Chiu, C., & Hong, Y. (2007). Cultural processes: Basic principles. In: A. W. Kruglanski, & E. T. Higgins (Eds.), *Social psychology: Handbook of basic principles* (pp. 785–806). New York, NY: The Guilford Press.

Choi, S., & Bowerman, M. (1991). Learning to express motion events in English and Korean: The influence of language-specific lexicalization patterns. *Cognition, 41*(1), 83–121.

Chun, K. T., Campbell, J. B., & Yoo, J. H. (1974). Extreme response style in cross-cultural research a reminder. *Journal of Cross-Cultural Psychology, 5*(4), 465–480.

Cialdini, R. B., Kallgren, C. A., & Reno, R. R. (1991). A focus theory of normative conduct: A theoretical refinement and reevaluation of the role of norms in human behavior. In: M. Zanna (Ed.), *Advances in experimental social psychology,* vol. 24, (pp. 201–234). San Diego, CA: Academic Press.

Clark, P., & Mills, R. (2013). *Masterminding the deal: Breakthroughs in M&A strategy and analysis.* London: Kogan Page Publish.

Clinton, B. D., & Chen, S. (1998). Do new performance measures measure up? *Strategic Finance, 80*(4), 38.

Colfer, L., & Baldwin, C. (2010). The mirroring hypothesis: Theory, evidence and exceptions. Harvard Business School Working Paper. Retrieved from: http://hbswk.hbs.edu/item/6361.html.

Collins, J. (2001). *Good to great: Why some companies make the leap…and others don't.* New York, NY: Harper Collins.

Connors, R., & Smith, T. (2011). *Change the culture, change the game: The breakthrough strategy for energizing your organization and creating accountability for results.* Portfolio Publishers.

Cook, R., & Jenkins, A. (2014). *Building a problem-solving culture that lasts.* McKinsey & Company.

Corporate Leadership Council (2004). *Driving performance and retention through employee engagement.* Washington, DC: Corporate Executive Board.

Cowen, R. (January 2, 2002). Galaxy survey sheds light on dark matter. *Science News.* Retrieved from: https://www.sciencenews.org/article/galaxy-survey-sheds-light-dark-matter.

Daley, B. (2001). Learning and professional practice: A study of four professions. *Adult Education Quarterly, 52,* 39–54. doi:10.1177/074171360105200104.

D'Andrade, R. (1995). *The development of cognitive anthropology.* Cambridge: Cambridge University Press.

D'Andrade, R. (2006). Commentary on Searle's "social ontology": Some basic principles. *Anthropological Theory, 6*(1), 30–39.

D'Andrade, R. (2008). *A study of personal and cultural values: American, Japanese, and Vietnamese.* Palgrave Macmillan.

de Bruin, L. C., & Kästner, L. (2012). Dynamic embodied cognition. *Phenomenology and the Cognitive Sciences, 11*(4), 541–563.

De Ruiter, J., Weston, G., & Lyon, S. M. (2011). Dunbar's number: Group size and brain physiology in humans reexamined. *American Anthropologist, 113*(4), 557–568.

Deal, T., & Kennedy, A. (1982). *Corporate cultures: The rites and rituals of corporate life.* Cambridge, MA: Perseus Publishing.

Denison, D. (1990). *Corporate culture and organizational effectiveness.* New York, NY: John Wiley & Sons.

Dent, K. (August 21, 2019). The risks of amoral AI: The consequences of deploying automation without considering ethics could be disastrous. *Techrunch.com.* Retrieved from: https://techcrunch.com/2019/08/25/the-risks-of-amoral-a-i/.

Descola, P. (2013). *Beyond nature and culture.* Chicago, IL: University of Chicago Press.

Diaz, M., Barrett, K., & Hogstrom, L. (2011). The influence of sentence novelty and figurativeness on brain activity. *Neuropsychologia, 49*(3), 320–330. doi:10.1016/j. neuropsychologia.2010.12.004.

Dougherty, D. (1992). Interpretive barriers to successful product innovation in large firms. *Organization Science, 3*(2), 179–202.

Drucker, P. F. (1973). *Management: Tasks, responsibilities, practices.* New York, NY: Harper & Row.

Dunbar, R. I. M. (1992). Neocortex size as a constraint on group size in primates. *Journal of Human Evolution, 22*(6), 469–493.

Dunbar, R. I. M. (1993). Co-evolution of neocortex size, group size and language in humans. Behavioral and Brain Sciences, 16(4), 681–735.

Dunbar, R. I. M. (2018). Network structure and social complexity in primates. *BioRxiv,* 354068.Retrieved from: https://doi.org/10.1101/354068.

Duranti, A. (2009). Linguistic anthropology: History, ideas and issues. In: A. Duranti (Ed.), *Linguistic anthropology: A reader* (2nd Edition) (pp. 1–60). Malden, MA: Blackwell.

Edvardsson, B., & Roos, I. (2001). Critical incident techniques: Towards a framework for analysing the criticality of critical incidents. *International Journal of Service Industry Management, 12*(3), 251–268.

Effectory. Effectory gobal employee engagement index 2016. *Effectory.com.* Retrieved from: https://www.effectory.com/about-effectory/.

Elliott, M. S., & Scacchi, W. (2003). Free software developers as an occupational community: Resolving conflicts and fostering collaboration. In: *Proceedings of the 2003 international ACM SIGGROUP conference on supporting group work* (pp. 21–30). New York, NY: ACM.

Engel, A. (2010). Directive minds: How dynamics affects cognition. In: J. Stewart, O. Gapenne, & A. Di Paolo (Eds.), *Enaction: Toward a new paradigm for cognitive science* (pp. 219–244). Cambridge, MA: MIT Press.

Engert, O., Gandhi, N., Schaninger, W., & So, J. (June 2010). *Perspectives on merger integration.* McKinsey & Company.

Epstein, S. (1998). Cognitive-experiential self-theory. In: D. F. Barone, M. Hersen, V. B. Van Hasselt (Eds.), *Advanced personality. The plenum series in social/slinical Psychology.* Boston, MA: Springer.

Erez, M. (1994). Towards a model of cross-cultural I/O psychology. In: M. D. Dunnette, L. Hough, & H. Triandis (Eds.), *Handbook of industrial and organizational psychology* (2nd Edition), vol. 4. (pp. 569–607). Palo Alto, CA: Consulting Psychologists Press.

Ericsson, K. A., Krampe, R. T., & Tesch-Römer, C. (1993). The role of deliberate practice in the acquisition of expert performance. *Psychological Review, 100*(3), 363.

Fealy, E., Oshima, M, Sullivan, M., & Arian, M. (2011). Culture integration in M&A (Aon Hewitt). Retrieved from: http://www.aon.com/human-capital-consulting/thought-leadership/m-and-a/reports-pubs_culture_integration_m_a.jsp.

Fiske, A. P. (2002). Using individualism and collectivism to compare cultures – A critique of the validity and measurement of the constructs: Comment on Oyserman et al. (2002). *Psychological Bulletin, 128*(1), 78–88.

Fleck, L. (1979). *Genesis and development of a scientific fact* (Fred Bradley and Thaddeus Trenn, Trans.). Chicago, IL: University of Chicago Press. (Original work published 1935).

Freeman, L. C., Romney, A. K., & Freeman, S. C. (1987). Cognitive structure and informant accuracy. *American Anthropologist, 89*(2), 310–325.

Friedman, T. L. (2016). *Thank you for being late: An optimists guide to thriving in the age of accelerations.* New York, NY: Picador.

Fitzgerald, G. A., & Desjardins, N. M. (2010). Organizational values and their relation to organizational performance outcomes. *Atlantic Journal of Communication, 12*(3), 121–145.

Fodor, J. (1975). *The language of thought.* New York, NY: Crowell.

Fonne, V., & Myrhe, G. (1996). The effect of occupational cultures on coordination of emergency medical service aircrew. *Aviation, Space and Environmental Medicine, 67*, 525–529.

Gallagher, S. (2001). Dimensions of embodiment: Body image and body schema in medical contexts. In: S. Kay Toombs (Ed.), *Phenomenology and medicine* (pp. 147–175). Dordrecht, NL: Kluwer Academic Publishers.

Gallagher, S. (2005). *How the body shapes the mind.* New York, NY: Oxford University Press.

Gallup (2016). State of the American workplace. Retrieved from: http://www.gallup.com/services/178514/state-american-workplace.aspx?g_source=EMPLOYEE_ENGAGEMENT&g_medium=topic&g_campaign=tiles.

Gelfand, M. J., Erez, M., & Aycan, Z. (2007). Cross-cultural organizational behavior. *Annual Review of Psychology, 58*, 479–514.

Gentner, D., & Colhoun, J. (2010). Analogical processes in human thinking and learning. In A. von Müller, & E. Poppel (Series Eds.) & B. Glatzeder, V. Goel, & A. von Muller (Vol. Eds.), *On thinking: Vol. 2. Towards a theory of thinking* (pp. 35–48). Berlin: Springer-Verlag.

Gentner, D., Lowenstein, J., & Thompson, L. (2003). Learning and transfer: A general role for analogical encoding. *Journal of Educational Psychology, 95*, 393–408.

Gertler, M. (2004). *Manufacturing culture: The institutional geography of industrial practice.* Oxford: Oxford University Press.

Gibbs, R. (2003). Embodied experience and linguistic meaning. *Brain and Language, 84*(1), 1–15.

Gibbs, R., & Matlock, T. (2008). Metaphor, imagination, and assimilation: Psycholinguistic evidence. In: R. Gibbs (Ed.), *The Cambridge handbook of metaphor and thought* (pp. 161–176). Cambridge: Cambridge University Press.

Gick, M., & Holyoak, K. (1983). Schema induction and analogical transfer. *Cognitive Psychology, 15*, 1–38.

Gladwell, M. (2000). *The tipping point.* New York, NY: Little, Brown and Company.

Glaser, V. L., Fast, N. J., Harmon, D. J., & Green Jr, S. E. (2016). Institutional frame switching: How institutional logics shape individual action. In: Michael Lounsbury (Ed.), *How institutions matter! (Research in the sociology of organizations)* (pp. 35–69). Emerald Group Publishing Limited.

Gomes, C. F., Yasin, M. M., & Lisboa, J. V. (2004). A literature review of manufacturing performance measures and measurement in an organizational context: A framework and direction for future research. *Journal of Manufacturing Technology Management, 15*(6), 511–530.

Goodwin, C. (1994). Professional vision. *American Anthropologist, New Series, 96*(3), 606–663.

Gordon, G. G. (1991). Industry determinants of organizational culture. *Academy of Management Review, 16*(2), 396–415.

Govindarajan, V., & Immelt, J. R. (2019). The only way manufacturers can survive. *MIT Sloan Management Review, 60*(3), 24–33.

Graham, J. R., Harvey, C. R., Popadak, J., & Rajgopal, S. (2017). Corporate culture: Evidence from the field (No. w23255). National Bureau of Economic Research Working Paper. doi:10.3386/w23255. https://www.nber.org/papers/w23255.

Greenhouse, S. (August 3, 2019). Yes, America is rigged against workers. *The New York Times*. https://www.nytimes.com/2019/08/03/opinion/sunday/labor-unions.html.

Gregory, K. (1983). Native-view paradigms: Multiple cultures and culture conflicts in organizations. *Administrative Science Quarterly, 28*, 359–376.

Griffin, D., & Tversky, A. (1992). The weighing of evidence and the determinants of confidence. *Cognitive Psychology, 24*(3), 411–435.

Griffiths, P., & Stotz, K. (2000). How the mind grows: A developmental perspective on the biology of cognition. *Synthese, 122*, 29–51.

Guenther, K. (2002). Memory. In: D. Levitin (Ed.), *Foundations of cognitive psychology: Core readings* (pp. 311–360). Cambridge, MA: MIT Press.

Guzman, I. R., Stam, K. R., & Stanton, J. M. (2008). The occupational culture of IS/IT personnel within organizations. *ACM SIGMIS Database, 39*(1), 33–50.

Halford, G., Bain, J., Mayberry, M., & Andrews, G. (1998). Induction of relational schemas: Common processes in reasoning and complex learning. *Cognitive Psychology, 35*, 201–245. Retrieved from: http://scholar.google.com/.

Hallowell, I. (1976). *Selected Papers of Irving Hallowell*. Chicago, IL: University of Chicago Press. Originally published in 1954.

Hamel, G., & Zanini, M. (August 10, 2017). What we learned about bureaucracy from 7,000 HBR readers. *Harvard Business Review*. Retrieved from: https://hbr. org/2017/08/what-we-learned-about-bureaucracy-from-7000-hbr-readers?utm_ medium=email&utm_source=newsletter_daily&utm_campaign=dailyalert&refer ral=00563&spMailingID=17853288&spUserID=MTM5NjExMzY1MTQzS0&spJo bID=1080656592&spReportId=MTA4MDY1NjU5MgS2.

Handwerker, W. P. (2002). The construct validity of cultures: Cultural diversity, culture theory, and a method for ethnography. *American Anthropologist, 104*(1), 106–122.

Handwerker, W. P. (2009). *The origin of cultures: How individual choices make cultures change*. Walnut Creek, CA: Left Coast Press.

Harari, Y. N. (2018). *21 Lessons for the 21st Century*. New York: Random House.

Harris, S. (1994). Organizational culture and individual sensemaking: A schema-based perspective. *Organization Science, 1*, 309–321.

Harter, J., & Mann, A. (January 7, 2016). The worldwide employee engagement crisis. *Gallup Business Journal, 7*. https://www.corporatejournal.com/resources/ Worldwide%20Employee%20Engagement%20Crisis%20-%20Gallup%202016.pdf.

Harter, J., & Mann, A. (2019). The right culture: Not just about employees satisfaction. *Gallup workplace*. Retrieved from: https://www.gallup.com/workplace/236366/ right-culture-not-employee-satisfaction.aspx.

Haudricourt, A. G. (1962). Domestication des animaux, culture des plantes et traitement d'autrui. *L'homme, 2*, 40–50.

Hayes, J. R. (1989). Cognitive processes in creativity. In: J. A. Glover, R. R. Ronning, & C. Reynolds, C. (Eds.), *Handbook of creativity*. New York, NY: Springer.

Heifetz, R., Grashow, A., & Linsky, M. (2009). *The practice of adaptive leadership: Tools, tactics for changing your organization and the world.* Boston, MA: Harvard Business Press.

Heifetz, R. A., & Laurie, D. L. (1997). The work of leadership. *Harvard Business Review, 75,* 124–134.

Helms Mills, J. (2003). *Making sense of organizational change.* New York, NY: Routledge.

Hensley, J. (August 31, 2019). John Harbaugh's T-shirt game is strong and motivating the Ravens. *ESPN.* Retrieved from: https://www.espn.com/blog/baltimore-ravens/post/_/id/50478/john-harbaughs-t-shirt-game-is-strong-and-motivating-the-ravens.

Hermalin, B. (1999). *Economics and corporate culture (draft).* Retrieved from: *https://ssrn.com/abstract=162549* or http://dx.doi.org/10.2139/ssrn.162549.

Heskett, J. (2011). *The culture cycle: How to shape the unseen force that transforms performance.* Upper Saddle River, NJ: FT Press.

Hofstede, G. (1998). Attitudes, values and organizational culture: Disentangling the concepts. *Organization Studies, 19*(3), 477–493.

Horowitz, M., Yaworsky, W., & Kickham, K. (2019). Anthropology's science wars: Insights from a new survey. *Current Anthropology, 60*(5).

Hui, C. H., & Triandis, H. C. (1989). Effects of culture and response format on extreme response style. *Journal of Cross-Cultural Psychology, 20*(3), 296–309.

Hui, H., & Triandis, H. C. (1986). Measurement in cross-cultural psychology: A review and comparison of strategies. *Journal of Cross-Cultural Psychology, 16,* 131–152. doi:10.1177/0022002185016002001.

Hummel, J., & Holyoak, K. (1997). Distributed representations of structure: A theory of analogical access and mapping. *Psychological Review, 104,* 427–466. Retrieved from: http://scholar.google.com/.

Huselid, M. A. (1995). The impact of human resource management practices on turnover, productivity, and corporate financial performance. *Academy of Management Journal, 38*(3), 635–672.

Hutchins, E. (1987). Myth and experience in the Trobriand Islands. In: D. Holland, & N. Quinn (Eds.), *Cultural models in language and thought* (pp. 269–289). Cambridge: Cambridge University Press.

Hutchins, E. (1995). *Cognition in the wild.* Cambridge, MA: MIT Press.

Hutchins, E. (2000). Distributed cognition. *International Encyclopedia of the Social & Behavioral Sciences* (4th edition, pp. 2068–2072). Amsterdam: Elsevier.

Hutchins, E. (2005). Material anchors for conceptual blends. *Journal of Pragmatics, 37,* 1555–1577.

Hutchins, E. (2010). Enaction, imagination, and insight. In: J. Stewart, O. Gapenne, & A. Di Paolo (Eds.), *Enaction: Toward a new paradigm for cognitive science* (pp. 425–450). Cambridge, MA: MIT Press.

Janis, I. L. (1971). Groupthink. *Psychology Today, 5*(6), 43–46.

Jaques, E. (2013). *The changing culture of a factory.* London: Routledge. Original work published 1951.

Johnson, G. (1990). Managing strategic change; The role of symbolic action. *British Journal of Management, 1,* 183–200.

Johnson, M. (1987). *The body in the mind.* Chicago, IL: University of Chicago Press.

Johnson, M. (2007). *The meaning of the body.* Chicago, IL: University of Chicago Press. B194.

Johnson-Laird, P. N. (1983). *Mental models: Towards a cognitive science of language, inference, and consciousness* (No. 6). Cambridge: Harvard University Press.

Jorgensen, J. G. (1979). Cross-cultural comparisons. *Annual Review of Anthropology, 8,* 309–331.

Kahn, W. A. (2001). Holding environments at work. *The Journal of Applied Behavioral Science, 37*(3), 260–279.

Kahneman, D., & Tversky, A. (1973). On the psychology of prediction. *Psychological Review, 80*(4), 237.

Kantor, J., & Streitfeld, D. (August 15, 2015). Inside Amazon: Wrestling big ideas in a bruising world. *The New York Times.* Http://www.nytimes.com/2015/08/16/technology/inside-amazon-wrestling-big-ideas-in-a-bruising-workplace.html?_r=0.

Keller, J. (2011). The limits of the habitual: Shifting paradigms for language and thought. In: D. Kronenfeld, G. Bennardo, V. de Munck, & M. Fisher (Eds.), *A companion to cognitive anthropology* (pp. 61–81). Chichester: Wiley-Blackwell.

Keller, S., & Aiken, C. (2015). The inconvenient truth about change management. In: J. Lane (Ed.), *Higher education reconsidered: Executing change to drive collective impact* (pp. 27–60). Albany, NY: State University of New York Press.

Kepner, E. (1980). Gestalt group process. In B. Feder, & R. Ronall (Eds.), *Beyond the hot seat: Gestalt approaches to group* (pp. 5–24). Montclair, NJ: Beefeeder Press.

Kimmel, M. (2008). Properties of cultural embodiment: Lessons from the anthropology of the body. In: R. Frank, R. Dirven, & T. Ziemke (Eds.), *Cognitive linguistics research: Sociocultural situatedness,* vol. 2. (pp. 77–108). Berlin: Mouton de Gruyter.

Kirsh, D. (2013). Embodied cognition and the magical future of interaction design. *ACM Transactions on Computer-Human Interaction (TOCHI), 20*(1), 3.

Kitayama, S., & Park, J. (2010). Cultural neuroscience of the self: Understanding the social grounding of the brain. *Social Cognitive and Affective Neuroscience, 5,* 111–129. doi:10.1093/scan/nsq052.

Kitroeff, N. (September 26, 2019). Boeing Underestimated Cockpit Chaos on 737 Max, N.T.S.B. Says. *The New York Times.* Retrieved from: https://www.nytimes.com/2019/09/26/business/boeing-737-max-ntsb-mcas.html.

Kitroeff, N. (January 9, 2020). Boeing employees mocked F.A.A. and "Clowns" who designed 737 max. *The New York Times.* Retrieved from: *https://www.nytimes.com/2020/01/09/business/boeing-737-messages.html?searchResultPosition=2.*

Knorr-Cetina, K. (1999). *Epistemic cultures: How the sciences make knowledge.* Cambridge, MA: Harvard University Press.

Kohut, H. (1977). *The restoration of the self.* Madison, CT: International University Press.

Koopman, P., Den Hartog, D., Konrad, E., et al. (1999). National culture and leadership profiles in Europe: Some results from the GLOBE study. *European Journal of Work and Organizational Psychology, 8*(4), 503–520. doi:10.1080/135943299398131.

Kotter, J. P., & Heskett, J. L. (1992). *Corporate culture and performance.* New York, NY: The Free Press.

Kourtzi, Z., & Kanwisher, N. (2000). Activation in human MT/MST by static images with implied motion. *Journal of Cognitive Neuroscience, 12*(1), 48–55.

Kroeber, A. L., & Kluckhohn, C. (1952). Culture: A critical review of concepts and definitions. *Papers.* Peabody Museum of Archaeology & Ethnology, *47*(1), Harvard University.

Kronenfeld, D. (2018). *Culture as system: How we know the meaning and significance of what we do and say.* Abingdon: Routledge.

Krosnick, J. A., Narayan, S., & Smith, W. R. (1996). Satisficing in surveys: Initial evidence. *New Directions for Evaluation, 70*, 29–44.

Kunda, G. (1992). *Engineering culture: Control and communication in a high-tech corporation*. Philadelphia, PA: Temple University Press.

Lakoff, G. (1987). *Women, fire, and dangerous things*. Chicago, IL: University of Chicago Press.

Lakoff, G. (2008). The Neural theory of metaphor. In: R. Gibbs (Ed.), *The Cambridge handbook of metaphor and thought* (pp. 1–35). Cambridge: Cambridge University Press.

Lakoff, G., & Johnson, M. (1980. Reprinted 2003). *Metaphors we live by*. Chicago, IL: University of Chicago Press.

Lakoff, G., & Johnson, M. (1999). *Philosophy in the flesh*. New York, NY: Basic Books.

Larwood, L., & Whittaker, W. (1977). Managerial myopia: Self-serving biases in organizational planning. *Journal of Applied Psychology, 62*(2), 194.

Lehmann, J., & Dunbar, R. I. M. (2009). Network cohesion, group size and neocortex size in female-bonded Old World primates. *Proceedings of the Royal Society B: Biological Sciences, 276*(1677), 4417–4422.

Leonardi, P. (2011). Innovation blindness: Culture, frames and cross-boundary problem construction in the development of new technology concepts. *Organization Science, 22*, 347–369.

Leonardi, P., & Jackson, M. (2009). Technological grounding: Enrolling technology as a discursive resource to justify cultural change in organizations. *Science, Technology and Human Values, 34*, 393–418. doi:10.1177/016224390832877.

Levinson, S. (1996). Language and space. *Annual Review of Anthropology, 25*, 353–382. Retrieved from: http://scholar.google.com/.

Levinson, S. C. (2006). Introduction: The evolution of culture in a microcosm. In: S. Levinson, & P. Jaisson (Eds.), *Evolution and culture: A Fyssen Foundation symposium* (pp. 1–41). Cambridge: MIT Press.

Lieberman, M., & Eisenberger, N. (2010). The pains and pleasures of social life: A social cognitive neuroscience approach. Retrieved from: http://web.mac.com/naomie-isenberger/san/Naomi_Eisenberger_SAN_Papers_files/Lieberman%20%26%20Eisenberger%20(2008)%20Neuroleadership.pdf.

Lieberman, M., Eisenberger, N., Crockett, M., Tom, S., Pfeifer, J., & Way, B. (2007). Putting feelings into words: Affect labeling disrupts amygdala activity in response to affective stimuli. *Psychological Science, 18*, 421–428. doi:10.1111/j.1467-9280.2007.01916.x.

Lindholm, C. (2007). *Culture and identity: The history, theory, and practice of psychological anthropology*. Oxford: Oneworld Books.

Lounsbury, M. (2007). A tale of two cities: Competing logics and practice variation in the professionalizing of mutual funds. *Academy of Management Journal, 50*(2), 289–307.

Mahon, B. Z., & Caramazza, A. (2008). A critical look at the embodied cognition hypothesis and a new proposal for grounding conceptual content. *Journal of Physiology-Paris, 102*(1), 59–70.

Malafouris, L. (2004). The cognitive basis of material engagement: Where brain, body and culture conflate. In: C. Gosden (Ed.), *Rethinking materiality: The engagement of mind with the material world* (pp. 53–61). McDonald institute for Archaeological Research.

Malmendier, U., & Tate, G. (2005). CEO overconfidence and corporate investment. *The Journal of Finance, 60*(6), 2661–2700.

Maltseva, K., & D'Andrade, R. (2011). Multi-item scales and cognitive ethnography. In: D. Kronenfeld, G. Bennardo, V. de Munck, & M. Fischer (Eds.), *A companion to cognitive anthropology* (pp. 153–170). Malden, MA: Wiley-Blackwell.

Mandler, J. (1983). *Stories, scripts, and scenes: Aspects of schema theory.* New York, NY: Psychology Press.

Mandler, J. (1992). How to build a baby: II. Conceptual primitives. *Psychological Review, 99*, 587–604. Retrieved from: http://scholar.google.com/.

Marciano, P. (2010). Carrot and sticks don't *work: Build a culture of employee engagement with the principles of respect.* New York, NY: McGraw-Hill.

Martin, J. (2002). *Organizational culture: Mapping the terrain.* Thousand Oaks, CA: Sage.

Martin, J., & Frost, P. (2011). The organizational culture war games: A struggle for intellectual dominance. In: M. Godwin, & J. Hoffer Gittell (Eds.), *Sociology of organizations: Structures and relationships* (pp. 559–621). Thousand Oaks, CA: Sage. Retrieved from: http://scholar.google.com/.

Martin, J., Sitkin, S., & Boehm, M. (1985). Founders and the elusiveness of a cultural legacy. In: P. Frost, L. Moore, M. R. Louis, C. Lundberg, & J. Martin (Eds.), *Organizational culture* (pp. 99–124). Newbury Park, CA: Sage Publications.

Martinez-Conde, S., Macknik, S. L., & Hubel, D. H. (2004). The role of fixational eye movements in visual perception. *Nature Reviews Neuroscience, 5*(3), 229–240.

Maturana, H. R., & Varela, F. J. (1991). *Autopoiesis and cognition: The realization of the living,* vol. 42. Springer Science & Business Media.

Mead, M. (1972). *Blackberry winter: My earlier years.* New York, NY: Kodansha America, Inc. (First published in 1972 by William Morrow and Company, Inc.).

Meltzoff, A. N., & Moore, M. K. (1983). Newborn infants imitate adult facial gestures. *Child Development, 54*(3), 702–709.

Merritt, A. (2000). Culture in the cockpit: Do Hofstede's dimensions replicate? *Journal of Cross-Cultural Psychology, 31*, 283–301.

Michelman, P. (2017, Summer). The end of corporate culture as we know it. *MIT Sloan Management Review.*

Miller, D., & Dröge, C. (1986). Psychological and traditional determinants of structure. *Administrative Science Quarterly, 31*(4), 539–560.

Misra, G., & Gergen, K. J. (1993). On the place of culture in psychological science. *International Journal of Psychology, 28*(2), 225–243.

Munby, H., Versnel, J., Hutchinson, N., Chin, P., & Berg, D. (2003). Workplace learning and the metacognitive function of routines. *Journal of Workplace Learning 15*(3), 94–104. doi:10.1108/13665620310468432.

Nadler, D. (1977). *Feedback and organizational development using data-based methods.* Reading, MA: Addison-Wesley.

Newman, W. R., Hanna, M., & Maffei, M. J. (1993). Dealing with the uncertainties of manufacturing: Flexibility, buffers and integration. *International Journal of Operations & Production Management, 13*(1), 19–34.

Nomura, S., Hutchins, E., & Holder, B. (2006). The uses of paper in commercial airline flight operations. In: *Proceedings of the 2006 20th anniversary conference on computer supported cooperative work* (pp. 249–258). New York, NY: ACM. doi:10.1145/1180875.1180914.

Nunez, R. (2008). Conceptual metaphor, human cognition, and the nature of mathematics. In: R. Gibbs (Ed.), *The Cambridge handbook of metaphor and thought* (pp. 339–362). Cambridge: Cambridge University Press.

Nunez, R. (2010). Enacting infinity: Bringing transfinite cardinals into being. In: J. Stewart, O. Gapenne, & A. Di Paolo (Eds.), *Enaction: Toward a new paradigm for cognitive science* (pp. 307–334). Cambridge, MA: MIT Press.

Ogbonna, E., & Wilkinson, B. (2003). The false promise of organizational culture change: A case study of middle managers in grocery retailing. *Journal of Management Studies, 40*(5), 1151–1178.

Olesen, C., White, D. G., & Lemmer, I. (2007). Career models and culture change at Microsoft. *Organization Development Journal, 25*(2), 31.

O'Reilly, C., Chatman, J., & Caldwell, J. (1991). People and organizational culture: A profile comparison approach to assessing person-organization fit. *Academy of Management Journal, 34*, 407–516. Retrieved from: http://scholar.google.com/.

Ormerod, P. (2005). *Why most things fail: Evolution, extinction, and economics.* Hoboken, NJ: John Wiley Sons.

Osborne, J. D., Stubbart, C. I., & Ramaprasad, A. (2001). Strategic groups and competitive enactment: A study of dynamic relationships between mental models and performance. *Strategic Management Journal, 22*(5), 435–454.

Ozcaliskan, S., & Goldin-Meadow, S. (2006), X is like Y: The emergence of similarity mappings in children's early speech and gesture. In: G. Kristiansen, M. Archard, R. Dirven, & F. Ruiz de Mendoza Ibanez (Eds.), *Cognitive linguistics: Current applications and future* perspectives, vol. 1. (pp. 229–262). Berlin: Walter de Gruyter.

Palfrey, J. G., & Gasser, U. (2008). *Born digital: Understanding the first generation of digital natives.* New York, NY: Basic Books.

Palmer, G. (1996). *Toward a theory of cultural linguistics.* Austin, TX: University of Texas Press.

Paoline, E. (2003). Taking stock: Toward a richer understanding of police culture. *Journal of Criminal Justice, 31*, 199–214.

Park, D. C., & Huang, C. M. (2010). Culture wires the brain: A cognitive neuroscience perspective. *Perspectives on Psychological Science, 5*(4), 391–400.

Patcheskvy, B. (2019, Novermber 11). I was fired from Deadspin for refusing to "stick to sports". The New York Times. Retrieved from: https://www.nytimes.com/2019/11/11/opinion/deadspin-sports.html.

Peng, K., Ames, D., & Knowles, E. (2000). Culture and human inference: Perspectives from three traditions. In: David Matsumoto (Ed.), *The handbook of culture and psychology* (pp. 245–264). Oxford: Oxford University Press.

Peng, K., Nisbett, R. E., & Wong, N. Y. (1997). Validity problems comparing values across cultures and possible solutions. *Psychological Methods, 2*(4), 329.

Pessoa, L. (2008). On the relationship between emotion and cognition. *Nature Reviews Neuroscience, 9*(2), 148–158.

Peters, T. J., & Waterman, R. H. (1982). *In search of excellence: Lessons from America's best-run companies.* New York, NY: Harper Collins.

Pfeffer, J. (2015). *Leadership BS: Fixing workplaces and careers one truth at a time.* New York, NY: HarperCollins.

Pool, G. J., & Schwegler, A. F. (2007). Differentiating among motives for norm conformity. *Basic and Applied Social Psychology, 29*(1), 47–60.

Porter, M. (1996). What is strategy? *Harvard Business Review, 74*(6), 61–80.

Quinn, N. (2005). How to reconstruct schemas people share, from what they say. In: N. Quinn (Ed.), *Finding culture in talk* (pp. 35–84).New York, NY: Palgrave.

Quinn, N. (2011). The history of the cultural models school reconsidered: A paradigm shift in cognitive anthropology. In: D. Kronenfeld, G. Bennardo, V. de Munck, & M. Fischer (Eds.), *A companion to cognitive anthropology* (pp. 30–46). Malden, MA: Wiley-Blackwell.

Raynor, M. (2011). Disruptive innovation: The Southwest Airlines case revisited. Retrieved from: http://www2.deloitte.com/content/dam/Deloitte/us/Documents/strategy/us-consulting-disruptive-innovation-southwest-airlines-09062011.pdf.

Reber, A. S. (1989). Implicit learning and tacit knowledge. *Journal of Experimental Psychology: General, 118*(3), 219.

Reeves, M., Faeste, L., Friedman, D., & Lotan, H. (2019). Beat the odds in M&A turnarounds. *MIT Sloan Management Review, 60*(4), 69–73.

Regier, T. (1996). *The human semantic potential: Spatial language and constrained connectionism.* Cambridge: MIT Press.

Rerup, C., & Feldman, M. (2011). Routines as a source of change in organizational schemata: The role of trial and error learning. *Academy of Management Journal, 54*, 577–610.

Restrepo, P. (2015). The Mounties and the origins of peace in the Canadian prairies. MIT Department of Economics Graduate Student Research Paper No. 15-01. Retrieved from SSRN: http://ssrn.com/abstract=2671980.

Robertson, K. (November 2, 2019). Deadspin isn't dead, owner says, as last staff member signs off. *The New York Times.*

Rodriguez, K. (2019). Companies, cultural values and success. *The Economist.* Retrieved from: https://execed.economist.com/blog/industry-trends/companies-cultural-values-and-success.

Rogoff, B. (1990). *Apprenticeship in thinking: Cognitive development in social context.* New York, NY: Oxford University Press.

Rohrer, T. (2006). Three dogmas of embodiment: Cognitive linguistics as a cognitive science. In: G. Kristiansen, M. Archard, R. Dirven, & F. Ruiz de Mendoza Ibanez (Eds.), *Cognitive linguistics: Current applications and future* perspectives, vol. 1. (pp. 119–1468). Walter de Gruyter.

Rosch, E. (2002). Principles of categorization. In: D. Levitin (Ed.), *Foundations of cognitive psychology: Core readings* (pp. 251–270). Cambridge, MA: MIT Press. (Reprinted from *Concepts: Core Readings*, pp. 189–206, by E. Margolis and S. Laurence, Eds., 1978, Cambridge, MA: MIT Press).

Rousseau, D. (2001). Schema, promise, and mutuality: The building blocks of the psychological contract. *Journal of Occupational and Organizational Psychology, 74*, 511–541.

Rumelhart, D. E., & Ortony, A. (1977). Representation of knowledge. In: R. Anderson, R. Spiro, & W. Montague (Eds.), *Schooling and the acquisition of knowledge* (pp. 100–132). NJ: Lawrence Erlbaum Associates.

Russell, J. A. C. (August 11, 2019). Celebrating each other to create an enjoyable work culture. *Forbes.* Retrieved from: https://www.forbes.com/sites/joyceearussell/2019/08/11/celebrating-each-other-to-create-an-enjoyable-work-culture/#54f38adb3944.

Saks, A. M., & Gruman, J. A. (2014). French and British top managers understanding of the structure and the dynamics of their industries: A cognitive analysis and comparison. *British Journal of Management, 3*, 61–78. doi:1045-3172/92/020061-18.

Schank, R., & Abelson, R. (1977). *Scripts plans goals and understanding.* Hillsdale: Lawrence Erlbaum & Assoc.

Scheiber, N. (July 3, 2019). Inside an Amazon warehouse, robots' ways rub off on humans. *The New York Times*. Retrieved from: https://www.nytimes.com/2019/07/03/business/economy/amazon-warehouse-labor-robots.html.

Schein, E. (1992). *Organizational culture and leadership* (2nd Edition). San Francisco, CA: Jossey-Bass.

Schein, E. H. (1984). Coming to a new awareness of organizational culture. *Sloan Management Review*, *25*(2), 3–16.

Schivelbusch, W. (1977). *The railway journey: The industrialization of time and space in the 19th century*. Berkeley, CA: The University of California Press.

Schmenner, R. W., & Vollmann, T. E. (1994). Performance measures: Gaps, false alarms, and the "usual suspects". *International Journal of Operations & Production Management*, *14*(12), 58–69.

Schneider, B. (1987). The people make the place. *Personnel Psychology*, *40*, 437–453.

Schneider, B., & Smith, D. B. (2004). Personality and organizational culture. In: B. Schneider, & D. B. Smith (Eds.), *Personality and organizations* (pp. 347–370). Mawah, NJ: Lawrence Erlbaum Associates.

Schultz, P. W., Nolan, J. M., Cialdini, R. B., Goldstein, N. J., & Griskevicius, V. (2007). The constructive, destructive, and reconstructive power of social norms. *Psychological Science*, *18*(5), 429–434.

Schwab, K. (2019). The Fourth industrial revolution: What it means, how to respond. World Economic Forum. Retrieved from: https://www.weforum.org/agenda/2016/01/the-fourth-industrial-revolution-what-it-means-and-how-to-respond/.

Schwartz, S. H. (1994). Are there universal aspects in the structure and contents of human values? *Journal of Social Issues*, *50*(4), 19–45.

Senge, P. (1992). Mental models. *Planning Review*, *20*(2), 4–44.

Sewell, W. H. (1999). Concepts of culture. In: V. Bonnell, L. Hunt, & R. Biernacki (Eds.), *Beyond the cultural turn: New directions in the study of society and culture*, vol. 34, (pp. 35–61). Berkeley, CA: University of California Press.

Sewell, W. H. (2005). *Logics of history: Social theory and social transformation*. Chicago, IL: University of Chicago Press.

Shweder, R. (1991). *Thinking through cultures: Expeditions in cultural psychology*. Cambridge: Harvard University Press.

Sidanius, J., Feshbach, S., Levin, S., & Pratto, F. (1997). The interface between ethnic and national attachment: Ethnic pluralism or ethnic dominance? *Public Opinion Quarterly*, *61*(1) Special Issue on Race, 102–133.

Sieck, W., Rasmussen, L., & Smart, P. R. (2010). Cultural network analysis: A cognitive approach to cultural modeling. In: V. Dinesh (Ed.), *Network science for military coalition operations: Information extraction and interaction* (pp. 237–255). Hershey, PA: ICI Global.

Siehl, C., & Martin, J. (1989). Organizational culture: A key to financial performance? *A CEO publication*. Retrieved from: *https://ceo.usc.edu/files/2016/09/1990_03-g90_3-Org_Culture_Key_to_Financial_Performance.pdf.*

Simon, H. A., & Chase, W. G. (1973). Skill in chess: Experiments with chess-playing tasks and computer simulation of skilled performance throw light on some human perceptual and memory processes. *American Scientist*, 394–403.

Singh, P. J., Feng, M., & Smith, A. (2006). ISO 9000 series of standards: Comparison of manufacturing and service organisations. *International Journal of Quality & Reliability Management*, *23*(2), 122–142.

Sinha, C., & Jensen de Lopez, K. (2000). Language, culture and the embodiment of spatial cognition. *Cognitive Linguistics*, 11-1/2, 17–41.

Siu, E. (2019). The statistical case for company culture (blog). https://growtheverywhere.com/management/statistical-case-company-culture/ Growth Everywhere.

Smith, J. R., & Louis, W. R. (2008). Do as we say and as we do: The interplay of descriptive and injunctive group norms in the attitude–behaviour relationship. *British Journal of Social Psychology*, 47(4), 647–666.

Smith, K. V., & Schreiner, J. C. (1969). A portfolio analysis of conglomerate diversification. *The Journal of Finance*, 24(3), 413–427.

Smith, L. B. (2005). Action alters shape categories. *Cognitive Science*, 29(4), 665–679.

Smith, M. E. (2003). Changing an organisation's culture: correlates of success and failure. *Leadership & Organization Development Journal*, 24(5), 249–261.

Smith, P. & Dugan, S. (1996). National culture and the values of organizational employees. *Journal of Cross-Cultural Psychology*, 27(2), 231.

Spender, J. C. (1989). *Industry recipes: An enquiry into the nature and sources of managerial judgment*. Oxford: Basil Blackwell.

Spender, J. C. (1996). Making knowledge the basis of a dynamic theory of the firm. *Strategic Management Journal*, 17, 45–62.

Steele, F. I. (1972). Organizational Overlearning. *Journal of Management Studies*, 9(3), 303–313.

Stening, B. W., & Everett, J. E. (1984). Response styles in a cross-cultural managerial study. *The Journal of Social Psychology*, 122(2), 151–156.

Stewart, A., & Aldrich, H. (2015). Collaboration between management and anthropology researchers: obstacles and opportunities. *The Academy of Management Perspectives*, 29(2), 173–192.

Strauss, C. (1992). What makes Tony run? Schemas as motives reconsidered. In: R. D'Andrade, & C. Strauss (Eds.), *Human motives and cultural models* (pp. 191–224). Cambridge: Cambridge University Press.

Strauss, C. (2012). *Making sense of public opinion: American discourses about immigration and social programs*. New York, NY: Cambridge University Press.

Strauss, C., & Quinn, N. (1997). *A cognitive theory of cultural meaning*. Cambridge: Cambridge University Press.

Suneson, G., & Stebbins, S. (May 28, 2019). These 15 countries have the widest gaps between rich and poor. *USA Today*. Retrieved from: *https://www.usatoday.com/story/money/2019/05/28/countries-with-the-widest-gaps-between-rich-and-poor/39510157/*.

Sur, S., & Sinha, V. K. (2009). Event-related potential: An overview. *Industrial Psychiatry Journal*, 18(1), 70.

Svenson, O. (1981). Are we all less risky and more skillful than our fellow drivers? *Acta Psychologica*, 47(2), 143–148.

Swidler, A.(2001). What anchors cultural practices. In: T. Schatzki, K. Knorr-Cetina, & E. Von Savigny (Eds.), *The Practice turn in contemporary theory* (pp. 74–92). London: Routledge.

Takata, T. (2003). Self-enhancement and self-criticism in Japanese culture: An experimental analysis. *Journal of Cross-Cultural Psychology*, 34(5), 542–551.

Triandis, H. (1996). The psychological measurement of cultural syndromes. *American Psychologist*, 51(4), 407–415.

Van den Steen, E. (2009). Culture clash: the costs and benefits of homogeneity. Harvard Business School Working Paper. Retrieved from: http://hbswk.hbs.edu/item/6254.html.

Van Maanen, J., & Barley, S. (1984). *Occupational communities: Culture and control in organizations (No. TR-ONR-10).* Cambridge, MA: Alfred P. Sloan School of Management. Retrieved from: https://scholar.google.com/scholar?hl=en&q=Occupational+communities%3A+Culture+and+control+in+organizations&btnG=&as_sdt=1%2C5&as_sdtp=.

Van Maanen, J., & Kunda, G. (1989). "Real feelings": Emotional expression and organizational culture. In: L. Cummings, & B. Staw (Eds.), *Research in organizational behavior*, vol. 11, (pp. 43–103). Greenwich, CT: JAI.

Varela, F. J., Thompson, E., & Rosch, E. (1991). *The embodied mind.* Cambridge, MA: MIT Press.

Vorhees, B., Read, D., and Gabora, L. (2020). Identity, kinship, and the evolution of cooperation. *Current Anthropology*, 61(2).

Walsh, J. P. (1995). Managerial and organizational cognition: Notes from a trip down memory lane. *Organization Science*, 6(3), 280–321.

Wapner, S., & Werner, H. (1965). An experimental approach to body perception from the organismic-developmental point of view. In: S. Wapner, & H. Werner (Eds.), *The body percept.* New York, NY: Random House.

Ward, R., & Robison, J. (2015). *How to build a thriving culture at work featuring the 7 points of transformation.* Kalamazoo, MI: IHAC, Inc.

Weick, K. (1995). *Sensemaking in organizations.* Thousand Oaks, CA: Sage Publications.

Westerman, G., Soule, D., & Eswaran, A. (2019, Summer). Building digital-ready culture in organizations. *Sloan Management Review.*

Weston, J. F. (1969). The nature and significance of conglomerate firms. *John's L.* Review, 44, 66.

White, D. G. (2017). *Rethinking culture: Embodied cognition and the origin of culture in organizations*, vol. 17. New York, NY: Routledge.

Wilson, T. D., Dunn, D. S., Bybee, J. A., Hyman, D. B., & Rotondo, J. A. (1984). Effects of analyzing reasons on attitude–behavior consistency. *Journal of Personality and Social Psychology*, 47(1), 5.

Wilson, T. D., & Gilbert, D. T. (2003). Affective forecasting. *Advances in experimental social psychology*, 35(35), 345–411.

Winnicott, D. W. (1965). *The maturational process and the facilitating environment.* New York, NY: International University Press.

Winnicott, D. W. (1971). *Playing and reality.* London: Tavistock/Routledge.

Wood, J., & Vilkinas, T. (2004). Characteristics of chief executive officers. Views of their staff. *Journal of Management Development*, 23(5), 469–478.

Yap, A. J., Wazlawek, A. S., Lucas, B. J., Cuddy, A. J., & Carney, D. R. (2013). The ergonomics of dishonesty: The effect of incidental posture on stealing, cheating, and traffic violations. *Psychological Science*, 24(11), 2281–2289.

Yates, J. F. (1990). *Judgment and decision making.* Englewood Cliffs: Prentice-Hall, Inc.

Index

Note: Page locators in *italics* denotes figures and tables.